T0322356

Private Inquiries

Private Inquiries

THE SECRET HISTORY OF FEMALE SLEUTHS

CAITLIN DAVIES

OTHER TITLES BY CAITLIN DAVIES

FICTION:

Jamestown Blues

Black Mulberries

Friends Like Us

The Ghost of Lily Painter

Family Likeness

Daisy Belle: Swimming Champion of the World

NON-FICTION:

The Return of El Negro

Place of Reeds

Taking the Waters: A Swim Around Hampstead Heath

Camden Lock and the Market

Downstream: A History and Celebration of Swimming the River Thames

Bad Girls: The Rebels and Renegades of Holloway Prison

Queens of the Underworld: A Journey into the Lives of Female Crooks

To Ruby, with my love

First published 2023

The History Press
97 St George's Place, Cheltenham,
Gloucestershire, GL50 3QB
www.thehistorypress.co.uk

British Library Cataloguing in Publication Data.
A catalogue record for this book is available from the British Library.

ISBN 978 0 7509 9888 8

Typesetting and origination by The History Press
Printed and bound in Great Britain by TJ Books Limited, Padstow, Cornwall.

Trees for LYfe

CONTENTS

Prologue: Case No. 480   9

1   A Consulting Detective   13
2   How to Become a Private Eye   17
3   Inspector Field and the Peephole Servants   23
4   A Special Detector   31
5   Clubnose   39
6   Secret Watchings   43
7   A Profession for Charlatans   49
8   Assessment Day   55
9   Antonia Moser: Detective Expert   61
10   Adventures of a Woman Detective   71
11   Kate Easton: 'I Can Shoot Straight'   79
12   A Dominant Face for a Woman   89
13   Lady Detective and Wizard   95
14   The Lady Copper   101
15   The Women 'Tecs of Baker Street   107
16   An Underground Job   113
17   A Clean Profession   117
18   May Storey: A Great Career for a Girl   123
19   A Modest Woman   131
20   Annette Kerner: The Mayfair Detective Agency   137
21   Truth and Lies   145

22 The Case of the Disappearing Whisky   151
23 A Woman Private Dick   159
24 Do You Want to Know a Secret?   181
25 Zena Scott-Archer: Scott's Detective Bureau   191
26 Merseyside's Mrs Sherlock Holmes   197
27 Duly Served   205
28 A Dangerous Profession   211
29 Anne Summer: 'I Couldn't Do That!'   217
30 A Toothsome Sleuth   225
31 Lady Gumshoe   235
32 'She-lock Holmes'   241
33 Private Lives   249
34 Death Investigator   257
35 Twenty-First-Century Detectives   265
36 Rogue Daters   269
37 The Art of Shadowing   277
38 The Best Disguise is a Woman   289

Sources   297
Select Bibliography   313
Acknowledgements   314
Index   315

CASE NO. 480

Early one September morning, shortly after the end of the Second World War, private detective Annette Kerner arrived at work to find an unexpected visitor. Jacques Vers of the French Secret Service had flown over from Paris on the night plane and now he was worriedly pacing up and down outside her London office. Annette knew him well; she had cooperated with French detectives on a number of criminal cases, but this was a particularly delicate mission and not even Scotland Yard was to know he was here. A New York bank was concerned about one of its wealthiest customers, an oil king called Jerome Y-. He was on his way to London on a business trip, where he was about to become the target for international fraudster Howard Robinson. The American bank needed someone to protect its customer's interests without his knowledge; they had to be efficient, dignified and charming. Would Mademoiselle accept the case?

Annette Kerner agreed and went at once to a nearby fashion house where she was fitted out with furs, evening gowns and diamond jewellery. Next, she headed to Claridge's, where the oil king was staying, disguised as 'Mrs Etherington', a rich, well-dressed widow in her late forties, kindly, lonely and a little eccentric.

When Annette caught sight of fraudster Howard Robinson in the hotel's foyer she drew her breath, he was one of the most handsome men she had ever seen. As Annette passed by his table, she 'accidentally' knocked over his glass of brandy, apologised with a charming smile and soon they were chatting over cocktails.

A few days later, the smooth-talking Howard Robinson invited her to an intimate party for an American business friend. Annette put on her furs and jewellery and went along. But Jerome Y-, the man she'd been hired to protect, ignored her, she was a female nuisance and not worthy of his attention.

The next morning Annette overheard the two men discussing an oil deal and knew she had to work fast. She approached Howard Robinson, pleading with him to help a rich widow who wanted to make money, and he agreed to sell her £8,000 worth of Standard Oil shares – equivalent to around £300,000 today. But he wanted a cash deposit straight away, so they jumped in a taxicab to a West End bank.

Annette was worried, she knew she needed documentary evidence of the bogus oil deal if she was to catch her man. When they arrived at the bank, Annette walked up to the counter; Howard Robinson handed her the transfer form and she gave him her cheque, when suddenly he realised it was a trap. His beguiling manner vanished and his eyes blazed with fury. The bank's alarm bell started clanging, and Annette's operative, ex-CID officer Eddie Parsons, pounced. As she watched the two powerful men locked in struggle, she knew that if Howard Robinson broke free, he would kill her.

Annette Kerner was no stranger to hazardous jobs; she was hailed as 'Britain's foremost woman detective', and newspaper readers were regularly treated to her daring adventures. She'd worked undercover in Soho opium dens in the 1920s, tracked down a baronet's son and a missing Van Dyck painting in the 1930s, and recently rescued an MP from blackmail and recovered £100,000 worth of stolen jewellery.

Annette was on close terms with senior officers at Scotland Yard, and she was also well known in the criminal underworld. Not long ago, Johnny Dannett, who ran a gambling joint in the West End, had sent two hoodlums to threaten her. They'd followed her down to the tube station, where she'd managed to jump on a train, and then they'd attempted to run her over outside her office. Annette had flung herself out of the way of their car with a moment to spare, and only regained consciousness in hospital with two broken ribs and a broken arm.

Now she had successfully trapped international fraudster Howard Robinson, who was convicted on a previous, lesser charge and jailed for three years. Annette had ended his career, and CID were quick to congratulate her – 'Nice work, Mrs Kerner'.

Annette modestly accepted the compliment. 'It was a case of a woman's intuition succeeding,' she explained, 'where the FBI and the Paris *Sûreté* had failed.'

Jerome Y-, the American buyer who'd underestimated her capabilities, apologised. 'You've helped me to avoid losing a small fortune,' he told her. 'How did you first tumble to this crook?'

Annette replied with a smile, 'I give myself away when I explain, results without causes are much more impressive.' This was no throwaway remark – the words had been spoken by her fictional hero, Sherlock Holmes, in *The Adventure of the Stockbroker's Clerk* – and not only was Annette a self-styled Mrs Sherlock Holmes, she too ran her detective agency from one of the most famous addresses in the history of detection: Baker Street.

1

A CONSULTING
DETECTIVE

Outside the Sherlock Holmes Museum on Baker Street there's quite a crowd. It's 11 on a Sunday morning and people are already queuing along this pretty stretch of Georgian townhouses on the edge of Regent's Park. A newsagent opposite boasts a silhouette of Sherlock Holmes on its shop front, while further down on the Marylebone Road there's a 10ft-high bronze statue of Sherlock outside Baker Street tube station. This is the London stomping ground of the most famous private detective who never lived.

I've booked my £15 museum tour online but the 'constable' at the head of the queue, wearing a black cape and facemask, sends me next door to get a ticket, so I'm forced to start my visit in the gift shop. It's packed. The carpeted floor creaks as people drift past inspecting the goods – Sherlock Holmes lollipops, teddy bears, rubber ducks, bow ties, aprons, pipes and bowler hats. I wait as a German couple pay in euros for a deerstalker hat, then the assistant scribbles a line on my booking form and off I go back next door.

It feels like entering a real house; the hallway is narrow and the light is dim, a row of coat hooks are lined up on the wall. I follow half a dozen people up the stairs where a woman dressed as a maid directs us into a small room, made even smaller because half of it is roped off. We all stand and wait.

'Welcome to 221b Baker Street,' begins a recorded voice. 'What you are about to see is exactly as it would have been when Sherlock Homes lived here.' This is his study, we are told, and there are real antiques in here, over 100 years old. As we're invited to look at his chemistry set, I glance at the other people in the room. They don't seem too concerned that Sherlock Holmes is a fictional character and so he didn't actually live here at all.

The world-renowned detective first appeared in print in 1887 in Arthur Conan Doyle's *A Study in Scarlet*. The tale was narrated by Dr John H. Watson, a former army medical officer who lodges with Sherlock at 221b Baker Street. Dr Watson is mystified by his friend's constant stream of visitors, until Sherlock explains he has 'a trade of my own. I suppose I am the only one in the world. I'm a consulting detective.' He possesses a scientific, inquiring mind, as well as 'a kind of intuition' that allows him to unravel mysteries, often without leaving his rooms.

When an American man is murdered, Sherlock Holmes visits the scene, deduces the order of events, identifies crucial clues and, three days later, the killer is caught. Sherlock Holmes and Dr Watson went on to solve numerous cases of mystery and intrigue, pitting their wits against criminal masterminds like Professor Moriarty. Sherlock has remained a legendary figure ever since, appearing in endless books, plays, TV shows and films, and every year around 70,000 people come to the museum on Baker Street to see how he lived.

The maid ushers more people into the study and so I move next door where three young women are standing by Sherlock's bed, their heads slightly bowed in respect. Upstairs in the landlady's room I flick through a visitors' book. So far this morning there have been Sherlock enthusiasts from China, Spain, Portugal, Greece and the Netherlands. Yesterday, there were visitors from Hungary, Venezuela, Russia, Latvia, India and Wales. There are some odd things on display in this room – a human 'voodoo fetish', a 'severed ear', a revolver, and a 'severed thumb'.

'It's a very good museum,' murmurs a woman from the doorway.

'Yes,' says her partner. 'Shall we go to the gift shop?'

I walk up to the villains' floor, where there's a massive dog's head jutting out of the wall and a plaque to the 'Hound of the Baskervilles. Dartmoor. Killed 19 October 1888'. I pick up a laminated book of letters. 'Dear Mr. SHERLOCK HOLMES,' writes a young Japanese woman, 'You are a gentleman of the first class as well as you are the greatest detective in the world.' But a fan from China has some bad news,

'Professor James Moriarty is BACK! Last Friday, I saw him in a supermarket near my house.'

A young boy comes into the room and crouches down to inspect a case of books. 'Do you like Sherlock Holmes?' I ask.

'Yes,' he beams. 'I've seen the film.'

'Did you know,' I say, 'that a real detective once worked on this road?'

The boy doesn't reply.

'She was a woman,' I say, 'and she had an office just there.' I gesture at the window behind us, with its view over Baker Street.

But the boy ignores me. 'Look!' he cries, before jumping up and dragging his mother to the other side of the room.

I return downstairs and ask the maid if there is any information on the history of private detectives. She shakes her head. 'People mainly come to see a Victorian house and how everything looked back then,' she explains. 'We're trying to replicate the era.'

'So, there's nothing on the history of private detection,' I ask, 'not even in Victorian times?'

The maid shakes her head.

'There was a real woman detective,' I say, 'who operated just down the road from here.'

The maid nods politely. 'Some people think Sherlock Holmes is real.'

'And do you tell them he's not?'

She smiles and shrugs, 'Some people prefer to believe.'

When Arthur Conan Doyle first introduced the world to Sherlock Holmes, there was no 221b Baker Street. It was only later that the road was extended, and the address became home to the Abbey Building Society. In the 1970s, an advertising assistant was given the job of replying to fan mail from all over the world. 'Sometimes I really do get the impression that they believe in him,' she told the press. 'I just say that he is very busy or is away resting at the moment.' Today, the Sherlock Holmes Museum has a plaque outside giving its address as No. 221b, but it's actually Nos 237–41.

As for Annette Kerner, the real-life detective who operated from Baker Street, very little has ever been written about her. I first came across her several years ago, while researching a book on female criminals, and I've just read her memoir, *Woman Detective*, published in 1954. Her tales sound melodramatic – such as the entrapment of handsome fraudster Howard

Robinson in a West End bank – but she was revered by the British press as the only woman in Britain to run a detective agency.

She sounds like an intriguing figure, so why isn't she known today? I wonder how she became a private detective, and how she managed to survive from the 1920s to the 1950s. Then I wonder about the women who came before her. Who were the very first female private eyes? Did real female sleuths exist in Victorian times, alongside the fictional Sherlock Holmes? I came to the museum hoping to find some clues about the roots of detection, because while I can name numerous imaginary female sleuths – from Agatha Christie's Miss Marple, to twenty-first-century Mma Precious Ramotswe – I know nothing about their real-life counterparts.

My knowledge of private eyes comes from watching TV as a teenager, as affable Jim Rockford sped around Los Angeles in his 1970s gold Firebird, Magnum PI set off in his red Ferrari to solve a murder in Hawaii, and the three glamorous *Charlie's Angels* tackled investigations provided by their mysterious male boss, and then changed into bikinis by the poolside. I want to know more about Annette Kerner, the Mrs Sherlock Holmes of Baker Street, and how she fits into the history of female private eyes. But first I need to understand what private detectives do.

2

HOW TO BECOME
A PRIVATE EYE

'Dear Caitlin, Congratulations on signing up for our BTEC Level 3 for Professional Investigators … Get ready to start learning!'

It's the end of April 2021 and I'm about to start my training as a private detective. I've just paid £275 to Bluemoon College, which runs training courses for the Association of British Investigators (ABI), the oldest professional organisation for private investigators in the UK. It's taken me a while to decide where to do this course, because a Google search for 'how to become a private eye' provided numerous options. One site offered me an online Diploma of Private Investigation for just £19, while another promised I could start my own agency in less than six weeks and earn up to £100 per hour.

I soon realised there is no set route into private investigation in the UK, because the industry is completely unregulated. Anyone can become a PI – a private investigator – whatever their skills, experience or criminal record. The industry is a 'free-for-all', warns the ABI, where unscrupulous, untrained operators are free to practise.

In 2013, the Home Office announced that regulation was on the way; those without a licence would face fines of up to £5,000 and up to six months in prison. This was the year of the *News International* phone-hacking trial, when private investigators were accused of listening in on private phone calls belonging to politicians, victims of crime, members of the royal household and celebrities. 'It is vital we have proper regulation,' declared Home Secretary Theresa May, 'to ensure rigorous standards in this sector and the respect of individuals' rights to privacy.'

However, a decade after the Home Office announcement, the industry has still not been regulated. No one even knows how many PIs there are in the UK, although the official estimate is around 10,000. But if licensing is introduced, then according to the ABI, the Level 3 Award for Professional Investigators will become the industry standard.

I'm doing the course online, because Covid restrictions mean the in-person courses aren't running, but my final assessment will be in Paddington, west London, where I'll meet the other trainee PIs. I've read that it usually takes thirty-nine hours to complete the Level 3 Award; it doesn't sound too long, and I'm used to reading documents and doing research. But I don't know if my background as a journalist and novelist will lend itself to detective work. I've always been nosey and have some experience in finding people from the past. I can track down a Victorian jewel thief who used a dozen aliases, but I don't know if I could shadow someone down Oxford Street without being seen.

Will it make any difference that I'm a woman? Annette Kerner believed that women were particularly suited to the job of detection. Women are quick to seize a situation, she explained, and act in an emergency. We possess 'wit, charm and intuition', and we're highly skilled at bluffing. It's true that as women we learn from an early age to read those around us, to approach situations in a different way from men, to stand back, be quiet and observant. We are experts at interpreting body language and looking for non-verbal clues. We are also used to watching out for danger, especially from men. But does this make us better detectives?

I pay my £275 to Bluemoon College, and I'm sent a username and password. Then I start to feel a bit anxious. What exactly am I going to have to do? The course is split into two units with twenty-nine different topics, and it's described as suitable for those with no prior experience or knowledge.

Ex-police and military usually make excellent private investigators, according to Bluemoon College, but their students have included publicans, television producers, social workers and limousine drivers. The work of a PI is diverse — it can include background checks, accident investigations, serving court papers, domestic surveillance, child custody disputes, industrial espionage, employee theft, tracing birth parents and finding stolen goods. PIs rarely investigate criminal matters; instead, they're more likely to work on civil cases, hired by solicitors, private individuals, insurance companies, businesses and local authorities.

Now I have a slightly clearer idea of the job, I'm ready to begin my studies. Unit 1 – planning and reporting investigations – covers sources of evidence and the importance of establishing what a client wants to achieve. Next comes an operational plan: what information will I need to solve a case, how will I get it, and how long will that take? The process sounds similar to writing a book. These are the same questions I'd ask myself at the beginning of a project.

It all seems quite straightforward, and I picture myself in a book-lined drawing room, behind a mahogany desk, wearing a tweed suit and a bucket hat, awaiting my first client. But then I see a button I hadn't noticed before, the course materials for Unit 1. I click on a link for the Criminal Procedure and Investigation Act of 1996, and it takes me to a government site. When I try to download the Act, a pop-up warns it 'contains over 200 provisions and might take some time to download. Would you like to continue?' I hesitate and press cancel; I'll look at it another time.

The next topic lists the legislation that needs to be followed when conducting an investigation. PIs aren't specifically included in any UK laws, so we're expected to follow the rules that apply to police officers. I scroll down the page and count the legislation that we need to be familiar with – there are twenty separate Acts, rules and regulations, covering fraud, bribery, theft, data protection, prevention of corruption, misuse of computers, sexual offences, freedom of information, health and safety and human rights. Private detection seems to be a legal minefield that potentially breaches all sorts of laws – whether the Human Rights Act, which ensures the right to respect for a person's private and family life, or the Stalking Protection Act, which covers loitering, watching, following and spying. Soon I'm so overwhelmed with wading through legal jargon that I'm having second thoughts about even attempting the course.

A few days later, I start Unit 2 – gathering and using information. I read about the importance of keeping notes, maintaining confidentiality of sources, avoiding conflicts of interest and how to conduct interviews. It sounds like the job of a journalist, although there is a lot of military language. PIs 'stake out' a 'target', 'recce' an area, conduct interviews 'in the field', and try to avoid 'Collateral Intrusion' – when information is gathered on someone other than the subject under surveillance. I'm also learning a lot of acronyms. A CROP operative is a covert rural surveillance expert; CHIS are Covert Human Intelligence Sources – undercover agents – and when planning a surveillance, we must always ask, is it JAPAN – justified, accountable, proportionate, appropriate and necessary? The terms 'ethics' and 'morals' crop up quite a bit and PIs must ensure their clients have 'lawful and ethical reasons to request an investigation' – but the terms are not defined.

There is a focus on evidence right through the course – collecting, recording, retaining and revealing it – because if the rules aren't followed, then it won't be admissible in court. But perhaps the most delicate area is surveillance, whether directed surveillance – such as following a target down a street – or intrusive surveillance – like planting a bug in someone's house, which would be illegal. The use of GPS trackers is a tricky area, but if I surreptitiously fit one onto the outside of someone's car in a public place, it's not intrusive surveillance.

It takes me about two weeks to work my way through the Level 3, studying court procedures, examining surveillance logs, learning how to keep data secure and confidential. Then I revise for the midway assessment. The last time I took an exam was fifteen years ago for a driving theory test, and I'm tempted to keep my notes in front of me while I answer the forty-eight multiple-choice questions. But that would be cheating.

Some of the questions are straightforward: 'When carrying out surveillance, which of the following is not a desired outcome – being hungry, being hot, being cold, or being compromised?' But most of the questions require a good knowledge of legislation, especially in terms of evidence, surveillance, interviewing suspects and data protection.

I finish the test, spend a while reviewing my answers and eventually press a button to await my results. I've passed with a score of 87.5 per cent. I'm a bit disappointed – I got six questions wrong and in half of those I'd changed my answer at the last minute and my first choice would have been correct. A few minutes later, I get an email, 'Congratulations Caitlin … You are ready to attend your assessment day.'

I book my place for the final exam in Paddington, already worried that in two months' time I'll have forgotten everything. The course has required far more reading than I'd expected, and while I've learnt a lot of theory, I'm not sure how much I've gained in terms of practicalities. The emphasis on legislation and the need to obey the law is a far cry from the popular image of PIs, who happily bug phones and hack computers, delve into people's bins and trespass on private property. 'Never be tempted to break any rules,' warns Bluemoon College, 'and especially laws to give your client the result they want.'

I wonder if the earliest female detectives had to study anything when they started out on their careers, and what laws they had to be aware of. Did they receive any training? Who hired the first female sleuths, what crimes did they solve and how did they do it?

3

INSPECTOR FIELD AND THE PEEPHOLE SERVANTS

In the summer of 1854, a former cook called Sarah Grocott was offered an unusual job. Retired police inspector Charles Frederick Field promised her 2 guineas a week if she would move into a household on Bryanston Street in London's fashionable Marylebone, to 'watch the conduct of a lady' lodging on the first floor. On 29 June Sarah started work, noting that 'there was not much cooking to do', instead she was kept busy watching her mistress.

A few days later, the retired police inspector came round and gave her a gimlet – a small, handheld tool – and explained how to bore two holes in the folding doors between her mistress' drawing room and bedroom. He peered through the holes to make sure he could see straight across the room, and then left the cook to get on with the job. According to some reports, Charles Field bored the holes himself. Either way, it was one of the earliest documented cases of a woman being paid for undercover investigation work in Britain.

Charles Frederick Field was a well-known figure in Victorian England, having enjoyed a long career as a high-profile and well-respected police detective. He had initially wanted to become an actor and had performed as a 15-year-old at a theatre on Gray's Inn Road, but then he'd joined the newly formed Metropolitan Police. In 1842, he was one of eight 'intelligent men' selected to form a new body, the Detective Police. They had no specific beat or round, explained the press, but were 'concerned with the investigation of specific cases, or the watching of particular individuals or classes of offenders'. According to one paper, they were employed 'for the express purpose of prying into men's secrets'.

Detective was still a relatively new word in Britain. The verb 'detect' came from Latin – to uncover or expose – and had been used to describe the apprehension of criminals since at least the early eighteenth century. But it was the formation of the Detective Police, and coverage of their exploits in the press, that meant 'detective' soon became a household word.

The new police 'spies' were viewed with suspicion at first, and *Punch* joked they were so inefficient they should be called the Defective Force. But their public image was far more respectable than that of police constables, who were routinely mocked in the music hall as inept and corrupt. Detectives had sharp minds and vigilant eyes – particularly Inspector Charles Frederick Field.

In 1846, he was appointed Chief of the Detective Division, and tales of his clever captures often appeared in the press. Novelist Charles Dickens accompanied the inspector on nightly tours of London's lodging houses, pubs and underground dens, and wrote about him in *Household Words* – a burly figure, who strides unperturbed into a cellar of robbers and ruffians, 'the Sultan of the place'. He was 'discretion itself', according to Dickens, 'and accustomed to the most delicate missions'. Charles Field inspired the figure of Inspector Bucket in *Bleak House*, published in 1852, who employs the services of his wife, 'a lady of a natural detective genius', to solve a murder. He instructs her to observe their lodger, Mademoiselle Hortense, 'My dear, can you do without rest, and keep watch upon her, night and day?' Mrs Bucket obliges, watching from her 'spy-place', securing letters and leading the police to the murder weapon.

The real police inspector, Charles Field, also employed women to catch crooks. He once paid a Mrs Jenkins to assist in the capture of two American coiners who were making counterfeit money at a house in High Holborn. Mrs Jenkins was the wife of a police sergeant and she'd grown suspicious about goings-on at the house and had reported her concerns to her husband. Inspector Field promised her 'a substantial reward' if she made use of her friendship with the landlady in order to search the premises.

The two coiners were caught, and a large quantity of gold and silver bars were found in the house, along with four fully loaded revolvers. The case 'reflected the greatest credit' upon Inspector Field, according to ex-Metropolitan Police chief inspector Timothy Cavanagh, but he would have remained in the dark had it not been for the sagacious Mrs Jenkins, 'the pioneer of female detectives'.

But who was Mrs Jenkins? Her full name was not given, and nor was her husband's. There were no clues as to her age or place of birth, or whether she was sent on further missions for Inspector Field. And what about his own wife, Jane Chambers, who he'd married in 1841? Was she ever required to assist in police investigations, just like her fictional counterpart, Mrs Bucket?

In 1852, Charles Field retired from the police force with a handsome annual pension of £126 and a first-class certificate of good character. But, as the *Illustrated Times* noted, 'From a life of truth and activity it is not to be supposed Mr Field could settle down "to a cow and a cottage".' Instead, he opened a Private Inquiry Office in Westminster 'to make inquiries and detect frauds'.

Soon he was boasting of solving 'some of the most extraordinary investigations of the day', including forgeries, horse poisoning and insurance frauds 'by the sordid relatives of drunken debauchees'. Charles Field appointed Ignatius Paul Pollaky, a Hungarian who'd arrived in London a few years earlier, as his foreign superintendent. Ignatius specialised in gathering intelligence on 'foreigners', and later established Pollaky's Private Inquiry Office in Paddington Green, earning the music hall nickname, 'Paddington Pollaky'.

Charles Field's detective agency was a relatively novel idea, although in 1833 Eugène-François Vidocq, an ex-criminal and former police officer, had opened *Le bureau des renseignements* – an office of intelligence – in Paris. The British press described him as a 'thief taker', and the jobs had much in common.

In the seventeenth century, before the days of formal policing, victims of crime had to catch an offender themselves and take them to court at their own expense. Wealthier individuals began to hire thief takers, both to catch crooks and return stolen goods. In the mid-eighteenth century, the Fielding brothers, John and Henry, employed former thief takers as 'runners', attached to their magistrates' court at Bow Street. The Bow Street Runners arrested offenders and served writs, carrying court documents inside their Tipstaff.

Some runners, like Henry Goddard, offered their services to private individuals, and his *Memoirs of a Bow Street Runner* described several dramatic investigations. Henry Goddard was frequently sent out 'to the scene of action', carrying a pocketbook, cutlass and handcuffs, to interview witnesses and search and examine premises. His clients included a Bond Street wine merchant, an actress whose purse had been stolen from her carriage and a foreign count who'd lost a diamond ring. Henry once received instructions from the king to keep the Duke of Brunswick 'under strict observation and note down all places he may go to', and he was hired by the Russian Consul to provide protection for His Imperial Highness in England.

Henry also handled more 'delicate' inquiries. In 1839, he was dispatched on 'an important errand of a confidential nature' for an unnamed lord who'd received 'very unpleasant' reports about his wife. Henry tracked the woman to Paris, where with the assistance of the Chief of the Paris Police, he kept Her Ladyship under observation.

He was also hired to keep a gentleman's daughter-in-law under surveillance, following her to a hotel in Dartford, questioning the landlord and chambermaid, and reporting back to the client's solicitor. Solicitors had a very long tradition of hiring detectives to find evidence of adultery for wealthy clients. In the early 1700s, during the divorce of Leonard and Charlotte Calvert, both sides employed 'semi-professional detectives', explains historian Lawrence Stone. These were probably bailiffs, who were hired to gather evidence and track down eyewitnesses.

In 1770, when Lady Henrietta Grosvenor was taken to court by her husband, accused of an affair with the Duke of Cumberland, she hired private detectives to find her husband's mistresses. She instructed them to 'go about into bawdy houses and other places' and offer handsome rewards in return for information.

But such investigations were costly and could take time – and divorce required an Act of Parliament, so it was only available to the rich and well connected. In 1801, Jane Campbell, the daughter of an MP, became the first of only four women to ever obtain a Parliamentary divorce when she successfully accused her husband of 'incestuous adultery'. A waiter provided the evidence; he'd bored a hole in the door of a bedchamber and peeped through it several times.

By the mid-nineteenth century, those seeking a divorce could call on the services of professional private detectives – men like ex-inspector Charles Field. In January 1854, he was approached by Ormwold Evans, a well-to-do gentleman in Cheltenham, who suspected his wife Mary Sophia of having an affair with Robert Robinson, a magistrate and a married man. The Evanses had wed four years earlier, but separated after a few months, and Ormwold had been paying his wife an annual allowance ever since. If she *was* having an affair, then he could stop paying the allowance, and he could sue her lover for damages over a 'criminal conversation'.

A 'crim.con' was a civil wrong in which a husband sued another man for 'debauching' his wife. It was a peculiarly English custom and received avid press attention. But in order to succeed, Ormwold Evans needed evidence. So, he offered Charles Field 15 shillings a day, plus 12 shillings for hotel expenses and an extra 6 shillings a day if he caught the couple in the act. It was a considerable sum; a police inspector earned less than 30 shillings a week.

Charles Field set off to Cheltenham, Gloucestershire, where he spent a couple of months watching Mary Evans and Mr Robertson. Then he followed the couple to London, where Mary took lodgings at No. 2 Bryanston Street in Marylebone. The ex-inspector rented rooms in the same house, paying the landlady Maria King £25 per month. 'I told her who I was,' he explained, 'and that I was employed to watch the conduct of the lady on the first floor, and would she assist me.'

But Mrs King refused. If her lodgers preserved outward respectability, then what they got up to 'was nothing to do with me'. But she did introduce him to Ann Price, who worked in the house, and she also informed him that her cook was leaving, and she needed a replacement. So, Charles Field engaged Sarah Grocott. She was in her late 30s, a former cook who was married to a butcher in St John's Wood and had two young children. She had not met the inspector before, she said, but knew his sister.

Sarah Grocott moved into Bryanston Street, where she saw Mary Evans alone with Mr Robinson several times, then she was told to bore two holes in her mistress' door. The following day, just after lunch, Sarah looked through one of the holes, and there was Mr Robinson sitting upon the sofa with Mary Evans by his side. She called her fellow servant Ann Price to 'come and look here', and Ann was so surprised she made a noise with her chair. This alerted their mistress, who rushed in and demanded to know what was going on.

The moment she left, Sarah looked through the hole again, and this time she saw a 'criminal connexion' taking place between Mary Evans and

Mr Robinson. Sarah was 'very much shocked'; in fact, she thought 'every modest woman would feel very much shocked to have seen the indecency they saw there'. Ann Price looked in a moment afterwards, and she too was shocked. She was 'looking out for a little indecency', she admitted, 'but not in that position'. Mr Robinson's 'person was exposed. He was sitting forward on the sofa. Mrs. Evans had a light gown on. She had her clothes up, and was sitting astride of him.'

It was a disgustingly vulgar and immoral case, according to the press, and naturally received enormous coverage, with *The Times* in particular reporting every detail. The crim.con was initially heard in Liverpool, where Ormwold Evans' attempt to sue Mr Robinson failed, but in a retrial the jury agreed he'd been wronged and awarded damages of £500.

However, the judge condemned the unscrupulous methods that had been used to gather evidence. When Charles Field insisted, 'I never knew Mrs King before, upon my honour', the judge responded, 'You are on your oath, sir. Don't talk of honour with a private business like yours.' The *Cheltenham Examiner* deplored the use of 'hired informers and salaried spies', and the Bryanston Street servants were closely examined on their own marital status. Mrs Price explained her husband was abroad, while Mrs King refused to say if there was a Mr King. Their characters were 'tainted', explained the defence, and if the jury relied upon the evidence of 'the fat cook Grocott', 'the flippant lady', Ann Price, or the 'kept woman', Mrs King, then 'no person in this country was safe'.

There would be two further trials before the Bryanston Street case was over. But at the end of 1858, Mary Sophia Evans was consigned to disgrace; she was guilty of adultery and the marriage dissolved. Her final trial took place in the new Court of Divorce in London, and her husband was one of the first men to obtain a divorce without an Act of Parliament. The court had been established under the 1857 Matrimonial Causes Act, which allowed male petitioners to divorce if they could prove adultery – a woman, however, also had to prove cruelty, rape, desertion, incest or bigamy.

The Bryanston Street case put private detectives firmly in the spotlight. The sacred privacy of domestic life was being undermined by 'agents of private vengeance', according to the press, who were hiring themselves out to 'hunt up private scandals'. Charles Field wrote to the *London Daily News* defending his job. As 'a private individual, and in a free country', he was 'at liberty to give my services to those who may honour me with employment'. But the paper questioned whether bribing servants and boring holes in doors could really be considered an honourable occupation. And what about the Detective Police, were they undertaking private inquiries on the side as well?

The saga of the Bryanston Street detectives, a tale of sex and spying, respectable society and undercover maids, established an image of the private eye that the profession would never quite shake off. But while Charles Field's female helpers were publicly lambasted as morally suspect, he continued to advertise his services until the early 1870s. Four years after his death in 1874, *The Globe* announced a new play, 'The Detective's Watch', based on incidents from his life.

When it came to female sleuths, their role in detection seemed to be clear – ex-inspector Field had needed an insider, someone who could infiltrate a household without being suspected. Women were ideally placed to watch other women, and gather evidence in matrimonial scandals. But, in reality, female detectives in Britain were already being used to investigate a whole host of criminal activity.

4

A SPECIAL DETECTOR

One November afternoon in 1855, a shabbily dressed man entered the first-class waiting room at the Eastern Counties Railway terminus at Shoreditch, east London. His shoes were old, and he carried no luggage, but he settled himself down on a sofa by the fire, next to a table on which passengers had placed their belongings. There was nothing underneath the table except for a travelling bag, which a reverend on his way to Colchester had left unattended while he'd gone to the ticket office. After a while, the shabbily dressed man got up from the sofa and went out onto the platform. Then he returned, grabbed the travelling bag, and ran. Unbeknown to him, however, a female detective had been watching his every move.

Elizabeth Joyes had been working undercover at Shoreditch Station for the past two weeks, following a series of 'adroit robberies' from first-class waiting rooms. Such was the outcry that it had become 'imperatively necessary', explained the press, 'to adopt more than ordinary measures of suppression'. Elizabeth had been sitting opposite the entrance to the waiting room since 10 that morning, but despite her vigilance, the shabbily dressed man had just stolen a reverend's bag from right under her nose.

A week later, however, the same man walked into the waiting room, only this time he was respectably dressed. Elizabeth watched as he sat down on one of the lounges, then she alerted the stationmaster. A few moments later, the Lost Property Officer sauntered into the first-class waiting room, disguised as a passenger. He deposited some valuable luggage under the table and retired to the refreshment room. It wasn't long before a man was arrested on his way out of the station, carrying a stolen dressing case and carpetbag. He was identified as John Curtis, a gentleman who had once worked in the City.

At the Old Bailey trial, Elizabeth Joyes sounded confident. She was 'perfectly certain' and 'quite sure' that this was the man who'd previously stolen the reverend's bag. John Curtis didn't take kindly to being apprehended by a female detective. He demanded to know why she hadn't immediately followed the shabbily dressed man. 'I could not swear at that time whether the man had stolen it or not,' she replied. Then she added, 'You were not dressed as you are now — you were dressed as you are now the second time you came.'

John's defence was unconvincing. He'd thought the man whose luggage he'd taken was a friend; he was simply taking it to him. It had all been a trap and the allegations were nonsense. Did anyone believe that this 'could be done before a woman, a special detector, appointed there for her acute knowledge of all these things'? How could any man come into a waiting room, take a package weighing 40lb, and walk away with it? But the testimony of Elizabeth Joyes was enough; John Curtis was found guilty and sentenced to twelve months in prison.

Was this the first time Elizabeth had been hired for undercover assignments, or was it a regular occurrence? If the police required her services, then they certainly knew where to find her. For the past few years, Elizabeth had been living at 119 Fleet Street, one of six City of London police stations, where she worked as a female searcher. Sixteen officers were listed at the address in the 1851 census, including a police sergeant, Walter Tyler.

Elizabeth's usual job was to search female prisoners, looking for stolen items and other incriminating evidence. A few years earlier, she'd searched a woman charged with stealing a purse in St Paul's Churchyard and found another purse and a stolen handkerchief.

Female searchers were the first women to be officially employed by the police, but they've been largely ignored in the history of policing, and little is known about their lives and careers. A Mrs Batcheldor – Sarah Pearson – worked as a female searcher at Liverpool's Central Bridewell, a police lock-up and holding centre, as early as the 1830s. Her husband was the Bridewell 'keeper' and a former constable, but Sarah received her own annual salary, and was described as a 'shrewd woman'.

Within police stations, female searchers were often constables' wives, who were barred from working in certain professions and were frequently employed as housekeepers and cleaners. But Elizabeth Joyes didn't have any obvious connection to the force. She was a 40-year-old widow, born Elizabeth Woolard in Cambridge, and her late husband had been a shoemaker. She appeared to be living in an extension next door to the police station, along with five constables and two prisoners – a printer and a 'prostitute', presumably housed in police cells. Elizabeth had several roles. Her occupation was 'Housekeeper & Female Searcher', while her relationship to the head of the house was 'Servant'.

The year after solving the railway theft, Elizabeth married Sergeant Walter Tyler. The couple had two children and moved to Bishop's Stortford in Hertfordshire, and their son Walter later became a railway guard. Elizabeth seems to have given up her job as female detective, and doesn't appear in the press again, spending her final years in an almshouse.

Elizabeth Joyes had played a far more active role than the Bryanston Street detectives hired by ex-inspector Charles Field. They'd been employed to gather evidence of illicit sex, but there'd been little actual detection work involved, other than looking through a peephole. The female police searcher, on the other hand, watched out for thieves and mingled with first-class passengers, and unlike the Bryanston Street servants, her evidence was taken seriously at court.

But who was Elizabeth working for? She may have been hired by the railway company on a temporary basis for surveillance duties, as she appeared to report directly to the stationmaster. Or the railways may have approached the City of London Police, and they'd suggested assigning a woman, who might create less suspicion than a male police officer. London's police forces were already employing women for undercover work – and not just Charles Field.

During the Great Exhibition of 1851, when visitors averaged 40,000 a day, female detectives had been 'taken into the police service', explained the press, 'to hang upon the arms of their apparent husbands or brothers'. Their role appeared decorative; they were 'ladies of elegant dress'. But it was still responsible work; the Great Exhibition included displays of military arms, lace, gold and the largest and rarest diamonds in the world.

Other women were enlisted by their police husbands. In 1860, Sarah Dunaway, 'a very intelligent woman', was sent to investigate the theft of large amounts of sugar from the West India Dock in London. Sarah, who was married to a detective police constable, followed a dockworker called

Edward Payne. She watched as he parked his van and horses, entered a beer shop and came out to collect a bag. She had 'no doubt it contained sugar', she told the court, it was 'like the smell of rum, and smelt very strong as I passed him'.

When the dockworker disappeared into the back entrance of a grocer's shop, Sarah went round the front and 'purchased a few trifling articles'. She saw the grocer empty the till and leave the shop. Then she returned to the back door to wait for Edward Payne, who emerged with an empty bag, got in his van and drove away. Two days later, Sarah watched him again, and this time two police constables caught him red-handed, selling stolen sugar. Her testimony at the trial was clear and confident. 'She has given her evidence very well indeed,' said the judge, 'and has acted with consummate tact and judgment. Female witnesses, as I have often had occasion to observe in my thirteen years' experience, generally give the best evidence.' According to *Reynolds's Newspaper*, Sarah Dunaway had 'shown herself capable of a man's work'.

Constables' wives were also used to lay traps. In Manchester, a Mrs Lawton was recruited to catch a suspected burglar. She was sent to an inn, where she pretended to be a broker looking for clothing. When the burglar offered to sell her two bundles of clothes, she accompanied him to a nearby house, gave him £1 and promised to pay the rest if he accompanied her to the railway station. When he arrived, he was promptly arrested.

Other women were sent to infiltrate households, not as a servant like Sarah Grocott but as a respectable lodger. In 1868, the assistant registrar of the Wolverhampton County Court, Samuel Foulkes, absconded with nearly £2,000. His family home was watched night and day, and a private detective was hired to track him down in Liverpool, Southampton, Boulogne, Calais, Paris and Switzerland. Then his family moved to London, where his wife took a house near the suburbs, describing herself as a widow. When the police saw a notice in her window advertising lodgings, they arranged for an unnamed woman detective of 'lady-like address' to be placed in the house. She pretended to be a governess and 'did her work so well' that when Samuel Foulkes – who'd been hiding in France – rejoined his family, the police were there to arrest him. According to one report, this undercover detective had been 'introduced into the service', while others described her as an amateur.

The British police appeared to have a wide range of female helpers. When an elderly woman named Judith Newton appeared in court in Bradford charged with loitering and refusing to leave the streets, a local superintendent testified to her good character. She had 'acted as detective' for the police on several occasions, he explained, and so the case was dismissed.

It's not clear whether Sarah Dunaway, Mrs Lawton, or the ladylike governess were formally hired by the police, or even if they were paid. And to what extent did they use their own initiative, rather than simply acting under instructions?

Female detectives often showed a real zeal for the job, and Mrs Williams, 'a good-looking, middle-aged Welsh woman', travelled miles in search of her target. She journeyed to Liverpool to track down William Roberts, who was accused of neglecting his family. He'd gone to America and left his son in the care of the parish, but now he was back in England.

Mrs Williams was married to a relieving officer, who was responsible for the welfare of the poor, sick and infirm. He had already been to Liverpool twice with an arrest warrant for William Roberts but hadn't been able to find him. So his wife 'took the matter out of his hands', explained the press, found the suspect at an inn and accompanied by a local police detective, apprehended him on the spot.

At the trial in 1857, Detective Smith from the Liverpool Police entered the witness box, while 'the female detective, Mrs. Williams, stood by the side of the witness box, her countenance beaming with satisfaction'. The prosecutor explained that William Roberts had been apprehended by 'this officer', but the magistrates were perplexed. Then one leaned forward, saw Mrs Williams, and exclaimed, 'Oh, she's the officer!' The discovery was followed by much laughter in court.

By the 1860s, the term 'female detective' was often applied to any plucky woman who caught a crook – especially if it was a man. When a rough-looking fellow broke into a house near Greenwich and stole some silver plate, the cook, Ann Smith, seized him by the shoulders, grabbed his collar and shook him violently until the police arrived. The magistrate was impressed, 'Young woman, you have behaved very courageously in this matter, and I think you would make a good detective. I only wish I had half your ability.'

However, while female detectives were often described admiringly by the British press, the tone was nearly always humorous. Victorian women were supposed to depend on the protection of men, not chase after suspects, seize back stolen goods and bring offenders to justice. The idea of women being capable of a 'man's work' was troubling, and when female detectives appeared in court their very existence caused confusion and laughter.

Over in America, however, the Pinkerton National Detective Agency was sending women on death-defying wartime missions. The Pinkerton Agency had been formed in 1850 by Glasgow-born ex-Chicago police officer Allan Pinkerton, whose 'operatives' were employed by railroad lines, attorneys and law enforcement departments.

One afternoon in 1856, a woman called Kate Warne came to his private office, and he assumed she was looking for a job as a secretary. Her features were 'decidedly intellectual,' he noted, and she seemed to possess 'the masculine attributes of firmness and decision'. Allan explained it was not the custom to employ women as detectives, but asked what she thought she could do. When Kate offered to 'worm out secrets' in places that male detectives couldn't access, he decided to give her a chance, and soon she became his 'lady superintendent'.

Kate was in her late 20s and reportedly a widow. She'd originally wanted to become an actress and now she put her performance skills to good use. In 1858, she investigated a freight company manager, Nathan Maroney, who was accused of stealing $50,000. She went undercover as 'Madam Imbert' and befriended Nathan's wife, who eventually led her to the stolen money.

Kate's most famous case came in February 1861, when President Elect Abraham Lincoln set out to Washington for his inauguration. Kate had been working undercover in Baltimore, befriending the wives and daughters of conspirators planning an assassination, and now she successfully secreted Lincoln into Washington, organising transportation, disguises and protection.

Kate Warne was not the only female operative employed by the Pinkerton National Detective Agency; others surreptitiously sketched submarines and uncovered weaponry plans, using a cipher code to pass on messages written in invisible ink. But it was the Abraham Lincoln case which became the stuff of legend. Allan Pinkerton reportedly came up with his agency's slogan – 'We never sleep' – as a result, as well as a logo featuring an open eye.

Kate Warne's role in the investigation, and in the agency itself, varies depending on who is telling the tale. But after her death in 1868, her obituaries made for inspiring reading. She was 'the first female detective in the United States, if not the world', and portrayed as a mythological figure – 'strong, pure, and devoted' – who set rigid rules of discipline and morality. Her career sounded a lot more exciting than the job of the female detective in Britain, where despite the variety of work, the profession was still associated with matrimonial scandals. But one woman was about to take on far more dangerous missions, by infiltrating criminal gangs for Scotland Yard.

5

CLUBNOSE

Late one winter's evening, somewhere in the depths of London's East End, a gang of thieves were hiding out from the police when suddenly one of their older members became worried. He had recently been released from prison and didn't recognise the new member of the gang, a boy sitting quietly in the corner. So he gestured at the boy and demanded the thieves' password.

When the boy failed to answer, the gang turned on him. They pulled off his hat, ripped off his coat and discovered he was none other than Clubnose, a notorious female detective. The furious thieves welted her with pokers, iron bars and legs of chairs until she was left a 'mess o' jelly'. But before they knocked her completely senseless, she managed to smash her hand through a pane of glass, blow her whistle and shake her rattle, and the police rushed in and rescued her. Clubnose had fourteen pieces of bone extracted from her head but, undaunted, she returned to work.

The mysterious Clubnose appeared in several reports in the late 1870s, including the *Pictorial World*, *Chamber's Journal*, *The Sporting Gazette* and *The Times of India*. There were several versions of her story, but the basics remained the same, and various journalists claimed to have known her. She was a 'female tough', with muscular strength and a harsh voice. She also possessed the 'most hideous and repulsive face' ever seen on man or woman, after surviving an attack by waterside ruffians. The police knew her as 'Clubnose' but her real name, according to *Chamber's Journal*, was Margaret Saunders.

Her career had started sometime in the 1850s, while working as a cleaner in London. One night her master was robbed, mutilated and left for dead, and Margaret was arrested. She was soon released because of lack of evidence but felt so horrified at the false accusation that she vowed never to rest until she'd brought the real offender to justice.

A few days later, Margaret ended up in hospital after falling down a flight of steps. Here she overheard a woman in the next bed talking about a friend who'd recently been charged with a crime. Margaret instinctively knew that this was the man she was after, and the moment she left hospital she tracked him all the way to Glasgow. Nearly eighteen months after the assault on her employer, Margaret Saunders had collected enough evidence and went to Scotland Yard; the assailant was arrested and sentenced to life.

Margaret was praised by the judge for her 'sagacity and acuteness' and told she was 'a born detective'. The press launched a public subscription to reward her courage, and a journalist was sent to interview Margaret, accompanied by an inspector from Scotland Yard. They found her living among some very unsavoury society in a filthy den near the London Docks.

She refused to have anything to do with a reward. She had caught the villains 'for my own sake, and nobody else's. I meant rightin' of myself, and I have righted myself.' But then she had an idea – if the inspector genuinely admired her skills, 'I'll tell ye what ye can do to show it … make me one o' yourselves. If I'm as good as you say, I might be worth something in your line. Make me one o' yourselves – a detective.'

The inspector was somewhat taken aback, but he approached the authorities at Scotland Yard and Margaret Saunders was duly 'enrolled' as a female detective. She tracked down a murderous gang of coiners, worked undercover in hospitals, nursing patients whose 'honesty was suspected by the authorities', and she also moved in wealthier circles.

One journalist met her after two of his lady friends had been robbed of valuable jewellery. He was sitting alone after dinner one evening when a servant announced a visitor, a respectable-looking woman wearing a thick veil. Once the servant had left the room, the woman threw back her veil and declared, 'I am Margaret Saunders, from the Detective Department.' She had discovered a very important piece of evidence, and before long, the jewellery thieves were caught.

Clubnose died in London in March 1877, according to the press, not long after she was attacked by the gang of East End thieves. But was she a real person, or just a figment of journalistic imagination? And how was a woman with such a 'remarkable physiognomy' not instantly recognised wherever she went?

Saunders was a common name, and yet there is only one matching death registered for a Margaret Saunders who died in London in March 1877, a 43-year-old woman in Islington. She'd been born Margaret Bentley and was married to a filter manufacturer, but her death certificate shows she'd actually died at the end of 1876.

Clubnose sounded like a fictional character, and she bore more than a passing resemblance to some of the female detectives beginning to appear in popular literature. They too were mysterious figures, and especially 'Miss Gladden', the star of Andrew Forrester's *The Female Detective*, published in 1864. 'Who am I?' she asks in the novel's opening line, 'It can matter little who I am.' Her background is kept deliberately ambiguous; she may have become a detective because she had 'no other means of making a living', or because she had a longing for detection that she simply couldn't overcome. She may be a widow, working to support her children, or she may be 'an unmarried woman, whose only care is herself'.

Her professional status is also unclear. She calls herself a police officer and 'one of the secret police', who is paid by the government. But she is an independent operator, who answers to no one in her quest for justice and retribution. Miss Gladden keeps her job a secret – her friends 'suppose I am a dressmaker' – and even her name is an alias that she uses while working undercover. But she stresses the advantages of being a woman, for it meant 'far greater opportunities than a man of intimate watching'.

This wasn't the first novel to feature a female detective. In 1862, Edward Ellis' *Ruth the Betrayer; or, The Female Spy* was an action-packed series of stories in which Ruth Trail works for the London Police and wears a whistle round her neck to summon them. She is 'a sort of spy we use in the hanky-panky way when a man would be too clumsy', explains one officer. But Ruth is also attached to a 'notorious Secret Intelligence Office', and ultimately, she works for herself, making use of the police to extract revenge on her enemies.

Ruth has delicate features and a profusion of golden ringlets, but she's a cold-blooded woman with 'a strangely savage expression' – and she seems to enjoy dicing with death.

William Stephens Hayward's *Revelations of a Lady Detective*, published the same year as *The Female Detective*, also featured a thrilling protagonist.

Mrs Paschal is a 'well born and well educated' widow, driven to detective work to support her children, and she occasionally carries a Colt revolver. She receives her assignments directly from Colonel Warner, the head of the London Detective Police. When she is sent undercover to investigate a dangerous secret society, she discovers their hideaway on the Isle of Dogs and alerts the police with a shrill whistle, just like Clubnose and Ruth Trail.

Female detectives were also appearing on the stage, such as in the long-running play *The Female Detective; or, The Foundling of the Streets*. Other stage shows included *Frolicsome Fanny* and *The Wrong Mr Wright*.

These were hardly conventional Victorian heroines. Miss Gladden, Ruth Trail and Mrs Paschal were assertive and active. They took risks and survived dangerous missions. But detective novels with female protagonists wouldn't become really popular until later in the century, when male private inquiry agents began openly boasting about female detectives for hire.

6

SECRET WATCHINGS

Thirty years after ex-inspector Charles Field had opened his Inquiry Office in Westminster, the world of private detection had grown considerably, partly fuelled by the change in divorce laws. By the mid-1880s, adverts for Private Inquiry Agents appeared regularly in newspaper personal columns, alongside lovers' messages, lost property and clearance sales. The agencies were often run by former police detectives, and some combined private inquiries with debt collecting, house sales or accounting.

One of London's largest and best-known agencies was Slater's Private Detective Offices, opened by Henry Slater around 1885 on Basinghall Street in the City. Henry was a self-proclaimed expert in 'secret watchings, ascertaining where people go, what they do, the company they keep etc'. His agency was the 'only acknowledged establishment of this description in the City of London', although newspaper adverts from other firms suggest this wasn't the case.

Henry Slater was a dashing figure, with a neat handlebar moustache and well-oiled hair. He was born George Tinsley, according to his own account, but he had an ever-shifting identity. 'How many different names have you had in the course of your career?' asked the Solicitor General, during one cross-examination. Henry admitted there had been 'a great many'.

He'd started off as a pawnbroker's assistant in Fleet Street and was something of a showman, who later lent his endorsement to St Jacobs Oil, said to cure rheumatic pain. Henry recruited his agents through newspaper adverts, but he didn't seem keen on those from the force – 'Ex Police Officers please not apply'.

The private detective industry was dominated by men, but there were occasional references to women working independently. In 1877, Mary Ann Rumper took a client to court over an unpaid bill after obtaining evidence for a Mrs Mullins, a music publisher in the City of London, who was seeking a divorce. Mary Ann Rumper had promised to provide evidence of Mr Mullins' affair with a servant girl, with whom he'd had a child. She had located a witness, kept watch over her and provided 'some necessaries', and she'd also watched Mr Mullins for eight months, with the assistance of another female detective. The court was told that private detection was a 'peculiar vocation' for a woman but 'in these days of agitation for women's rights', there was no reason she shouldn't receive payment, and Mrs Mullins was instructed to pay a further £12.

Caroline Smith, a machinist from Kent, also worked for herself. She was married to an ex-police officer turned private inquiry agent, who deserted her and their children and ran off with the family income. So Caroline established herself as a private detective as well, carrying out inquiries for solicitors.

In the summer of 1880, she went to court to ask for a protection order against her husband, to protect her goods, furniture and earnings. The order was granted, and the following year Caroline was living on the Holloway Road, with her five children. Her occupation was still Private Inquiry Agent, but she doesn't appear to have advertised her services in the press.

Henry Slater, meanwhile, was eager to promote his use of women detectives and by 1887, he boasted of an unlimited staff of experienced female agents. But while he saw himself as a pioneer, he wasn't the first to do this. A dozen years earlier, Arthur Montagu, who offered confidential inquiries and 'family difficulties adjusted' from his City of London agency, had a 'large staff' of experienced female detectives. Ernest Leslie in High Holborn also employed women agents – but it wasn't until the end of the nineteenth century that references to female staff became standard practice.

One of the reasons for this new interest was a series of murders in and around Whitechapel in 1888, which the press blamed on 'Jack the Ripper'. If the authorities wanted to capture the 'demon of Whitechapel', argued writer and suffrage campaigner Frances Power Cobbe, then why not employ women? On 11 October, she wrote to *The Times*, arguing that 'a clever woman of unobtrusive dress and appearance ... would possess over masculine rivals not a few advantages'. A woman could move unsuspected through the streets, extract gossip from other women, and 'employ that gift of intuitive quickness and "mother wit" with which her sex is commonly credited'. *The Globe* found 'much good sense' in the suggestion. The plain-clothes officer was too familiar to the habitual criminal, but the female detective would bring the peculiarly feminine trait of 'instinct' rather than reason.

The roots of female intuition lay in the 'subhuman stage', according to Victorian scientists. It was part of women's 'maternal instinct', and its purpose was to protect a mother and her offspring from danger. While men relied on the 'masculine' skills of intellect and abstract reasoning, women possessed the instinctive skill of intuition, which was closely linked with emotion. There was no time for reflection or deliberation, explained American sociologist Lester Frank Ward, 'she must act at once or all is lost'. But this action was only defensive, for women were naturally conservative and cautious, never took risks and always chose the safest option. Intuition was an almost miraculous gift, explained one commentator, although others dismissed feminine instinct as simply jumping to conclusions.

By the time of the Whitechapel murders, there were plenty of female sleuths available for hire in London, according to the *Echo*, either in the 'regular or casual employ of the Private Inquiry and Investigation Offices'. A few days after Frances Power Cobbe's letter to *The Times*, the *Echo* sent a journalist to visit an eminent firm in the City. 'Women are often useful to us here,' explained the agency's owner, 'I employ numbers of them in, say, divorce or money cases, and I can meet the wants of all classes by providing them with women of all ranks, from a Russian Princess or a Polish Countess down to a factory girl.' This, presumably, was Henry Slater, based in the City and never shy about talking to the press. A good female detective, he explained, was 'the cruelest, most devilish creature under the sun'. She had to drop her beautiful womanly attributes and be 'fiendishly calculating and foreseeing'. But the job sounded worth it, some women were paid £200 a year – four times the average annual wage in England – and they were provided with 'unlimited money' in case of emergency.

Henry Slater introduced the journalist to one of his agents – a woman in her mid-20s who'd joined the agency as a copying clerk. She wore a neatly made black dress and jacket and a pretty black bonnet adorned with coloured flowers, and she looked like a typical shop girl or middle-class governess. 'I thought that the detective work seemed interesting,' she explained, 'and would be easy to me.'

She'd been sent to a Nottingham lace factory which suspected that a rival house had obtained their designs. A staggering sum of £25,000 was at stake, and after joining the workforce, she soon identified the culprit. She also worked undercover in private houses as a lady's maid and nurse-maid, 'I have been in all sorts of domestic scenes, some of them terribly rough ones'.

She had tracked guilty parties to Berlin, and had 'often been dogged myself by detectives on the other side'. Only the night before, she'd been followed to an underground station and had to give her pursuers the slip. When the journalist asked, 'Have you no compunction in telling the secrets, or convicting the guilty one?', she replied, 'Not in the slightest. It is my business to do so.'

The *Echo* journalist also visited the head of a detective agency near Charing Cross, who was less enthusiastic about female detectives. It was true that a woman could enter a house, shop or factory, but she was 'of little use' for outdoor watching and tracking. A female attracted too much attention; she wouldn't be the slightest use in the Whitechapel murder cases.

The unnamed detective then raised the issue of respectability. How would a woman who was 'morally all that she ought to be' behave on night duty? If a man offered her a drink and she refused, he would wonder what she was doing out alone after dark. If she accepted the drink, she would be among very dubious company, and they would spot her true calling at once. Women had been 'tried enough already as detectives' and aside from investigations of a domestic nature, men were 'the best at this class of work'. Female detectives could be compromised and corrupted, they just weren't up to the job.

Yet according to the press, female sleuths were springing up every-where. They were smiling seductively over the counters of West End shops, waiting tables as demure domestics, even titled ladies were 'not above turning an honest penny at this delicate occupation'. Soon, the Londoner would be tempted to doubt every female who 'seeks to make herself pleasant'.

There was something very duplicitous about female detectives, even more so than their male counterparts. Women were deceitful by nature, according to criminologist Cesare Lombroso, whose hugely influential book *Criminal Woman, the Prostitute, and the Normal Woman* was published in English in 1895. 'Lying is habitual and almost physiological in women,' he declared. It is 'so organic that they are unaware of it'.

One unnamed female detective, 'Miss –', insisted there were very few women in the profession, and only one in London who worked 'on her own account'. 'Miss –' had begun her career working for the Paris Police, before being recruited by a London agency. She had shadowed a South American general, disguised herself as a French Sister of Mercy to follow a bomb-carrying anarchist and investigated a great bank robbery by pretending to fall in love with the bank manager. While an ordinary woman might think this 'very unwomanly', she regarded it as 'a mere matter of business'.

The Charing Cross detective had dismissed the abilities of women, but detection was beginning to be seen as a viable job. An 1894 handbook of women's employment, *What Our Daughters Can Do for Themselves*, surveyed around fifty occupations, from dressmaking, embroidery and knitting to more modern professions like medicine, journalism, clerkships, telegraphy and shop work. The shortest section in the book was devoted to private detectives, and the author was astonished to find the occupation so overcrowded. One firm had recently advertised for assistants – and received 1,800 applications.

In fiction, meanwhile, professional female detectives were becoming more common. Leonard Merrick's *Mr Bazalgette's Agent*, published in 1888, featured 28-year-old Miriam Lea, a former actress and governess, in dire need of a job. She is a 'lady of brains', explains a fellow lodger, who brings her attention to a newspaper advert for Alfred Bazalgette's Inquiry Office in High Holborn, which has 'agents of both sexes'.

Miriam is an 'adventuress', sharp-witted and with a longing to be successful, but acutely aware this isn't a job for a lady. Private detection is 'not honourable', it will ostracise her from society, and she will be an object of 'general abhorrence'. Miriam is sent to find a clerk who is accused of fraud and sets off to Hamburg with a colleague, Emma Dunstan, who pretends to be her maid. 'The work is not so bad as I had feared,' she muses. 'There is an excitement about it, and you live like a lady.' The two 'female police-agents' end up in the diamond mines of South Africa, where Miriam's fledgling detective career comes to an abrupt halt when she falls in love with the man she is supposed to bring to justice.

Five years later, another fictional sleuth made her debut, the indomitable Loveday Brooke, who works for a Fleet Street agency. She first appeared in a series of stories in *The Ludgate Monthly* in 1893, *The Experiences of Loveday Brooke, Lady Detective*, by Catherine Louisa Pirkis. Loveday is in her early 30s, neat and prim, with 'nondescript' features and always dressed in black. She has a shrewd brain and plenty of common sense, and like her forebear Sherlock Holmes, she methodically follows the links in the chain of reasoning. But while one reviewer praised the stories, he was 'just afraid Miss Brooke is too clever in catching criminals ever to catch a husband'.

Miriam Lea and Loveday Brooke were just two of several fictional female detectives to appear at the end of the nineteenth century – although most remained amateurs, not paid professionals. The period saw a boom in magazines and periodicals, many of which carried crime stories, as well as the emergence of the 'New Woman', an independent, educated figure, with increasing control over her own life.

Public debates about the 'Great Woman Question' raised issues of suffrage, education, equality and emancipation. Women were earning university degrees, becoming dentists and doctors, and lobbying for the right to vote. Nearly a third of the female population were now employed in the workforce, and women were increasingly visible in public spaces. What better figure to express this new social order than a female detective? There were more stage plays as well; *Bilberry of Tilbury* even featured an all-female detective agency, run by actress Miss Stella Dashwood.

Henry Slater capitalised on this interest in female sleuths. By the mid-1890s, his lady detectives came in 'all' ages and sizes, as well as all nationalities. 'WOMEN – Many men say women have been their downfall,' declared his advert in the *Daily Telegraph*, 'but HENRY SLATER owes his success to his lady detectives work of which he is the pioneer.' Henry also attempted to recruit women to join Slater's Army of Cyclist Detectives, 'Must be expert riders, well up in the art of disguising, and write shorthand'. But the image of real-life female detectives remained morally dubious, and especially those with links to men like Henry Slater, two of whom were about to stand trial for entrapment and blackmail.

A PROFESSION FOR CHARLATANS

In the spring of 1892, a young woman called Gertrude Barrett found herself friendless in London and sorely in need of a companion. She was in the process of going through a messy divorce from Edward Barrett, a civil servant she'd met in India. A few weeks after their wedding in London, she'd left him after a 'disagreement'. She had then filed for divorce, accusing Edward of cruelty, and her solicitors sent her to Slater's Detective Agency. Now she was alone in the capital waiting for her day in court, and so she was delighted when a woman called Countess Carina sought her acquaintance.

When Gertrude moved to a boarding house in Earls Court, she made another friend – Mrs Watson, a society lady who 'spoke very well'. Mrs Watson's husband was an electrical engineer and away a great deal; she had a lonely life, having no children. 'She told me all her troubles,' explained Gertrude, 'and I told her mine, and she asked if I would be her companion.'

The two women seemed to have a lot in common, and both had 'bad' husbands. One day, while walking near Victoria Station, Gertrude saw her estranged husband, Edward, in the street. Mrs Watson offered to follow him and bring back evidence 'if he went anywhere where he ought not', and Gertrude gratefully agreed. Mrs Watson watched Edward all day long on top of an omnibus, and she could tell he was a cad because he 'winked and blinked at her all the time'.

The two women moved to new lodgings together in Pimlico, and one evening, Mrs Watson suggested a trip to the theatre to cheer them up.

She introduced Gertrude to a Mr Stephens of the Stock Exchange, and he asked her to go to a private hotel. But she refused, so they all went for supper and champagne.

Mrs Watson seemed very keen that Gertrude should meet a man. She introduced her to two gentlemen at the Alhambra Theatre and suggested if Gertrude went to a hotel with one, she would go with the other. When Gertrude declined, she was introduced to Charles Wilson, the son of an MP, and he too pressed her to go to a private hotel.

Charles seemed like a gentleman, with a good appearance and good manners. He spoke like an educated man and Gertrude saw 'nothing caddish about him'. Charles took her for supper, promised her diamonds and a trip in his yacht, and confessed he had 'taken a fancy' to her. Gertrude agreed to spend the week with him in St John's Wood, but then she changed her mind. The risk was too great; she was still a married woman, what if her husband found out? Mrs Watson called her a fool, and Gertrude felt so 'over persuaded' that she agreed to return to Charles, although she insisted nothing improper took place.

Then the two female friends fell out. In April 1892, Gertrude Barrett accused Mrs Watson of stealing a diamond ring, as well as the pawn tickets for three more rings. It appeared to be around this time that Gertrude realised her friend and confidante, the lonely society lady looking for a companion, was in fact an undercover private detective. The stockbroker she'd been introduced to at the theatre was actually Henry John Clarke, a private inquiry agent based on Cockspur St in Charing Cross, who also used the name George Clarke. He'd been hired by Gertrude's husband, and with the help of Mrs Watson, he had tried to persuade Gertrude to 'misconduct herself'.

Mrs Watson stood trial over the missing diamond ring and was acquitted, but the prosecution hinted of a wicked conspiracy afoot. When the Barretts' divorce petitions came to court a few months later, Gertrude accused her husband of hitting her with a parasol, locking her in a room and threatening to poison her. But this was dismissed, as were her husband's allegations of adultery, for it was now all too clear that private detectives were involved.

In January 1895, Mrs Watson and Henry Clarke were charged with conspiracy to pervert the course of justice and attempting to persuade Gertrude to have a 'carnal connection' with another man. 'As God is my judge,' declared Mrs Watson, 'I never had anything to do with such a thing, but I am very sorry indeed for Mrs. Barrett.' She initially gave her name as Lawrence, but then identified herself as Ellen Lyons (or Lyon), a 30-year-old lodging housekeeper in Westminster. When the police queried this, she replied, 'That is the name I am known by in this case.' Ellen explained that her husband was a private detective and they often had to change their names. She had worked on a good many cases for Henry Clarke, 'but I only go where a stylishly-dressed person is required'.

Henry Clarke, meanwhile, dismissed the allegations as preposterous. 'My business has always been conducted properly; I do not believe there is an inquiry office in London more respectable than mine; I am quite innocent of any conspiracy.' But the couple were found guilty. Henry was sentenced to two years' hard labour, while Ellen was sent to Holloway Prison for twelve months.

Once again, the methods of private detectives were under scrutiny. *Lloyd's Weekly* provided an illustration of Mrs Gertrude Barrett, looking fresh-faced, youthful and worried, while Ellen Lyons, the stern-faced lady detective, resembled a fairy-tale witch.

Ellen had gone to great lengths to entrap young Gertrude and the case had involved a lot of planning, arranging and patience. She had located her target, become a fellow lodger in her house, persuaded Gertrude they should live together, devoted nearly two months to befriending, listening and talking to her new friend, quite apart from numerous visits to the theatre. Did she have any misgivings about the entrapment, or did she see it as simply her job? And who exactly was Ellen Lyons?

There are no clues in the press reports about where she came from. She was apparently born around 1865, but so were many other Ellen Lyons. Was Lyons her birth name, or was it Lawrence? If she was married to a private detective, then what was his first name?

A couple of months after Ellen's conviction, another woman detective was in court. Paulowna Upperley also had links to Henry Slater. She had worked for his agency before starting her own inquiry business under the name 'Madame Paul'. In 1891, she'd been hired to investigate Elizabeth Price, who lived with her husband near Bristol. Paulowna introduced herself as a baroness, and while 'worming' her way into Elizabeth's confidence, she discovered a previous affair and apparently used it to blackmail the couple. When they refused to pay up, she took them to court, suing them for unpaid debts of £81.

Paulowna was described in court as Polish, and the wife of Major Upperley of the Bengal Cavalry. But, as with Ellen Lyons, her real identity is impossible to pin down. The judge dismissed the case, and *Lloyds Weekly* again provided court sketches; Mrs Price looked regal and ladylike, while Paulowna the lady detective looked haggard.

Female private detectives provided perfect fodder for the press, especially when it came to adultery. In August 1896, the *Illustrated Police News* carried a huge front-page illustration with the headline 'Caught! A Guilty Pair Tracked by a Female Detective'. The picture showed a dishevelled woman in bed, a man grabbing his clothes and a furious lady detective at the doorway, ordering him to leave. An inset also showed the female detective crouched in the hallway, her eye pressed against a keyhole.

The smartly dressed, 'sun-browned little woman' was the wife of an inquiry agent and ex-police constable. She'd been hired to follow a Mrs Hughes, whose husband suspected she was having an affair with his friend, Tudor Williams, an inventor of patent medicines. The lady detective had been on watch as the couple checked into a hotel in south Wales, and informed the landlord, who 'assembled the domestics' and they proceeded to the room. When they threw open the door, Mrs Hughes was in bed in her dressing gown, while Tudor Williams was clad in 'extremely light attire'. 'My God, we are discovered,' declared Mrs Hughes. At which the lady detective handed Tudor her husband's business card and retired. Mr Hughes obtained the divorce and £600 damages.

Female detectives seemed to be very successful at catching adulterers, but according to the American police they weren't much good at anything else. 'My experience,' declared one Californian police detective, 'is that they are a failure.' Women were led by their passions, working from 'intuition', not reason based on facts. They couldn't keep their mouths shut and were too elated at their 'secret power'. They were only useful in spying out evidence for divorce cases, 'and that is not exactly detective work'. No respectable woman would engage in keyhole peeping and eavesdropping.

The British press agreed. Private detection meant associating with thieves, profligates, dissipation and debauchery, explained *Ally Sloper's Half-Holiday*, and 'a female who enters this profession with that knowledge ceases to be a woman any longer'. It was a 'most objectionable' job for well-brought-up girls, according to *Hearth and Home* magazine, which was appalled that so many well-educated ladies had written to enquire about private detection.

Henry Slater dismissed such slurs and continued to advertise his detective services until the early 1900s, offering 'any character in life from his Staff of Female Detectives'. But then in 1904, he was again charged with conspiracy to pervert the course of justice, along with three of his detectives and a solicitor. This time, they'd attempted to get a man to 'procure' himself, plying him with alcohol and taking him to a house of bad repute. The press called for agencies like Slater's to be 'stamped out'; their methods were loathsome, dangerous and a 'terror to private life'. But Henry Slater was found not guilty and left the Old Bailey a free man.

It had been nearly half a century since ex-inspector Charles Field had hired a former cook to spy on her mistress in Bryanston Street, and private detectives were still invading privacy – as well as perverting the course of justice, using entrapment and fabricating evidence. Henry Slater insisted that his was a respectable business, and so did Henry Clarke, yet it was clearly an industry in which any crook could succeed. Britain's private detectives continued to operate outside the rules, and despite criminal trials and public outrage, they had little regard for the law.

8

ASSESSMENT DAY

'Dear Students, Your Assessment Day is confirmed as Thursday 15th June, 2021. Registration commences at 0930 hours.'

It's a boiling hot morning and I'm standing opposite Micky's Fish & Chips in Paddington, waiting to begin a revision session for the Level 3 Award for Professional Investigators. It's been two months since I passed my online assessment and for the past few days, I've been hurriedly going over reams of legislation.

We've been asked to stand by a gated alleyway opposite Micky's Fish & Chips, where our trainer Will Clayton will meet us. He's the co-owner of Bluemoon Investigations and has been training PIs for the Association of British Investigators (ABI) for the past ten years. I'd pictured a retired police inspector in his late 60s, but the man waiting by the alleyway is at least a decade younger, casually dressed in jeans and a checked shirt. I think of my brother asking me last night what I'm wearing for the exam; he suggested a raincoat, hat, pipe and slippers.

There were supposed to be four people sitting the Level 3 today, but two have just dropped out citing Covid. I'm disappointed, I was hoping to chat to other trainee PIs to find out why they've chosen this career.

Will unlocks the gate, and we walk across a courtyard and into what appears to be the offices of a TV production company. I thought we'd be doing the Level 3 at the offices of Bluemoon Investigations, but Will explains they are at an 'undisclosed location', and this is the venue they use for exams. We climb a spiral staircase up to a small, top-floor boardroom, where leather armchairs are placed around a table.

The BTEC course was designed ten years ago as a way for PIs to prove competency and to make sure they act lawfully. It hasn't changed much since then, aside from the addition of data protection regulation. Will explains he prefers the title Professional Investigator rather than Private Investigator; the latter has negative connotations because there's still no regulation.

'Anyone who fancies it can become a PI,' he says, sitting down on a swivel chair. 'We're less regulated than brothels.'

Will's detective career began while working at a pub, when he was seconded to a stock and audit department. Barrels of beer were going missing, and he was asked to investigate. 'It was my first UC work,' he says.

'UC?' I ask.

'Undercover,' Will laughs. 'Oh, we do love TLAs.'

'TLAs?'

Will laughs again, 'Three letter acronyms.'

He worked overseas, then returned to England and joined Bluemoon Investigations, eventually buying the company. Around a quarter of the inquiries they receive are matrimonial, 'but once they get a quote,' says Will, 'they usually give up'. Today, he does a lot of close protection work – body guarding – as well as surveillance and investigating fraud. He's just telling me how to spot when someone's about to get aggressive, when the other examinee arrives and he presses a buzzer to let her in.

A young woman comes up the stairs, she's in her late 20s and looks efficient and well prepared, with a takeaway coffee in one hand and a bottle of water in the other. As she sits down at the table, I notice a tattoo on her forearm. How interesting, I think, that someone so young wants to be a PI.

'Why do you want to be a private investigator?' I ask, as Will goes downstairs to close the door.

The woman smiles, 'I already am one.'

'Oh,' I say, embarrassed. 'Who do you work for?'

'I'm a case officer,' she says. 'I work for a specialist legal intelligence provider.'

'Oh,' I say again, not really sure what this means. 'Who are your clients?'

'High net worth individuals,' she says, taking a sip of coffee, 'and multi-national businesses.' Her employer is a member of the ABI, she explains, and has sponsored her training. Once she has the qualification, she can become an individual member of the ABI as well.

'Have you always been interested in detective work?'

The case officer smiles, 'Ever since I was a kid. One Christmas, I asked for a pair of binoculars because I wanted to spy on my brother. I also had a plastic gun,' she laughs, 'with a microphone to listen in on my parents. And I loved the movie *Spy Kids*! I'm nosey; I want to know what's going on.'

'Are people surprised at what you do for a living?'

The case officer sighs, 'They're shocked and surprised; they've usually never met a PI before. *Everyone* asks how I got into it, that's always the first question. They think I follow people who are having affairs, that it's all cloak and dagger surveillance. Some of it can be, but it's more about fraud, corruption and global risk.'

I'm just about to ask her more when Will Clayton comes back into the boardroom; it's time to start our three-hour revision. He hands us a mock exam and explains that the pass mark for the final exam is 70 per cent. We work our way silently through the questions, then take turns reading out our answers.

We're both doing well, and the case officer barely gets any wrong at all. We discuss some of the issues raised – data protection, privacy, corroboration of evidence, using a GPS tracker on private property and the need to caution an interviewee if they start to incriminate themselves in a criminal matter. Will stresses that as PIs we should follow the regulations for the police.

'What authority do PIs have?' he asks. 'None. As a professional investigator, I know where to look, and what to ask.' Then he laughs, 'Although people often think I have a special database, codes and buttons.'

He tells us to put ourselves in the shoes of the people we watch and think about when they would expect privacy. If they're coming out of a pub holding hands, there's no expectation of privacy. But if they're in their bedroom, then there is. I ask about Matt Hancock, the health minister who has just resigned after being filmed on CCTV 'snogging' an aide and breaching Covid rules. Will says the minister would have expected privacy in his own office, but the full details of the case – and who leaked the CCTV footage – are unlikely to ever come out.

He gathers in our mock papers and tells us about the final exam. We won't have exactly the same questions, as they come from a pool.

Examinees only pass or fail, there are no grades, and we won't know which questions we got wrong. Every year, around 100 people complete PI training through Bluemoon College, and while it's been erratic during the Covid pandemic, Will says numbers are on the rise. 'You'll do well,' he says. 'Normally, I get people to tot up their scores in the mock exams and you didn't even have to do that.'

When we return after our lunch break, an exams officer has set up two laptops on the table, while another man is ready to photocopy our ID and proof of address. Will leaves, the exams officer shows us how to do a test run on our laptop, then we enter a password and we're ready. At the end, he explains, we'll be able to see all the questions and answers, so we can review everything before we finish.

I'm feeling nervous now. This is the final stage of weeks of reading and research, and after three hours of revision my mind isn't feeling too sharp. It's so hot in the room, the air is muggy even with the window open, and I have to read the first question several times.

'You're investigating a case of adoption ...' it begins. 'Which of these should you do first?' I don't think we've covered any cases of adoption on the course, and I'm not sure of the right answer. There are also lots of questions on video surveillance, even what type of camera to use. I can't see any questions on acronyms, but there are plenty on conflict of interest. I peep over my laptop at the case officer, she's also frowning at her screen.

I decide to work through the exam quickly, knowing I'll have plenty of time to go back through my answers at the end. After I've answered the last question, I wait for all the questions to come up on the screen, as they did in the midway assessment. But instead, there are a series of boxes, green ones indicate unanswered questions, and as none are green and I've answered them all, I press 'finish'.

And that's it, my exam is over. The results go off to Pearson. I haven't had the chance to reread a single one. I've just done a forty-five-minute exam in eight minutes.

In a panic, I put my hand up. The exams officer comes over, confirms that there is nothing I can do. If I'd wanted to see my answers, then I should have clicked on each individual box. The case officer is still busy with her exam, so I quickly drink half a bottle of water and start the second paper. But many of the questions feel unfamiliar, and at this point there is little I can do; I've already messed up the first exam.

'That's almost a record,' says the exams officer when I put my hand up for the last time.

Less than twenty minutes after starting my BTEC Level 3 Award for Professional Investigators, I'm back outside Micky's Fish & Chips, trying to get an Uber home.

'How are you?' the driver asks as I get in the car.

'Awful,' I burst out. 'I think I just failed an exam.'

'What are you studying?' he asks.

'Private investigation.'

'What?' the cab driver turns around.

'Private investigation, you know, like a private detective? Well, actually they call it *professional* investigation, but ...'

'Oh, so you like go into a business and see if they're following the law?'

'Not really,' I say. 'It's more like, you know ...' But my mind is so jumbled I can't think how to explain it. 'You know, like a detective, but not with the police. A *private* detective. So, theft, fraud, missing people ...' I deliberately don't say marital affairs.

'Hmm,' says the driver, 'we call that "*dedektif*" in Turkish. Interesting. So how do you become one?'

'Well, you don't need anything at all,' I say. 'No training, no qualification ...' I trail off, because I'm describing myself; I'm not going to have any qualification. How can I investigate the history of PIs if I can't even get the basic Level 3 award?

I look out the car window. We're travelling down the Edgware Road heading towards Marble Arch. We pass Lebanese restaurants and a shisha bar and then on my left, I see a familiar name – Bryanston Street. This is where ex-inspector Charles Field handed a gimlet to Sarah Grocott and told her to bore two holes in a door to spy on her adulterous mistress.

I think of the other female detectives I've found so far: Victorian police searcher Elizabeth Joyes, constables' wives Sarah Dunaway and Mrs Lawton, the mysterious Clubnose, who infiltrated a robbers' gang, and Ellen Lyons who entrapped poor Gertrude Barrett. Female detectives had become better known by the end of the nineteenth century; their names and pen portraits appeared in the press, they worked for the police, solicitors and Private Inquiry agencies, their fictional counterparts starred in novels and plays. But very few worked for themselves, and none seemed to run agencies with business offices and employees. They didn't advertise in the press like Charles Field and Henry Slater or boast of solving 'some of the most extraordinary investigations of the day'. Surely, it was time for a woman to take on the men at their own game.

ANTONIA MOSER:
DETECTIVE EXPERT

I'm walking up Southampton Street, a pretty flagstone road just off the Strand in Covent Garden, lined with coffee shops and bars. I pass the offices that once belonged to *The Strand*, the magazine which first introduced the world to Sherlock Holmes, and then the eighteenth-century home of theatre manager David Garrick. I can't see No. 31 Southampton Street anywhere, so I stop a Covent Garden security officer in a yellow high-vis vest.

'Are you looking for an office?' he asks.

'No,' I say, 'not really, Number 31 is where an office used to be. It was one of London's best-known private detective agencies, back in the 1880s.'

The security officer raises his eyebrows. 'Wow, the 1880s?'

'Yes, and it was partly run by a woman, Antonia Moser.'

'Wow,' he says, 'a woman?' The security officer leads me across the road and points at a store belonging to The North Face, the outdoor clothing company. 'This is it,' he says. The open door on the corner of the street is unnumbered and inside there are rows upon rows of T-shirts.

When Charlotte Antonia Williamson arrived here in the autumn of 1888, this was home to Moser's Detective Agency, run by ex-CID inspector Maurice Moser. He was originally from Warsaw, Poland, although he sometimes gave his birthplace as Yorkshire, and often altered his date of birth as well. He'd joined the Metropolitan Police at the age of 22, and found the life profitable, interesting and exciting, even if he was mocked in the streets for his squeaky boots.

Maurice developed an extensive network of contacts, from friendly pub landlords to 'pretty servants' in neighbourhood houses always up for a gossip. He came to know London well, walking some 20 miles on every shift, with his regulation cape, lantern and stave. Maurice made 'a very large number of arrests', according to his own account, and once accompanied the Prince of Wales to Paris, receiving a handsome breastpin in reward. He was also a skilled linguist who could speak and write five languages, composed waltz tunes in his spare time, exhibited crayon sketches and invented an automatic burglar alarm.

Before long, the talented Maurice Moser was drafted into the Criminal Investigation Department (CID), formed in 1878 following the 'Great Turf Fraud' in which senior Scotland Yard officers were convicted of corruption. As a result of the scandal, the Detective Branch was reorganised into the CID. 'A detective is no longer a detective,' commented one paper, 'but a "crime investigator".'

Maurice Moser appeared in the press on numerous occasions, sent undercover to buy 'objectionable photographic prints' from a shop near Drury Lane, as well as investigating a Russian bonds robbery and an extraordinary case of child stealing. Within four years, Maurice was appointed CID inspector, 'one of the quickest promotions ever made'. He was known for his role in uncovering the Fenian dynamite plots of the 1880s, a bombing campaign against British rule led by Irish republicans who were exiled in America. When Maurice was sent to Liverpool, after a tip-off that suspicious cargo was arriving from the States, he correctly identified eight barrels which contained smuggled dynamite.

But he grew increasingly infuriated by police bureaucracy, unable to stand the general incompetency of CID and its 'rampant red-tapeism'. There were too many unnecessary reports, and inspectors were unable to work independently. Maurice had nine suggestions for improvement, and number five on the list was the 'employment of a competent staff of female detectives'.

He resigned from the force in 1887 and, like his forebear Inspector Charles Field, he set up a Private Inquiry Office at 31 Southampton Street. The Strand was an ideal location. It was a short stroll to Somerset House, which held all birth, death and marriage certificates, and lay just half a mile from the Royal Courts of Justice. The Old Bailey was in walking distance too, while Charing Cross Station was just across the road, with boat trains direct to the Continent should a foreign trip be required.

Moser's Detective Agency was 'prompt, secret, and reliable'. It promised agents in 'all principal cities of the world' and could provide translations in 'all languages'.

There were several other detective agencies in the area and had been for some time – a Mr Ward on Buckingham Street, Abbott's Private Detective Office on Essex Street, and Attwood's Confidential Inquiry Office on Catherine Street. Henry Slater, Maurice's main rival, operated less than 2 miles away on Basinghall Street. The two men's adverts appeared next to each other in the *London Evening Standard*, as they bid for customers among the paper's daily circulation of a quarter of a million readers.

Maurice Moser was in his 30s when he opened his detective agency, married with two children and living in Clapham. He would be his own master now, free from police regulations. But was it really 'red tapeism' that had sparked the move? According to one American report, Maurice had been forced to resign from Scotland Yard for 'crookedness in connection with the division of a reward' from a victim of crime. He was also accused of 'large mouthedness', and of constantly boasting of his intimacy with the Prince of Wales.

Maurice's version of events was rather different. A grateful Russian client had given his wife a handsome sealskin jacket with a £100 note inside. It wasn't his fault that the note turned out to be stolen, and in a 'weak moment', he'd asked the sergeant not to report the find to headquarters.

A few months after Maurice opened his private detective agency, a lady called Charlotte Antonia Williamson came to call. Her husband objected to her trip to No. 31 Southampton Street, but she had a burning ambition – she wanted to be a detective. Perhaps she'd seen adverts placed by Henry Slater and other inquiry agents. She may have enjoyed the fictional adventures of Miss Gladden or Miriam Lea, and she would certainly have heard lurid reports on the recent Whitechapel murders. So, like her American predecessor Kate Warne, thirty years earlier, she simply knocked on the door and asked for a job. It wasn't long before she was one of the best-known lady detectives in the business.

Charlotte Antonia Williamson was born on 19 February 1856, one of eleven children. The family were well off. Her father, Welburn Wilks, was a mechanical engineer who designed and sold washing machines, demonstrated daily at a showroom in the family home at 133 High Holborn. His American floating ball washing machine was said to do 'the work of women in a surpassingly beautiful manner'. His prize-winning washing, wringing and mangling machines were soon being used in naval and military hospitals. Welburn was an inventive man, he'd previously worked as an engineer on the construction of the Great Western Railway and would register several patents. By the early 1860s, he was a master mechanical engineer, employing twenty-six men and eight boys.

Charlotte's mother, Sarah Antonia Wagner, came from an illustrious line of royal hatters. Her father Anthony was a descendant of Melchior Wagner, who'd arrived in England from Coburg, Germany. He'd become hatter to King George I and was given the Crown lease of a house in Pall Mall. Sarah was also related to the Wagners of Brighton, 'a remarkable family', according to their biographers, who wielded influence in Brighton for nearly a century. Sarah's cousin, Reverend Henry Michell Wagner, a former tutor to the sons of the Duke of Wellington, was Vicar of Brighton for over forty years, while her brothers included two attorneys and a surgeon.

The young Charlotte Antonia grew up in style. The Williamson home lay on one of London's great thoroughfares, between the fashionable West End and the City of London. The family were part of a growing middle class, and the daughters were taught 'accomplishments' such as music, singing, drawing, dancing and languages. But then in 1875, Charlotte's mother died – and the same year, her father declared bankruptcy. He decided that the younger daughters should be baptised with their mother's name, and at the age of 19, Charlotte became Sarah. But professionally, she would always use her middle name, Antonia.

She reportedly worked as a commercial clerk and then, slightly unusually, in 1882 she married her first cousin, Edward James Clarendon Williamson. He was an engravers block manufacturer – a method used to produce illustrations for books and magazines – while his father, and Antonia's uncle, Peter was an evangelical Baptist minister. The couple had two children. Margaret was born seven months after the wedding – perhaps she'd been the reason for the marriage in the first place – while Richard was born in 1884. As a middle-class married woman, Antonia was expected to be loyal, demure and obedient. Paid work was frowned upon and her duty was to ensure the happiness and comfort of the family, and to respect her husband's authority.

Six years into the marriage, however, Antonia informed her husband that she intended to become a private detective. She appeared to have grown tired of the domestic life and was looking for a challenge. At the age of 32, married and with two children, Antonia was taken on by private detective Maurice Moser.

The couple grew close very quickly. She told her husband she wanted to go to Constantinople with her new employer, to which Edward unsurprisingly refused. He also objected when she brought home a portrait of Maurice and wanted to hang it up in her bedroom. 'You did not wish to have the detective eye always on you?' Edward was later asked by a judge. 'No, I did not,' he replied, which was met with laughter in court.

When Edward returned from a business trip to find his desk had been broken into, he decided he'd had enough. He hired Maurice's arch-rival Henry Slater, no stranger to domestic intrigues, to watch his wife. In September 1889, Edward petitioned for divorce, accusing Antonia of adultery at several hotels and private homes in London, claiming damages of £1,000 from Maurice and custody of the two children.

Antonia, in turn, accused her husband of assault, violent and abusive language and repeated acts of cruelty throughout the marriage. She also accused him of adultery with her younger sister Ada, in the family home at High Holborn. Antonia didn't ask for custody of her children, which she would have been unlikely to get, for only wives of 'good character' gained custody after divorce.

The case of Williamson vs Williamson came to the Royal Courts of Justice in July 1890, but Antonia offered no corroboration of her husband's cruelty and her lawyer tried to persuade her not to proceed. The evidence was stacked against her.

Private detective Louisa Sangster testified that she'd seen Antonia with Maurice Moser at apartments in Garrick St and Sussex Mansions and had frequently taken tea up to them in bed. The papers were full of the scandalous affair between 'Mr Moser and his Female Detective'. Edward Williamson was granted the divorce and given custody of the children.

It seems odd that Louisa Sangster had given such damning evidence when she was employed by Maurice Moser's own agency. But perhaps Henry Slater, hired by Antonia's husband, had found a way to convince her.

Antonia now focused on her new career, running the detective agency alongside Maurice. She called herself Antonia Moser and would continue to do so for the rest of her life, although there is no evidence that they ever married.

Maurice was a savvy self-promoter, just like ex-inspector Field and Henry Slater. The year of Antonia's divorce, he published a book, *Stories from Scotland Yard*, which was serialised in the press, followed by *True Detective Stories*. Both were 'as told by Inspector Moser' and recorded by journalist Charles Rideal.

Maurice frequently gave interviews, and he was keen to sing the praises of lady detectives. Diplomacy was a recognised woman's skill, he told *The St James Gazette*, and detective work was simply another branch of diplomatic service. He also pointed out that, contrary to public opinion, women were only rarely employed in divorce cases.

Antonia was equally eager to correct the popular image of female inquiry agents, and on joining Moser's agency she too gave interviews, but on an anonymous basis. *The St James Gazette* described her as a 'lady who knows perhaps more on this subject than anyone else in London'.

When the paper asked how any woman could become a detective unless she were 'utterly *declassee*', she replied:

> That is as unjust and as wrong a thing to think as was the assertion the other day that all ballet girls were immoral. Most people run away with the idea that all the work done by women detectives must be of the dirtiest and basest nature. But it is not necessarily or always so.

Suppose an innocent woman had been slandered and needed to vindicate her character, or a wealthy lady was asked for charity and wanted to know if a person was genuine before she helped them? And what about shopgirls who were pilfering little objects? Wasn't it kinder to save them before they embarked upon a career of crime?

Most private detectives weren't interested in watching or shadowing suspected persons; they liked the *finesses* of more complicated transactions. Trustworthiness and discretion were essential and so a woman of loose character would not be employed in the first place.

The St James Gazette seemed convinced; it noted that a well-organised inquiry office usually had a lady or two 'in society' and not 'merely acting counterfeits, but the actual persons'. It decided the job was not 'invariably degrading' but was often of 'real public utility'.

Antonia also appears to have been interviewed in another article, described as 'Mrs. Williams', the 'lady manageress of Mr. Maurice Moser's staff of women detectives'. She was 'a woman of the highest culture and refinement', spoke several languages and had the 'gentlest, sweetest manners'. Once again, she explained that a woman had to prove herself discreet, trustworthy and of good moral character before she could become a private detective. It was little wonder that Antonia wasn't using her real name, considering she was about to be found guilty of adultery at the divorce court.

But despite Maurice and Antonia's efforts to publicise their agency and improve the image of private detectives, the business wasn't a success. Maurice appeared to have financial problems. In the spring of 1890, his wife Harriet Ellen had sued him for divorce, and a few months later, he was ordered to pay alimony of £2 a week.

The following summer, Harriet accused a warrant officer of bribery. Instead of serving a warrant on her husband for unpaid maintenance, the officer was seen drinking champagne with Maurice and Antonia in a restaurant on the Strand. Maurice was then back in court after failing to pay alimony, when he explained that his 'partner Mrs Williamson' had sold her jewellery to cover his debts. He then accused his wife of adultery with a solicitor based on the Strand and demanded £1,000 in damages.

This was eventually dismissed, and Maurice was ordered to pay costs. He also lost his position as a Freemason. He'd been initiated into the Cripplegate Lodge in 1889 and now he was excluded, presumably because of the scandalous divorce. On 16 February 1892, Maurice and Antonia placed a notice in the *London Gazette* – their detective partnership was dissolved and she was responsible for all debts.

But the couple were still together when Antonia's son Richard died in 1899, at the age of 14, possibly as a result of influenza. The family were living in Clapham Common and Richard was described as 'son of Maurice Moser a retired Police Inspector', who was present at the death. By 1901, Antonia was living apart from Maurice, in Battersea with her 18-year-old daughter, Margaret.

The following October, Maurice Moser was summoned to Bow Street Police Court for assaulting his 'wife'. He was now based on Craven Street, near the back of Charing Cross Station, and Antonia came to his office to remind him that 'under their deed of separation', he owed her a considerable sum of money – about £50 – for maintenance. Maurice appeared friendly and asked her to call again the following morning. She did, repeating her request and pointing out he had taken her jewellery, furniture and money, and left her practically penniless.

After 'abusing her a great deal', Maurice informed her that he had a pistol in his drawer and that if she didn't leave, he would shoot her and then himself. When Antonia refused to go, he slapped her on the face and then kicked her in the stomach after she'd fallen on the floor.

Maurice called a policeman and a doctor and informed them his wife had attempted to kill herself. But Antonia had 'done nothing of the kind', she'd simply gone to the window because she felt faint. She was told she'd be taken home, but instead she was forcibly put in a cab and driven to the St Giles Infirmary, where she was confined as a lunatic for forty-eight hours.

St Giles Workhouse Infirmary, around a mile away in Covent Garden, was a large institution with separate wards for 'imbecile' inmates, and two padded rooms. It often took emergency cases, such as a man who'd wandered off while being hypnotised and lost his memory. In November 1901, a wealthy American, Miss Vanderbilt Wackerman, had been taken to St Giles after behaving in a 'very hysterical' manner at the London offices of a well-known New York newspaper, where she was 'found to be demented'.

Until the mid-nineteenth century, men were believed to be most liable to disorders of the mind. But by the 1890s, most patients were women, often institutionalised because of 'female illnesses' such as 'hysteria'. Doctors frequently described their female patients as disobedient, rebellious and sexually immoral.

There were several cases of women being wrongly confined as insane in the early 1900s. Mrs Clarkson, a 'clever and exceptionally intelligent woman', spent four days in an asylum in Surrey, having been 'carried off' by her husband and two nurses, despite the angry objections of her friends and neighbours.

As for Antonia Moser, she was examined by doctors, certified as perfectly sane, and, after paying her 'maintenance' costs, she was released. When her daughter Margaret called on Maurice Moser and asked him for an explanation, he threatened to treat her in the same way if she ever came again.

Maurice, of course, told a very different story. On the day in question, Antonia had called at his office at about ten o'clock in the morning and kept repeating, 'Where's Mr Moser?' She did not appear to recognise him, and remained all day, becoming very hysterical and irrational. He absolutely denied having assaulted her in any way.

An Inspector Mount testified that he had gone to Moser's office with a relieving officer, and if the officer hadn't removed Antonia to the St Giles Infirmary, he would 'certainly have had her sent away as insane'. Three of Maurice's clerks provided further corroboration.

The judge wasn't convinced that any assault had been committed. Maurice Moser was 'entitled to the benefit of the doubt' and the charges against 'the well-known private detective' were dismissed.

It would have been easy enough for Maurice to convince a court that Antonia was 'hysterical'. She was already a morally suspect figure – a private detective, an adulteress and a divorcee. She was also in her late 40s, and menopausal women were regarded as being especially susceptible to nervous disorders. They were likely to 'fall into loathing and disgust for men', explained criminologist Cesare Lombroso, and then into a state 'similar to madness'.

Dr Clare Clarke, who is writing a biography of Maurice Moser, believes it's entirely possible that he was violent and that he'd assaulted Antonia. She describes him as duplicitous, with 'a natural gift for exaggeration and braggadocio', and a man who was 'extremely driven by money and self-promotion'.

Once again, Antonia had failed to provide any evidence or witnesses, just as in her divorce. She had never actually married Maurice, so how did they have a deed of separation, drawn up between a husband and a trustee of the wife? She told the court they had married in Chicago in 1891, which sounds unlikely, and she also described herself as 'a widow' when her husband Edward was very much alive. But while she may not have told the truth about her marital status, she could well have been penniless. She'd had costs to pay in her divorce, had sold her jewellery to pay Maurice's alimony to his ex-wife, and when the detective agency closed, she'd been left responsible for all its debts as well. She'd also inherited nothing from her father, who died not long before her appearance at the Royal Courts of Justice. Welburn Wilks had left his considerable wealth of £380 to her estranged sister, Ada.

Antonia was apparently right about her allegations of adultery, for her sister and her former husband had a daughter together in 1900 and would eventually marry. But despite the significant financial difficulties Antonia was facing, the abuse she'd suffered at the hands of Maurice Moser and the loss of her young son, she wasn't deterred from her chosen career. Instead, she decided to open her very own detective agency.

ADVENTURES OF A WOMAN DETECTIVE

In January 1905, a new advert appeared in the *Morning Post*, 'Antonia Moser, Detective Expert, 37 and 38 Strand. Consultations free. Prompt, secret, and reliable.' It was listed amid rewards for lost jewellery, pleas from ladies in dire straits – 'for pity's sake, oh, please do help' – and notices from buyers of second-hand teeth. A few weeks later, Antonia Moser added a phone number, and by the following year she was promising 'agents in all cities of the world'.

Antonia was clearly taking advantage of her former partner's name – which was far better known in the world of detection – and she was borrowing his wording too, for he too was 'prompt, secret and reliable'. Maurice seemed rattled, he placed a notice for Mr G. Maurice Moser's Bureau for Detective Business and stressed it had 'no connection with any other office in London'.

Antonia was determined to keep herself in the public eye, and in June 1907 she wrote a series of detective stories for the *Weekly Dispatch*. 'The Adventures of a Woman Detective' were not everyday cases of theft and divorce, but intriguing tales of foreign noblemen, gentlemen burglars and gold brick swindlers.

Antonia began by revealing the roots of her detective career. She had 'family connections' to the police, she explained, and the very atmosphere of her childhood had been 'laden with the secrets and mysteries of crime detecting'. Her grandfather, Charles Wilks Williamson of the Strand, had counted Charles Dickens and William Makepeace Thackeray among his 'intimates', and the men had taken a deep interest in police mysteries. As a little child, Antonia had 'hung upon every word', listening while the men discussed the murder of 'a poor creature of the street' in Great Coram Street, and the terrible Canon Street murder in which William Smith had escaped the death penalty at the very last moment. Antonia was deeply affected by the idea of a miscarriage of justice, and this had eventually motivated her to become a detective.

But what exactly were her 'family connections' to the police? She was presumably referring to ex-CID inspector Maurice Moser, although her brother-in-law George Elliot may have had police connections too, as he worked as a private detective in the early 1900s. Was her grandfather Charles Wilks Williamson really good friends with Dickens, Thackeray and 'their set'? He was a skilled manufacturer of wood blocks for engravers and had worked and lived in the Strand in the mid-1850s and '60s, among a population of artisans and traders. His customers may well have provided illustrations for publications linked to Dickens and Thackeray, but the extent of his relationship with the great novelists of the day is hard to know.

The Canon Street Murder, meanwhile, happened in 1866, by which time Thackeray was dead, and the Great Coram Street murder of 1872 occurred two years after Dickens' death. So they could hardly have been discussing the cases in front of a young Antonia. But she was cleverly building a picture of herself as someone with a lifetime interest in and knowledge of crime.

She also paid tribute to the 'grandfellowship' that existed in the private detection profession. 'It is said that men are jealous of women treading on their grounds,' she wrote, 'and that they try in every way to thwart any effort a woman may make out of the beaten track. Such has not been my experience.' Instead, she had always been met with the greatest kindness and good comradeship.

This was plainly untrue. Maurice Moser had shown her neither kindness nor comradeship. He'd taken her money, threatened her with a pistol, punched her in the face and tried to have her certified as insane. But he would be aware of her series of seven tales running in the *Weekly Dispatch*, it was Britain's biggest selling Sunday newspaper, and so perhaps she had made her point.

Did Antonia pen the stories herself, or was it the work of a journalist? After nearly ten years as a private detective, she would have had plenty of stories to tell, and she'd always been a confident writer. As a 17-year-old, she'd written to an uncle in Canada, after the death of his brother, 'What a strange thing it seems Uncle that you did not know poor Uncle Melchior had a wife when he has been married over nine years but as I was telling Mama none of you are very communicative – Now are you?' Her tone was equally bold and cheery when it came to detective tales. Maurice Moser's memoir style had been long-winded and pompous, hers was far more entertaining. Antonia Moser was the first female private detective in Britain to publish 'true-life' crime tales – and she would set the bar high for those to come.

'A Case of Identity' opens in her inner office on the Strand when Robert Drane, a successful businessman, arrives to see her. He wants to know who he is – he lost his memory three years ago and is about to get married. Antonia searches news reports and carries out inquiries at asylums, then she notices mysterious lettering on a matchbox, which leads her to a witness to a terrible train crash. She discovers that Robert Drane was a bank cashier who'd stolen money and gone on the run. At the end of the tale, her client repays the stolen money, gets married and enjoys a happy ending.

In 'The Lady Who Disappeared', Antonia is hired to find Miss Kennedy, a wealthy woman who has disappeared from her home in Maida Vale. There have been 'family differences', and her brother-in-law wants to know where she is. Antonia tracks down former servants, interviews a barmaid and a landlady, gets the serial numbers of banknotes and follows Miss Kennedy to Scotland. There, she finds her wild-eyed, dirty and drunk, having run off with a philandering 'Captain'.

Were any of these tales true? The cases had echoes of Antonia's own experiences, especially marriage break-ups and family differences, and they often featured duplicitous, crooked, bigamist men.

In one case, she follows a scheming foreign count through Berlin, St Petersburg, Paris, Venice, Vienna, Budapest, Milan, Nice and Monte Carlo. Eventually, she tracks him to Cannes, where she learns he's married with a child. Then she crosses the Atlantic and determinedly trails him from Chicago to Winnipeg – a three-day trip on the back of a pony.

The *Weekly Dispatch* had no qualms about publishing these tales, no matter how implausible. But if Antonia's purpose was to earn money from her thrilling adventures, it didn't succeed. In 1908, she declared bankruptcy; she owed £482, and her assets were 'NIL'. She had no cash in hand or at the bank, no jewellery, life policy or property, and none of the furniture in her office on the Strand belonged to her. For once, she told the truth about her marital status with Maurice Moser and was recorded as 'unmarried'. But she insisted she'd taken the name Moser by deed poll 'about 20 years ago', when there's no evidence that she did.

The adventurous female sleuth was very adept at blurring the lines between fact and fiction. When she was asked to state her full and true name and age, she replied, 'Charlotte Antonia Moser, aged 50' – when her surname was Williamson, and she was nearer 53. She also rewrote her role in the Southampton Street detective agency. 'Mr Moser was never the proprietor of the business,' she declared, although he 'assisted her therein at times'. How Maurice would have fumed if he'd heard her.

As for her financial problems, Antonia blamed these on the costs incurred when she'd taken her estranged sister Ada to court over their father's will. She'd disputed his signature and alleged that Ada had 'set up' the will in order to inherit everything. There don't seem to be any records on this dispute over the will, but according to Antonia, she eventually abandoned the case and still owed her sister £67. She also owed several solicitors, one of whom she'd borrowed money from, and was penniless once again.

Antonia was living with her daughter Margaret, and her only furniture had been repossessed. Margaret had already become a partner in the detective agency and now she took over, apparently using her mother's name. She rarely appeared in the press, but in March 1909 she sued Mr Luck, a music hall artiste and one of the Six Brothers Luck, over an unpaid bill of £6 for watching his wife. There was some confusion as to which woman had been hired. Antonia said she'd known Mr Luck for fifteen years and had worked for him before, but he knew perfectly well her daughter owned the agency.

Antonia Moser was now directing her considerable energies elsewhere, as a vocal supporter of suffrage. In 1908, the year she declared bankruptcy, the Women's Social and Political Union (WSPU) had held a demonstration in Hyde Park with seven processions, twenty platforms and eighty speakers, attended by up to half a million people. When Prime Minister Herbert Asquith ignored the suffragettes' demands, stones were thrown at No. 10 Downing Street in one of the first examples of violence against property. The following year, suffragettes in prison went on hunger strike and endured the state-sponsored torture of 'forcible feeding'.

Antonia Moser supported the cause financially. In 1905 she'd donated 10*s* 6*d* to the Central Society for Women's Suffrage. Its committee members included Frances Power Cobbe, who'd once called for the employment of female detectives during the 'Jack the Ripper' murders. Antonia then donated 2 shillings to the national fund of the Women's Freedom League, formed in 1907 after a split from the WSPU. She also launched a new enterprise, the Women's Business and Legal Agency, which she advertised in *Votes for Women*, the official newspaper of the WSPU. Antonia's advert appeared in the miscellaneous column, and it sounded like a cross between a Private Inquiry Office and a citizen's advice bureau: 'ADVICE FREE – Where to go when in trouble, whether of a social, business, or private nature.' Was this altruistic work to help women in need, or had she seen a new market for her detective skills?

Antonia Moser had certainly become well known again. The year her advice agency opened, *Reynolds's Newspaper* reran one of her thrilling detective tales, this time accompanied with a photograph of Antonia, 'one of London's lady detectives', looking businesslike in a simple, high-collared dress. She was also back living on High Holborn, at No. 317, just half a mile from her childhood home. In 1910, an advert appeared for a 'Moser Detective Agency' at the same address – Maurice responded by placing an advert noting that his 'only address' was Bridge Street.

Antonia tried running an estate agent's, registering a business in 1911, with her daughter as director and capital of £500. But a few years later she was in trouble, the Board of Trade threatened her with a fine of £5 a day if she didn't provide a list of company members. Official letters sent to 317 High Holborn went unanswered; instead, they were marked 'Gone away' and returned to sender. Towards the end of 1915, a letter addressed to 'Sir' warned that the company would be struck off, and by the following year, Antonia Moser Ltd was no more.

Her old detective partner Maurice Moser, meanwhile, had died in Boulogne in 1913. His obituary, which appeared in numerous papers, described him as a famous royal detective who'd enjoyed a remarkable career. He had been guided by one principle: 'When you have no clue, try an intelligent guess.'

Antonia Moser continued to support the suffrage campaign through a stream of letters to the local and national press. Women needed the vote, she explained, in order to claim equal wages for equal work; otherwise, they would always fight a losing battle. *The Vote* published several letters from the 'able pen of Mrs Antonia Moser', as did *The Referee*. She criticised laws relating to marriage, divorce, breach of promise and probate, all of which were 'built upon the theory that the woman is the property of the man'. If a woman had full legal status, then her husband would 'not be able to traffic in his wife's shame' by obtaining damages in the divorce court for the 'loss of his wife's services'.

Antonia knew all about the divorce court, through both personal and professional experience, and she too had been shamed. Her former husband Edward had condemned her as an adulteress and run off with her sister, while Maurice Moser had exploited her financially, physically and emotionally. In a letter to the *Pall Mall Gazette* in 1913, the year that Maurice died, Antonia outlined 'Man's Duty Towards Woman'. It was time for 'candid criticism of the male half of humanity'. She listed the ways in which dishonourable men treated women. 'He may cheat her commercially, break his word to her, underpay her work, cozen her with false promises, accept any sacrifice at her hands without repayment, but yet retain his "honour".'

Antonia was a firebrand and her letters on suffrage sparked discussion and debate. In June 1914, she wrote to *The Vote*, responding to an article in *The Times* and suggesting a 'united protest'. The paper explained that 'steps are now being considered to carry this idea into effect'.

Antonia also drew on her knowledge and contacts as a private detective. When the government denied that police were employing spies and agent provocateurs at suffrage meetings, Antonia fired a letter off to *The Vote*. She had recently attended a suffrage procession when a gentleman started booing and hurling abuse. So she had turned round and called him a 'police nark' to his face, until he'd slunk away.

In 1913, Antonia was interviewed by the 'Woman's Platform' in the *London Evening Standard*, which called her the 'doyen of women detectives'. Women made as good detectives as men, she explained, and were often better. A woman's instinct and 'powers of intuition' were an asset, and her individuality and resourcefulness were unfettered by official training and red tape. Private detectives with police training, she noted, tended to fall to pieces when something unexpected happened. Antonia did 'not recommend the profession to women as a whole', but only because of the incessant work and uncertain hours, 'not because they are incapable mentally; this is nonsense'.

Antonia was still apparently running her advisory service in 1914, when she wrote to *The Vote* about the death of Joan Lavender Guthrie in a letter which had been 'suppressed' by other newspapers. Lavender Guthrie – who used 'Laura Grey' as her suffragette and stage name – had been found dead in her London flat after taking an overdose of veronal, a barbiturate. Her death was widely reported; she'd allegedly succumbed to a world of nightclubs, drugs and militant suffragettes. Two years earlier, Lavender had taken part in a WSPU window-smashing campaign and was sentenced to six months at Holloway Prison for wilful damage. She went on hunger strike, was forcibly fed and began taking veronal after her release, presumably to ease the pain.

At the inquest, the coroner described her as 'absolutely degraded', and she was also revealed to be pregnant. The jury decided her death was suicide during temporary insanity, and according to the press, she'd been a victim of the WSPU.

Antonia Moser was incensed. The poor woman's death had nothing to do with the leaders or teachings of the WSPU. Lavender had led a perfectly moral and upright life while she was a member, 'according to her own statement to me'. Eighteen months before her death, she had sought Antonia's advice 'in reference to a certain man who had obtained an improper influence over her'. Lavender's experience of being forcibly fed, coupled with the man's desertion, had 'caused her to take drugs – I have a similar case in hand now'.

Antonia Moser was still helping women who'd been exploited and corrupted by men, just like Miss Kennedy in her 'true' detective tale, seven years earlier. But she was also becoming increasingly xenophobic. She wrote sympathetically about women sent abroad into 'dens of infamy and vice'. But she described 'foreign' women as infesting the streets of England and poisoning 'the minds and bodies of our own peoples'. By the end of the First World War, she was urging women to form an 'anti-German League' and warning about 'the German spy danger' in Britain, a system of which she had 'personal knowledge'.

Antonia died on 19 September 1919 at St George's Hospital in Westminster, at the age of 63. Her death was recorded under the name

Charlotte Antonia Moser and her occupation as 'Private Enquiry Agent. Widow of Maurice Moser.' So she had kept hold of her former employer's name until the very end. Her daughter Margaret, however, had reverted to the surname Williamson, and by 1939 she was no longer a private detective but a private general nurse.

★　★　★

Antonia Moser had never made much money from detective work, but she had successfully raised the profile of female detectives, forming her own agency, giving interviews to the press and writing detective stories. She kept going through scandal, divorce, assault and bankruptcy. She ignored those who said women weren't cut out to be detectives and who disputed their morals, and she went on to be a funder and fighter for women's rights – particularly the right to work. However, very little has ever been written about this adventurous lady sleuth or her pioneering work within the world of private detection.

According to the authors of the *Wagners of Brighton*, she was married to a Scotland Yard detective, 'after whose death she was in business as a "detective expert"'. But Antonia hadn't been a widow when she'd first paid a visit to Moser's Detective Agency on Southampton Street in 1888; she'd been a married woman and the mother of two young children. She hadn't been motivated by financial need; she wanted to be a detective.

And she was proud of her business. After she set up her first agency on the Strand, she sent a relative, Henry Wagner, a wealthy bachelor, her business card. But her family seemed to regard Antonia with unease. One Canadian cousin, Mollie Wagner, couldn't understand the 'troubles and disunion' between Antonia and her sisters, who 'all seemed to go down'.

Antonia Moser survived a twenty-five-year career as a private detective, during which she ran agencies from five different addresses in and around the Strand. She showed the British public that private detection was a job for women – but she wasn't the only one, for another female sleuth had her office just a minute's walk from Antonia's advisory service, on the opposite side of High Holborn in Warwick Court. She, too, was a suffrage supporter; only she tackled more dangerous cases and she carried a gun.

KATE EASTON:
'I CAN SHOOT STRAIGHT'

As I step into Warwick Court, the noise from High Holborn slips away, and before me is a little slice of old London. The seventeenth-century lane curves slightly, paved with dust-coloured stones, while a Victorian streetlamp stands in the middle of what is a very short street. The offices of Tanfield Chambers, which specialises in commercial and property law, are on my right, and there's a sign for a literary agency at No. 6. But the rest of Warwick Court seems to have disappeared; perhaps it's part of the City Law School, which lies at the end of the lane and is currently covered in scaffolding and plastic sheeting.

A man comes into the street, jogging slowly after a Sunday morning run. 'Excuse me,' I say, as he stops at a front door next to Tanfield Chambers. 'Do you know where No. 10 used to be? Is it part of the law school?'

'It's not the law school any more,' says the man. 'They're turning it into a primary school. What are you looking for?'

'A detective agency,' I say. 'A famous detective, Kate Easton, had her offices here in the early 1900s, but I can't find No. 10.'

'Ah,' says the man, 'you're doing a little detective work to find a detective?'

'Are you a lawyer?' I ask.

He laughs and opens his front door, 'No, I work in security. Good luck with your research.'

Kate Easton moved into Warwick Court in the summer of 1909, where she advertised herself as 'LONDON'S LEADING WOMAN in every branch of Detective Work'. She branded herself more than Antonia Moser had done, giving herself a strapline – 'The Lady Detective' – providing an endorsement from *Vide Press* – 'Efficiency by dint of arduous and dangerous work' – and using box adverts rather than a few lines in the classified columns.

Kate had one of the most important clientele in the UK, according to the *American Register*, and had already saved many unblemished names from disgrace and ruin. The *Register* was a weekly publication aimed at wealthy Americans in Europe, which listed the most reliable shopping places in London – American table delicacies at Fortnum and Mason, evening gowns at Peter Robinson, and detective work at No. 10 Warwick Court.

Kate was the same age as her contemporary, Antonia Moser – she was born Kate Augusta Mead Easton in Lambeth, south London, on 18 June 1856, the youngest of three children. But she didn't have a wealthy background. Her father, William, was a fireman, who later worked as a waterman and tobacconist, while her mother, Sarah, was the daughter of a shoemaker. The family lived on the Waterloo Road, in one of the poorest districts in London.

By the time Kate was 14, the Eastons had moved to nearby Stamford Street, which would become notorious for its disorderly houses and criminal gangs. Kate described herself as a curious child, her favourite hobby was people-watching, and she haunted railway stations and other public places, imagining the lives of passers-by.

After her father's death in 1883, she lived with her mother in Bloomsbury where she gave her occupation as 'vocalist music'. Other family members also worked in the arts, her brother William was a professor of music, while her niece, Madeleine Lucette, was a highly successful actress and playwright. In the late 1870s, Madeleine toured Britain with Carte's comedy opera company, and then travelled to the States to perform in New York and Boston. She became a playwright, praised for her 'clean, wholesome comedies', which were hugely popular on both sides of the Atlantic. She married singer and actor J.H. Ryley and became vice president of the Actresses' Franchise League.

The extent of Kate Easton's theatrical experience isn't so well documented. The press don't seem to have covered her performances, and she may have used an unknown stage name. But in 1901, she was living at

No. 24 Great Russell Street and her official occupation was actress. It was an unreliable career, even for those who were decades younger. That year, two young actresses 'of great beauty' poisoned themselves in their rooms on Great Russell Street. They'd been engaged at a London theatre but had been out of work for some time and had failed to get a passage to America.

In June 1904, at the age of 48, Kate Easton suddenly appeared in a very different kind of theatre, giving evidence at the High Court of Justice in Ireland – as a lady detective. Sir Robert McConnell, a property developer and former Lord Mayor of Belfast, had accused his wife Elsie of committing adultery with a Londoner named Alfred Archer.

It seemed to be a clear-cut case. The couple had been seen in London and Brighton, they had a child together, and letters had been intercepted. Kate Easton's job was to follow Lady McConnell to Brighton, where she booked into the same hotel. During the trial, Kate was closely cross-examined by the Solicitor General – had Alfred actually been staying at the same hotel? By what name had Lady McConnell addressed him? What did the couple say to each other?

Kate handled the questions with self-assurance, just like her female detective forebears. She had identified Alfred Archer a few months later, she explained, when she saw him in London.

But how had Kate Easton transformed herself from struggling actress into lady detective? Was she working for Sir Robert McConnell's solicitor, or for a private inquiry agency? According to Kate, she'd started her career while employed as a correspondence clerk for a large wholesale merchant, when she was asked to 'undertake certain private inquiries'. She then worked for a solicitor and picked up 'a certain amount of legal knowledge', and 'obtained a great many practical wrinkles' from an unnamed ex-detective.

Was this the first time Kate had been cross-examined in court? And was it daunting or thrilling? She apparently had experience of public performance, and here was a courthouse packed with spectators, eager to witness a high-profile scandal.

Lady McConnell didn't contest the case, and her husband was granted a divorce. Kate Easton had done the job she'd been hired for; she'd caught an adulterous woman.

The following year, in October 1905, Kate launched forth on her own. She established a detective agency at No. 241 Shaftesbury Avenue, less than a mile from Antonia Moser's office on the Strand, which opened that same year. Kate's adverts in the *Daily Telegraph* sounded impressive: 'LADY DETECTIVE, thoroughly experienced, undertakes private and confidential inquiries.' She had the highest references from solicitors 'as to ABILITY and INTEGRITY', and also operated in Paris, although no address there was given.

A few lines above Kate's advert was the notice 'BEWARE of SELF-STYLED DETECTIVE AGENCIES'. It was placed by Maurice Moser, who was not impressed by the competition. 'How can they possibly possess the necessary sagacity of a life-long trained Detective like Mr Moser?' he asked. The following month, Kate's advert appeared above Antonia Moser's. The lady sleuths were competing for clients, and yet strangely, neither appears to have ever mentioned the other, and the press portrayed them as unique and never as rivals.

Kate's Shaftesbury Avenue office lay on an island of buildings at the corner of New Oxford Street, just behind James Smith & Sons Umbrellas. Today, its Victorian shop front still advertises ladies' umbrellas, stacked in the window like striped sugar canes.

In May 1907, *Lloyd's Weekly* sent a journalist to interview Kate Easton at her 'snug little' Shaftesbury Avenue office. She was pretty, practical and plucky, and she'd been engaged in some of the riskiest detective work in London. 'Blackmail, divorce, evidence, robbery. I undertake it all,' she declared. 'I have touched everything but murder.' Danger was inevitable, and she'd pursued her inquiries in the lowest parts of London. 'I do not know what fear is,' she told *Lloyds Weekly*, 'and I can shoot straight.'

Kate must have been asked to compare male and female detectives, and her reply was defiant: 'I have always done a man's work, and I always will, and I have succeeded.' She had once rented a room in west London to secure evidence in a blackmailing case, when a fellow lodger went 'absinthe mad' and attacked the proprietor with a carving knife. Kate had also spent time in an infectious diseases hospital, and while she didn't have permission from 'the proper authorities', she found out 'what I wanted to find out'. She sounded like Clubnose, the mysterious female sleuth from the 1870s, who'd worked undercover for Scotland Yard.

Kate's investigations also involved 'family secrets', just like Antonia Moser, whose stories were about to be serialised in the *Weekly Dispatch*.

She tracked down a missing daughter who'd run away with a married man and located a missing bride who'd disappeared with her bridegroom's money and jewellery and got married to someone else. Kate spent six months on a 'celebrated case', shadowing a couple, living beside them and spending up to five hours at a time secreted behind a door. It sounded very much like the Victorian image of the lady sleuth – eyes to the keyhole, ready to pounce on an adulterous couple. 'It is in private not in public life that the greatest secrets are revealed,' Kate told *Lloyds Weekly*, and for this reason, women were ideally suited to the job. By 1908, her adverts stressed her skills in private affairs: 'KATE EASTON, THE LADY DETECTIVE, personally undertakes matters requiring a woman's delicacy and tact; successful in divorce.'

Unlike Antonia Moser, Kate's actual investigations did appear in the press. In 1908, she was hired by company director Francis Wigglesworth, who accused his wife Violet of an affair with a clerk named Frederick Simpson. The marriage had been unhappy, owing to Violet's 'extravagance and intemperance' and she'd admitted to being indiscreet with a gentleman. Her husband agreed to take her back if she behaved herself, but Violet's conduct became even worse.

Mr Wigglesworth hired a male detective, W. James, who 'gained admission' to Violet's home in Chiswick, 'but nothing came of it'. So Kate Easton was hired, and she sent one of her assistants, a Mrs Bardrick, who took lodgings in Violet's house under the suitable name of 'Mrs Bland'. Then Violet received an alarming letter from the male detective:

> Kate Easton, the woman detective, has been engaged to watch you. If she or one of her satellites has managed to get into your house, get Mr. P. or one of your gentleman friends to chuck her out immediately. So beware of any strange woman who tries to make your acquaintance. They are anxious to find out what takes place at night at your apartments. Beware!

The male detective was so furious at being replaced by a female detective that he was alerting the very woman he was supposed to be watching. It was 'professional jealousy,' explained the press. A woman detective had succeeded where an 'enraged rival' had failed. Violet Wigglesworth showed the alarming letter to her lodger, 'Mrs Bland', unaware that she was a private detective, and asked for advice. Mrs Bland then arranged for 'representatives' of Violet's husband to enter the house, and they caught the adulterous couple together.

By the following summer, Kate Easton had moved offices to Warwick Court, and now she too began writing features for the press. In 'My Work as a Lady Detective', published in *London Mainly About People*, she described catching the perpetrators of a 'certain big silver robbery', and sending her staff on election work in the build-up to the general elections.

She also described the perils of the job. One day, a woman arrived at her Warwick Court office and attempted to throw a bottle of sulphuric acid in her face. Kate quickly 'covered her with a little revolver', which she always kept in her bureau drawer, and the woman disappeared in a hurry. 'I am afraid this sounds rather like melodrama,' Kate confessed, 'but it's perfectly true.'

She also appeared to write for *Pearson's Weekly* as the anonymous author of 'Why I Shadow People'. Shadowing was the 'kernel of the profession,' she explained, and three-fourths of her time was devoted to it. One night she might be on the tracks of a wealthy lady of title, the next day, following a commercial traveller suspected of fraud. She had once shadowed a lady 300 miles from King's Cross to Edinburgh, simply to find the address of her hotel.

Like Antonia Moser, Kate also supported the suffrage movement. In 1911, she took part in the Women's Freedom League's campaign to disrupt the census. On the night of 2 April, tens of thousands of women refused to complete the forms, writing slogans such as 'I don't count so I won't be counted'. Kate Easton declined to provide her details, but the enumerator knew enough about her to note that she was a Private Inquiry Agent, single, aged about 45 – nine years younger than she was – and resided at Warwick Court. 'N.B.', he wrote on the form, 'Information Refused by Miss Easton'.

Kate also had at least one suffragist client. In 1912, she was hired by Edith Wheelwright, a botanist, novelist and Secretary of the Bath Branch of the National Union of Women's Suffrage Societies. Edith was attacked while walking home one evening, and Kate Easton successfully tracked down the assailant.

While Kate refused to complete the 1911 census, many other women did complete it, and the profession of private detection showed signs of growing. Nearly a dozen women described themselves as inquiry agents, five as lady detectives, four as private detectives, and two as private inquiry agents – although a few used more than one title. Some worked as clerks at private detective offices, one was 'actress and detective', while other occupations are harder to decipher – one woman was a 'detective servant' and another was a 'detective maid'. But according to *London Mainly About People*, Kate Easton was 'the first woman to adopt seriously the profession of Lady Detective'. Antonia Moser wouldn't have been amused by this claim – she'd joined the profession back in 1888 – and nor would another famous female sleuth: Maud West.

Maud West was a good twenty years younger than Antonia Moser and Kate Easton. Her true-life detective tales would be even wilder and soon she would eclipse them both.

Maud was born Edith Maria Barber on 15 September 1880, in Deptford, south-east London. Her mother, Mary Ann, was a domestic servant, and as there was no father named on her birth certificate, Maud invented one, telling the press her 'barrister father' had encouraged her into detective work. Maud would spin a lot of stories during her career, as her biographer Susannah Stapleton has discovered. Maud's father, for example, was, in fact, a sailor.

Maud initially worked as a sales assistant in a drapery store, and her ambition was to be a milliner and run her own business. But instead, she took to the stage as a male impersonator, although she doesn't appear in the press and her stage name is unknown. In 1901, she married Harry Elliott, the son of a carpenter from the East End, who later worked as an advertising agent, and sometimes as Maud's office manager and private detective. The couple would have six children together, but Maud kept her personal life private and tended to portray herself as a single woman.

Her first case came when a 'solicitor relation' asked her to help solve a hotel robbery, by posing as a waitress. She apparently set up her own detective agency in 1905 – the same year as Antonia Moser and Kate Easton – but her first known adverts didn't appear until early July 1909. One ran on the front page of the *Sunday Times*: 'MAUD WEST, LADY DETECTIVE. Are you worried? If so, consult me!' Maud offered private inquiries into delicate matters and shadowings, and her 'high class firm' was based in Albion House, No. 59 New Oxford Street – right by Kate Easton at No. 241 Shaftesbury Avenue. For a brief time, the two women were virtually neighbours, they could easily have bumped into each other as they set off on their private inquiries.

On 29 July 1910, the capital's three leading female sleuths all placed adverts in the *Daily Telegraph*. First came Kate Easton at Warwick Court, then Maud West on New Oxford Street, and then Antonia Moser's Women's Business and Legal Agency on High Holborn. The women clearly knew each other, the private detection world was still small, and they would have known the same contacts – solicitors, police officers, other inquiry agents – appeared before the same magistrates and judges, and read each other's adverts, casebook tales and interviews.

Maud may even have started as Kate's protégé, as Susannah Stapleton suggests, for she had learned the nature of detective work from someone. Perhaps Kate had deliberately moved out of Shaftesbury Avenue and into Warwick Court to be further away from Maud.

Unlike her contemporaries, Maud West did not publicly support the suffrage cause. Instead, she kept watch on suffragettes. 'I have had practically all my staff employed at big social functions during the last six weeks,' she declared in May 1913, watching out for militant women disguised as guests or servants with suffragette sympathies. Maud focused on disguise far more than London's other female sleuths, boasting she could play any part from shabby old scrubwoman to factory hand, flower girl, fortune teller, housemaid, mother's help, Salvation Army 'lassie' and gold-digging temptress. She could alter the shape of her face simply by 'pushing a piece of orange peel beneath my upper lip'.

She also disguised herself as a man. Some female detectives had already adopted male disguise, such as Clubnose in the 1870s, but the role became central to Maud's identity as a private detective, whether a titled Englishman at a fashionable Paris hotel or a dandy lounging in a West End smoking room. 'Mannish' dress was in vogue for women in the early 1900s, as was the idea of the masquerade, and Maud seemed keen to stress her suitability at the role. She had been 'very boyish' as a child and was known as Jack by her family. In one case, she visited a nightclub disguised as a wealthy man in order to trap a woman accused of serial blackmail. The woman soon began to flirt, and Maud obliged. 'I kissed her,' she confessed. 'Being a detective has its dark side.'

The American press were captivated by Britain's latest female sleuth, and Maud enjoyed a more international image than her contemporaries.

If readers thought the woman detective was a figure of fiction, then, announced a San Francisco paper, 'Prepare to be astonished; greet one in real life!' It provided photographs of Maud 'making up as a man' but reassured its readers that her offices were distinctly feminine – they resembled a 'boudoir' rather than a detective bureau – and she was a 'modest woman with soft rosy cheeks, fair hair and a good figure'.

This modest woman was certainly having some thrilling adventures. When a blackmailer rushed into her office one day and threatened to shoot her, Maud was unfazed. 'I have my fingers on a pistol now,' she told him, 'that can spit ten bullets while you are firing one.' But there was another side to detective work for women in the early 1900s and it had little of the glamour of private inquiry work. There was no snug boudoir in which to receive wealthy clients and no need to carry a gun in an overnight bag, and yet the women who took up the job had to be just as fearless.

A DOMINANT FACE
FOR A WOMAN

In April 1910, Matilda Mitchell appeared in court with a sticking plaster on her face, after she'd been hit by a shoplifter attempting to resist 'lawful apprehension' at Selfridges department store. The shoplifter had stolen a customer's handbag and when Matilda confronted her, she'd 'started banging about', kicking the store detective and scratching her face. But Matilda Mitchell simply got on with the job.

A few months later, she caught a 28-year-old French waiter who'd stolen an item from the bronze department and hid it in his waistcoat. She described it as one of her 'cleverest captures'. She'd 'caught him quick, and no man had his waistcoat undone smarter than he had'.

Selfridges had only opened two years earlier. It was so grand that it occupied an entire block on Oxford Street, and like other department stores, it offered a new way of shopping. Customers could browse the items on sale – cosmetics and dresses, fur coats and silk stockings – rather than ask an assistant to bring them. Not surprisingly, theft was a problem right from the start, and the professional female shoplifter – or 'hoister' – could prove a dangerous opponent. 'I have known them carry scissors to stab the arm with,' explained Matilda, 'or pepper to throw in the eyes.' One woman had torn her hat and coat to pieces and Matilda had a hard time keeping her temper, but once the shoplifter was 'alone with me in the searching room, I soon let her know who was master'. The Selfridges detective was a tough woman, and she was often praised for her courage and pluck.

Female detectives had been employed at larger British shops since the late nineteenth century, especially during sales. In 1890, Florence Alexander, a private detective employed by Messrs. Crisp during their annual sale in Holloway, caught a woman stealing a jersey, fur trimmings, nine flowers, birds and children's shoes. She'd seen the suspect walking in a 'suspicious manner' and followed her for an hour before confronting her.

Some London establishments also hired female detectives to keep an eye on their staff. One store employed a lady 'whose business is merely to be on terms of private intimacy with the families of all of its hands'. She then provided regular reports on whether they were living within their means.

Over in America, male detectives didn't appear to think much of their department store counterparts. In 1892, a reporter from the *San Francisco Chronicle* asked a city detective, 'Are women a success as detectives in stores?' The response was, 'No, they are a detriment'. Store detection was 'not first-class work'; it was simply 'spotting'. Female detectives had frowning faces and contracted eyebrows, and they gazed at everyone as if they were a thief.

By the early 1900s, shoplifting was endemic in London, partly due to the activities of the Forty Elephants, an all-female gang under the leadership of Alice Diamond. Professional hoisters used ingenious devices from dummy bags with trap openings to hidden pockets under skirts, a garter fitted with hooks and wax stuck on the soles of shoes. Bourne & Hollingsworth on Oxford Street lost £2,000 worth of goods a year to shoplifting, and the activities of professionals like Alice Diamond led to increased demand for female detectives.

Only female sleuths could catch female hoisters. A man wandering around a lingerie department would arouse far too much attention. 'A woman has a thousand better opportunities than a man of watching unobserved,' explained *Cassell's Saturday Journal*. 'She can make her appearance at the same counter as the suspected lady and make ostensible purchases.'

Store detectives often worked in disguise, pretending to be a customer or the head of department, and Matilda Mitchell excelled at the job. She had also had a very colourful life in private detection before moving into shop work.

Matilda was a south Londoner like Kate Easton, born in Lambeth on 17 August 1873. She too had a theatrical background and by the age of 15, she was performing at the Royal Opera House in Covent Garden, 'taking part in several operas'. She then appeared in 'several pantomimes' at the Drury Lane Theatre Royal, under the stage name Ethel Chester, although she doesn't seem to have been named in any press reports. Matilda also attended local fancy dress balls 'in all sorts and conditions of disguises' and won many first prizes.

It was these early theatrical experiences that led to her career as a lady detective. Her first case was a divorce suit, when she located an adulterous couple at a big West End hotel. She booked into the room next door to where the erring wife and her lover 'were doing their billing and cooing', and then telegraphed the husband. In the morning, when Matilda heard the chambermaid arriving with the breakfast tray, she snatched the poor woman's cap, put her hand over the chambermaid's mouth and pushed her to one side. Then she ushered the husband into the room. The lovers were sitting up in bed, reading a newspaper, 'like a pair of soiled turtle doves', and the husband 'won his case hands down'.

Matilda Mitchell made a specialty of 'matrimonial misfits'. When a man of means and 'foreign extraction' ran away with a young 'supposedly innocent' girl, Matilda tracked them to a hotel near Caversham, Berkshire, and hid under the bed all night. The chambermaid screamed when she saw Matilda, and the landlord threatened to have her arrested as a lady burglar, but she'd solved the case and 'it ended profitably for me'. Matilda's true-life detective tales were often more salacious than her predecessors', and the wording sounded suspiciously like the work of a male journalist.

According to Matilda, she was also involved in the Hartopp divorce case of 1902, an infamous trial that lasted thirteen days. She wasn't named in the press coverage, and as both divorce petitions were dismissed it was hardly a case to boast about, but she apparently earned 'many compliments from Bench and Bar'. She was then engaged by an actress to investigate her fiancé, who'd set up a 'love nest' in Pimlico. Matilda disguised herself as a male decorator and began painting window frames. How this deterred the actress's rival wasn't explained, but she was disposed of, and the couple were happily married.

Matilda also worked undercover on the railways, as her predecessor Elizabeth Joyes had done in the 1850s. But her investigations took place on the trains rather than in waiting rooms and she sometimes disguised herself as a man. Most major railway companies now employed female detectives, often disguised as lady travellers. They were 'always on the watch,' explained the press, listening to stray pieces of conversation that could point to ticket fraud or corruption among staff.

Matilda then 'entered the service' of the Royal College of Veterinary Surgeons, riding about the country detecting unlicensed vets. But by 1909, she'd settled down at Selfridges, as one of three in-house detectives.

Selfridges was designed for well-to-do ladies to browse in leisure, and female detectives had to be very careful about who they accused of theft. In 1910, Matilda watched a woman of 'good position' put a robe and camisole in her bag and confronted her. 'What nonsense!' the lady replied. 'I have nothing at all.' Female store detectives faced two major problems: privileged ladies who were outraged at the suggestion of shoplifting, and hardened hoisters who were liable to punch them in the face. But Matilda seemed to enjoy the job, she was one of five women to give her occupation as Lady Detective in the 1911 census, and by the following year she'd become head of Selfridges' 'secret service'.

Ada Alice Humphries also worked for Selfridges, and she too had to deal with lady thieves. In April 1912, she observed Mrs Catherine Warham of West Kensington pick up a pair of knickerbockers and place them in her bag. Ada followed her to another department, where Mrs Warham picked up three fluffy toy chickens, before moving to a lace table where she took a piece of embroidery. Ada gave 'the well-known signal to a male assistant' and politely asked Mrs Warham to come to the manager's office. But according to Mrs Warham, a former governess to a 'number of titled families', she was dragged to the office, thrown in a chair, shaken, insulted, searched and accused of theft. She was then forced to listen while the lady detective – 'a wicked woman' – told 'falsehoods'.

Mrs Warham was so furious that in 1913 she sued Selfridges for assault, false imprisonment and slander. The store didn't exactly leap to its lady detective's defence. If any slanderous words had been spoken, then they'd been uttered by employees 'without their authority'. Ada then had to undergo a grilling in court. Didn't Selfridges promise its customers 'Freedom to handle and inspect the articles without obligation'?

'Yes,' she replied, 'but my suspicions were excited because the lady was acting in a suspicious manner.'

Mrs Warham insisted she'd been leaving Selfridges' basement 'when this wretched woman caught hold of me'.

'Where is she?' asked the judge, Justice Darling. 'If there is one woman more wretched than another let her stand up.'

The court erupted into laughter, and then store detective Ada Humphries was forced to stand up to be identified. But Ada handled herself well. The jury found that Mrs Warham had indeed taken the goods without intending to pay for them, and she lost the case.

Matilda Mitchell, meanwhile, had apparently grown tired of detective work. In January 1914, she married Surrey batsman Tom Hayward at Wandsworth Register Office. The press described her as one of 'England's most famous women detectives' and 'in her own way, as remarkable a personality as her husband'.

They were a celebrity couple. Tom was 'not badly off' and had recently scored his 100th century, the first cricketer to equal the record of W.G. Grace. Matilda told the *Mail* that her husband was about to retire, and so was she – 'Am I happy? Oh yes, ever so much.' A photo of the beaming couple hurrying out of the registry office appeared in *The Sketch*, under a feature entitled 'We take our hat off to ...' The caption ran: 'Tom Hayward – for taking a wife who can keep him under observation, and Mrs. Tom Hayward, for catching a great bat.' Tom looked happy and bashful, while Matilda strode ahead, a large fur stole round her shoulders.

She then told her story to the press, recounting some of her amusing adventures to *The People*. 'How did I become a lady detective?' she began. 'That is a question which I have often been asked.' The paper described her as 'a tall, striking blonde with a commanding figure and steady blue eyes' – although this wasn't borne out by the accompanying photograph. She had 'mobile features', according to another journalist, and 'an altogether dominant face for a woman'.

Female store detectives, as a whole, were dominant women. They might call male shop managers or police constables once they'd caught a thief, but they were relentless in their surveillance, trusted their instinct to spot suspicious behaviour, and often gave expert testimony at court.

By the time of her marriage, Matilda Mitchell had spent at least a dozen years in private detection and, according to one Scotland Yard detective, she was 'without doubt the cleverest lady detective in the world'. But here she was in 1914, about to retire.

'Am I glad that my detective days are over?' she asked. 'Well, yes ... a lady detective's life is a trying and risky one.'

Matilda died in 1945 in Hove, six years after her husband's death, leaving a considerable estate. But while Tom Hayward, the pre-war cricketer, is still remembered today, his Wikipedia entry does not even mention that he was married, let alone to a lady detective.

Store detection provided plenty of openings for female detectives, but they weren't glamorised in the same way as sleuths like Kate Easton and Maud West. It was not 'first-class' work, but 'simply spotting'. Their adversaries were usually other women, and they operated in the feminine space of department stores. But for female detectives keen to use their acting skills, there were opportunities in other fields – and one in particular required inventing a whole new persona.

LADY DETECTIVE
AND WIZARD

When Annie Betts arrived at the Regent Street rooms of world-renowned palmist Professor Keiro, she had two questions on her mind: would she travel and would she have children?

Annie was greeted by Madame Keiro, the celebrated clairvoyant, and asked to sit behind a screen to await Professor Keiro. The fee would be 10s 6d, but first she needed to sign a notice: 'Keiro ... has no intention or desire to deceive or impose on anyone. Any consultant is at liberty to believe or not his statements as to character, past life, otherwise.' He had to be very careful, he explained, and protect himself from prosecution. Some palmists, he added, were frauds.

Annie received a palm reading from Madame Keiro and was told her health would be good until the age of 44. Then the clairvoyant closed her eyes, concentrated on her soul, and invoked the aid of the Great Spirit. She gazed into a crystal ball and described a man – medium height, blue eyes and a moustache – and Annie agreed this was her husband, an engineer. She was delighted to hear that she'd have a chubby little baby in eighteen months, followed by four or five more children, one of whom would be a genius. Finally, she was told that a relative in a hot country would leave her a staggeringly large inheritance of £8,000.

Annie Betts left the Regent Street rooms a satisfied customer. But two weeks later, the Keiros were charged with obtaining money by false pretences and telling fortunes under the Witchcraft Act of 1735. Mrs Annie Betts wasn't an innocent customer after all – she was a lady detective.

Telling fortunes was illegal if money was involved or if there was intent to make money. Those 'pretending' to use 'witchcraft, enchantment or conjuration' faced a year in prison. On 9 August 1904, Professor Keiro – otherwise, Charles Stephenson, an ex-journalist – and his wife Martha, a former nurse, appeared in court. A third person was also charged, the intriguingly named Charles Tricker, a 'character reader' known as Yoga who also operated on Regent Street.

The case provided excellent entertainment for the press. The trial in October that year featured on the front page of the *Daily Mirror*, there were headlines such as 'Lady detective and wizard' and the proceedings frequently erupted into laughter. Annie Betts was described as a stylish, aristocratic-looking lady in a big black hat. But she was also portrayed as being a little shamefaced about her job. She told the court that Madame Keiro had not only predicted her fortune, she had 'also told me that I would deceive no one'.

'Did that make you blush?' asked the magistrate.

'Yes, a little,' confessed Mrs Betts.

Fortune telling had long been a staple area of work for female detectives, either investigating clairvoyants or pretending to be one. American Kate Warne had gone undercover as a clairvoyant in 1861, when a client suspected that his sister Annie had tried to poison him under the direction of her lover. Kate Warne quickly taught herself astrology, clairvoyance and mesmerism and transformed herself into L.L. Lucille, a fortune teller based at the Temple of Magic in Chicago. Annie was persuaded to have her fortune told, broke down and confessed, and her lover was found guilty of murder.

In Britain, undercover female detectives had been employed to catch fortune tellers since at least the 1870s, although not always successfully. In 1871, Harriet Courts testified that she'd visited a fortune teller in Birmingham but she seemed reluctant to go into details. She had looked through a globe, been given some cards and told her future looked bright. She then admitted, under cross-examination, that the police had sent her to lay a trap. The defence argued that the accused woman was a respectable dressmaker, and the charge was dropped. Fortune tellers might be frowned upon, but so too was the use of entrapment.

Fortune telling was in vogue in the early 1900s. Palmistry was a popular drawing-room game, while professional fortune tellers offered to find lost persons and property, diagnose and cure disease and pass on messages from the spirit world. But there was increasing concern about spiritualist charlatans. The *Daily Mail* had recently run a series of articles exposing West End palmists and the Keiro trial was a test case and part of a police crackdown.

Professor Keiro was enraged by the charges, telling the *Mirror* that he'd been operating in London for four years and had seen roughly 2,000 clients. 'Black art, indeed! [...] I am a palmist, and if people wish to come and consult me, what is it to do with anyone else?' He argued that the whole affair was a plot hatched up by the *Mail*'s wealthy owner, Sir Alfred Harmsworth – and it was the *Mail*'s solicitors, Messrs. Lewis and Lewis, who had hired lady detective Annie Betts.

She was in her late 20s, born Annie Lange on 27 November 1876 in Pimlico. Her father, Henry, was a coachman, and she was one of twelve children.

The year before the Keiro trial, Annie had married Robert Betts, a widower and clerk of works, and gave her occupation as Lady Detective on the marriage certificate. Aside from investigating fortune tellers, Annie also worked as a store detective, employed at the Army & Navy Stores in Westminster.

Annie insisted that she hadn't been aware of any potential prosecution when she'd visited the Keiros, but then she changed her mind – which was met with mutterings from the public gallery. If 'the truth had been told to her', she argued, then she wouldn't be in court giving evidence. 'I don't know about that,' said the judge. To which Annie quietly responded, 'I do.'

She appeared conscious that she, too, was on trial. According to Madame Keiro, Annie had spun quite a story. She'd arrived for her palm reading very smartly dressed, and 'spoke of being possessed of much money'. But the session had been short because Annie was anxious to get to Monte Carlo, and she wanted to know the winning numbers. 'If I could tell them,' Madame Keiro replied, 'I should be at Monte Carlo, not in Regent-street.'

Annie Betts wasn't the only detective sent by the *Daily Mail*'s solicitors. Retired police inspector Charles Richard also paid them a visit – and was told he'd live to be 100 – as did another lady detective, Dorothy Tempest. Professor Keiro examined her hands, gazed into a crystal ball, and told her she had a weak heart and bad nerves, but would live to 75. She would marry in two years – although Dorothy said she did 'not intend to' – and have one son. She would also be in danger on the sea, travel to Australia and be ill with diphtheria. Dorothy then consulted Madame Keiro, who suggested she needed more exercise.

Like many lady detectives, Dorothy Tempest was an actress. She was born in Dublin, according to Dr Nell Darby, author of *Sister Sleuths*, and received several brief mentions in *The Era* in the mid-1890s, appearing in travelling pantomimes *Aladdin* and *Dick Whittington*. By 1901, she was also working for Lewis & Lewis, the solicitors retained by the *Daily Mail*.

In one case, she was hired to watch Sir Archibald Lennox M. Napier's wife, Mary, after he'd received anonymous letters that she was having an affair. Dorothy travelled to London on the same train as Lady Archibald several times and noted that she was always met by her lover, 'who invariably kissed her'. In 1903, Sir Archibald was granted a divorce, with costs and custody of the couple's child.

But while Dorothy was named in press reports, when she gave evidence in the Keiro trial, she requested that her name and address were not made public. Her bid for anonymity failed. The *Daily Mail* carried a photo of 'Miss Dorothy Tempest the detective', arriving to give evidence wearing a large, ribboned hat, on its front page. The *Penny Illustrated Paper* published a court sketch of Dorothy, showing her looking forlorn but composed. She was a 'smart businesslike girl detective', according to one reporter, while another described her as a handsome lady detective in a crushed strawberry costume and black hat.

Dorothy explained she'd been a private detective for five years and could not be described as an 'ignorant person'. She didn't believe in witchcraft and sorcery, and she didn't believe what the Keiros had told her – it was all 'humbug'. But Dorothy then admitted that she knew a number of palmists and she herself had read hands, but only for amusement because 'people gave me their hands'. She also admitted writing to a Mrs Fisher, a palmist who'd just been acquitted of fortune telling in Aberystwyth, saying she knew more about palmistry than either of the Keiros. 'Oh Dorothy, dear,' replied Mrs Fisher, 'how you must have sunk to take up these horrible spying cases! Do, Dorothy, withdraw your charge!' But Dorothy explained she'd been 'starving for months, and then this case comes along. I did not start it, it was the "Daily Mail".' When she'd received instructions to visit the Keiros, 'I could not very well refuse'.

Dorothy Tempest was clearly under immense pressure. In the midst of being questioned about 'hard times', she suddenly staggered forward in the witness box and fainted. A gentleman standing nearby caught her in his arms, and she was carried from the court. After an adjournment of an hour and a half, she continued her evidence.

Madame Keiro described Dorothy as 'a poor, wretched little thing', but she was later accused of trying to contact the prosecution solicitors and recalled to the stand, 'her dark eyes burning with indignation'. Dorothy appeared to be quite a defiant woman. She'd told Professor Keiro she had no intention of marrying, and now she was apparently trying to pervert the course of justice. Had she fainted because of the shame? Had her collapse been a ploy to earn sympathy? Or was she so hungry she could no longer stand up in the witness box? Acting remained a precarious job, some women were paid as little as 18 shillings a week, whereas Dorothy received around 10 shillings a day as a private detective.

Professor and Madame Keiro were found guilty and bound over not to tell any more fortunes. A couple of weeks later, however, they were advertising 'free readings' in Piccadilly. That same year, Professor Keiro published a book, *Practical Palmistry*, followed, three years later, by an autobiography of his family's tabby cat. Madame Keiro also wrote a book, *Clairvoyance and Crystal Gazing*, and eventually resumed trading in Regent Street, selling embroidered portraits and hair remover.

Dorothy Tempest returned to the stage. In the autumn of 1906, she was playing Countess Anstruther in the musical comedy *The Orchard*, and the *Era* described her as 'sufficiently aristocratic'. Four years later, she was 'a delightful' Queen of the Fairies in *Sinbad the Sailor*, praised for her charm and singing voice. But by the census of 1911, she was back in London and living in Hampstead, where she worked as a lady's companion and gave her birthplace as Brighton. She was also advertising herself in *The Stage*, 'disengaged pantomime. Miss Dorothy Tempest. Experienced. Offers invited. Fairy Queen (Soprano).'

Annie Betts, meanwhile, went on to give evidence at several more occult trials. In 1911, she went undercover to catch Professor Zodiac, 'a well-groomed man of colour' from Jamaica, who operated on Bond Street. Professor Zodiac used numerous identities – Conrad Duhleep, Doctor Mahomed and Rupert Eric Costello De Montgomery – and would be convicted several times.

Annie was also hired by the police to visit Madam Ziska, who operated in Brixton and whose press advert read a little like a private detective's: 'If you are in doubt or difficulty, consult Madam Ziska ... Advice given in all matters of your prospective career.'

By 1914, Annie Betts was working as a store detective, and in one notable case she caught two women, Hannah Kelly and Lizzie Morris, stealing 381 yards of silk from a drapery sale in Kensington. When Annie grabbed 68-year-old Hannah, she objected, 'Take your hands off me – you ought to be a man.' Hannah described her arms as black and blue, 'it was like a navvy pulling me about instead of a woman'.

The two hoisters were professionals and had links to organised gangs. Lizzie Morris's niece was Alice Diamond, the leader of the Forty Elephants, while Hannah Kelly had recently come out of jail.

Annie Betts continued to alternate between store detection and investigating fortune tellers. She became resident detective at Whiteleys in Bayswater, where in 1914 she made six arrests in ten days and the press dubbed her 'Lady Sherlock Holmes'.

Annie Betts' image in the press had changed over the years from the stylish, aristocratic lady during the Keiro trial of 1904 to a woman whose grip was so strong it left bruises. Store detectives were often portrayed as masculine figures – with dominant faces and the desire to be 'master' – as were the suffragettes, who were frequently accused of wanting to 'be like men'. Traditional gender roles were under threat, women were demanding the vote, wearing 'masculine modes' of dress and revelling in doing 'a man's work'. So imagine the anxiety when women took to the streets as uniformed police officers.

14

THE LADY COPPER

Three months after the outbreak of the First World War, eight Women Police Volunteers (WPVs) marched single file through London's Hyde Park, smartly dressed in tunics, long skirts and wide-brimmed hats. The WPV 'posse' was led by an officer, explained the *Leeds Mercury*, and while their numbers were small, their activities were being watched with keen interest.

The patrol members seemed to be aware of the attention. Their gait was confident and three were looking directly at the press photographer. This was emergency wartime work, which would be carried out by various groups of volunteers across the country. The women helped keep order during bombing raids, supervised crowds in parks and tube stations, made inquiries about missing girls and monitored female workers at munitions factories. Some kept an eye on railway property and theft from allotments, others patrolled townships at night with bulldog lanterns and truncheons.

The volunteers also stopped street rows, explained the *League for Women's Suffrage*, 'using tact and the respect due to the lady copper'. But while the women wore uniform, they did not have the power of arrest. Their role was preventative and protective, and largely meant monitoring the behaviour of women and girls.

It could still, however, be exciting work. A journalist with the *Free Church Suffrage Times* described visiting a friend who joined up in 1915. 'Fancy!' she declared, 'I'm a woman patrol.' When the journalist asked, 'Do you like the work?', her friend replied, 'Who wouldn't? Everybody likes being awesome, and I can tell you we are. Nobody knows what powers we have or have not, so they look at us with curiosity very much tempered with fear.'

The idea of women police officers had been slow to catch on in Britain, although female searchers had been employed by the force since at least the 1850s. Thirty years after Elizabeth Joyes was hired to catch a railway thief, the Metropolitan Police started recruiting matrons, to search, transport, chaperone and guard female suspects and prisoners. They sometimes took statements as well and were used as informers and in undercover observations. But their status was semi-official, the work tended to be temporary and wages were low.

Women had also, of course, been working undercover for Scotland Yard since the mid-nineteenth century – 'recruited' into the force to patrol the Great Exhibition, helping police officer husbands to catch crooks, and employed to trap burglars, thieves and fortune tellers. But it wasn't until the early twentieth century that the idea of female police constables started to be taken seriously – and there was plenty of opposition.

When a Canadian soldier caught sight of a police volunteer patrolling in Weybridge one night, he 'advised me to stay at home and bring up my family instead of walking the streets in a way no decent woman should'. In October 1916, Portsmouth Town Council dismissed the very suggestion of female constables as a 'monstrous and awful mistake'. Policing was a masculine job, even more so than private detection, and it required physical strength and the use of force. But campaigners for women police took advantage of wartime conditions. Male officers were away in the trenches and there were increasing fears about 'immoral' behaviour around army barracks, as well as the 'white slave trade' with women trafficked into prostitution abroad.

Towards the end of 1915, a Training School for Women Police and Patrols was opened in Bristol. It was a four- or eight-week course, depending on experience, and cost around £3. Trainees received instruction in civil and criminal law, especially Acts relating to women and children, as well as lectures on 'sex biology', solicitation, prostitution and public indecency. They learned to collect evidence and write reports and studied the procedure and rules of evidence in police courts. They also learned first aid, Swedish drill – a popular form of gymnastics – and self-defence. These new recruits would be professionals, and, unlike private detectives, they received specific training.

The police school offered its graduates 'good posts', according to an advert in the *Gentlewoman*, but it appeared to be an exclusive club, because 'only educated women' could apply. The voluntary patrols were recruited mainly from the middle and upper classes, and few women could afford to live on the £1 a week during training or the starting salary of £2 a week.

In November 1918, Lilian Wyles, a former nurse who'd attended a finishing school in Paris, applied to join the newly formed Metropolitan Police Women Patrols. 'One of the last strongholds held exclusively by men,' she wrote, 'had been stormed.' Lilian attended Peel House Training School, receiving six weeks' instruction in police duties, first aid and drill. Then it was straight to Harrods, to be fitted for her new uniform. A photograph of Lilian shows her looking distinctly restrained, her hair entirely covered with a hat that resembled an 'inverted soup plate', a tunic buttoned up to her chin, a thick 2in-wide belt, a skirt as stiff as board and solid leather boots laced up to the knee.

In February 1919, Lilian Wyles took to the streets for the first time as a sergeant in charge of the whole of central London and the East End. The reaction from male colleagues was hostile, and her squad was told to 'go back to their washtubs'. Male constables objected to women being assigned observation jobs; they were used to employing their wives or girlfriends and pocketing an extra allowance in the process. Men were also reluctant to let women enter the witness box during court cases, preferring to use each other for corroboration.

The public was suspicious too and as Sergeant Wyles patrolled the London streets, she became familiar with muttered comments – 'how queer' and 'how unwomanly'. Female officers were an experiment, she explained. It was deemed dangerous to give them too much authority. Women with the power of arrest let loose on the streets of London might 'arrest all and sundry according to their whims and fancies'. The women had to patrol in pairs and, as they emerged from a police station, they were accompanied by two male officers, following a few yards behind and with instructions to keep them in sight.

In 1919, the Sex Disqualification (Removal) Act was passed, allowing women to join professional bodies. The world of law was changing. Women were becoming barristers, solicitors, magistrates and jurors. Women aged over 30 had also won the right to vote, although it would be several years before women had the same voting rights as men.

By the summer of 1920, the Metropolitan Police had 100 women patrols, and while they still could not make arrests, they were credited with 140 police court convictions in six months. But there were still doubts that women were up to police work – and what about if they were married? The main responsibility of a wife, one sergeant explained, was 'the propagation of children'.

Some local constabularies had already appointed women as constables with powers of arrest, such as Edith Smith in Lincolnshire in 1915. But it wasn't until 1923 that all female officers were sworn in as constables. Recruits had to be aged 25–30, at least 5ft 4in and with no dependent children. They received four-fifths of the men's pay – 60 shillings a week – and were expected to resign if they got married.

As for police detective work, that was still seen as too risky – except in fiction. In 1910, Baroness Orczy, already famous as the author of the *Scarlet Pimpernel*, published *Lady Molly of Scotland Yard*, a collection of tales featuring police detective Molly Robertson-Kirk. The stories are told by Molly's former maid, Mary Granard, a Dr Watson-like character who has become her assistant and friend. Lady Molly heads Scotland Yard's Female Department, who are 'dreadfully snubbed by the men' but who have 'ten times as much intuition as the blundering and sterner sex'. When the two women are assigned a murder case, Lady Molly displays ingenious ways of extracting information – whether clever questioning or placing a false report in the press. She is the 'most wonderful psychologist of her time', detecting crucial clues 'which no amount of male ingenuity would ever have obtained'. But it is later revealed that Lady Molly, the daughter of the Earl of Flintshire, only joined the detective staff to prove her husband's innocence after he was wrongly convicted of murder. Once she hands over proof of one of the dastardliest crimes ever committed, she gives up police work.

Lady Molly was ahead of her time. The Lancashire Police force had formally employed female detectives since 1918, although historian Joan Lock describes their work as mainly clerical and secretarial. Detective Inspector Lilian Naylor, however, did work on murder investigations, policed royal visits and may have worked undercover during investigations into Fenian activity in London. But, in general, the government wasn't keen on female detective officers. 'Detective work is by far the most dangerous work of the lot,' declared a Home Office representative, it involved 'considerable danger, culminating with the arrest of the criminals'.

However, according to the *Leeds Mercury*, in 1914 there was already a specially trained corps of women detectives 'doing police work in

London'. They carried a card issued by Scotland Yard, 'which quickly puts at rest any doubts as to the bona-fides of the lady investigator'. The paper cited several cases in which these female detectives had been involved – information on the activities of the suffragettes and the campaign against West End fortune tellers. But these investigations had been carried out by private detectives – such as Maud West, Annie Betts and Dorothy Tempest – who were often employed by solicitors, private inquiry agencies and individual clients. Female sleuths had paved the way for the acceptance of women in the police force, both as constables and as detectives.

At least one policewoman was also working as a detective on the railways. In 1916, Annie Martin was employed by the Great Western Railway and became known as the 'Terror of Station Thieves'. Annie was 'a little woman, with a pleasant face', according to the press, and she looked 'as unlike a policewoman as one could imagine'. She assisted women passengers who 'complained of molestation', identified, confronted and interviewed fare dodgers, and gave evidence in court. Like her Victorian forebear Elizabeth Joyes, she also sat watch in waiting rooms, 'If I am sitting in there in a hat and coat, they never dream that I'm a detective'.

But unlike her predecessor, she had a warrant and was able to make an arrest. In one case, she was sent undercover after reports of jewellery thefts from women's luggage on a Somerset line. Annie set out with cash and jewellery in her bag, which she placed in the luggage compartment. On arrival in Yatton, she knew her bag had been tampered with because 'the case was packed as a man would pack it' and a piece of gauze was poking out the side. A railway carriage cleaner was arrested, and when police searched his home, they found the stolen jewellery hidden inside his piano.

By the mid-1920s, some local authorities also had 'a small body of clever women detectives', according to one report, 'little is said of this, the fact that their office and work is so little-known helping towards its success'.

In 1922, Lilian Wyles became the first female CID officer at the Met Police, but her work was restricted to women and girls, and her specific job was as a 'sex statement' taker. She was the only woman among 3,000–4,000 men and had no office or room to work from.

CID women were gradually entrusted with a more varied workload – inquiries, observations, tailing and shadowing suspects. But female officers continued to face criticism and humiliation in the courts, and they could be ordered out if a judge decided a case would offend their feminine sensibilities.

What did female private detectives think of their police counterparts – both uniformed and undercover? It's unlikely they were consumed with envy over their sisters in blue. Private detectives worked far more independently than those in the force, especially women like Maud West who ran their own agencies. They had more freedom, were better paid and suffered less grief from male colleagues. They also recruited, hired and gave orders to men.

Private detectives were not confined to dealing with women and children; they chose their own cases. They weren't hampered by bureaucracy or red tape and they had not been 'drilled', given a number, made to wear a restrictive uniform or banned from wearing make-up in public. There were no entry requirements for private detection in terms of class, age or height and women were not barred because they had small children nor expected to resign if they got married. But private detectives did not have official authority, they didn't carry a warrant and couldn't make an arrest – however much some seemed to think they could.

Women police officers were trained professionals. They belonged to an institution and were invested with the power of the state. But it wasn't too long before lady detectives were receiving more formal training as well.

15

THE WOMEN 'TECS
OF BAKER STREET

At the top of some rather dingy stairs in Baker Street, not far from Sherlock Holmes' fictional home, lay the offices of Charles Henry Kersey, a burly 6ft trainer of lady detectives. When *Britannia and Eve* sent a journalist to visit his College for Feminine Undergraduates of Crime Investigation, a class was in progress. 'If he seizes you by the throat,' Mr Kersey told his pupils, 'DO THIS', and with a bloodcurdling gesture, he showed them the best way of breaking a little finger. This was followed by a demonstration of 'the death grip', which rendered suspects completely helpless.

British women appeared very keen to learn the death grip. Charles Kersey's trainees included 'all sorts' – shop assistants, private secretaries, clerks, women who ran tea shops, managers of hotels and restaurants and ladies of title and wealth. The trainees visited police courts, practised evidence giving, learned how to shadow and received detailed instruction on laws and 'worldly wisdom'. They also learned how to handle obstreperous shoplifters, and ju-jutsu techniques for self-defence.

Ju-jutsu had been popular in Britain since the early twentieth century. In 1909, Edith Garrud, who ran the School of Ju-Jutsu on Regent Street, had included a display as part of a suffragette exhibition in Knightsbridge. She then trained a thirty-woman protection unit, the Bodyguard, for the WSPU.

Students at the College for Feminine Undergraduates of Crime Investigation learnt their ju-jutsu skills from Charles Kersey, an ex-Metropolitan Police officer and military 'hero'. He'd retired from the force after twenty-five years and opened a detective agency and training school at No. 130 Baker Street. Like Victorians Maurice Moser and Henry Slater, he created publicity through his use of lady detectives, and when the crime investigation college opened in 1927 it attracted plenty of attention.

'In these days of women barristers, doctors, steeplejacks, and deep-sea divers,' wrote the *Sunday Post*, 'it is not surprising to hear that there are now women detectives.' It was another example of the 'latest invasion of the sacred domains of man'.

In reality, women had been working as private inquiry agents for over fifty years, but it was being presented as a novel career path. Private detection was a 'new' profession for women, according to *The Graphic*, and the *Weekly Dispatch* said the same – the 'new' profession of detection was 'claiming its fair share of recruits' and numbers were 'ten times' higher than before the war.

Pathé News produced a short film on the Baker Street training school, where a group of fashionable, bobbed-haired young women took notes from Mr Kersey, and then enthusiastically tried out a restraining hold. But the focus of the film was the students' ability to transform themselves. 'Disguise is, of course, a necessary acquirement,' explained *Pathé*, as two newspaper boys removed their hats and shook out their hair to reveal they were female detectives.

Women were on the look-out for excitement in post-war Britain, and detection seemed to fit the bill. Young girls besieged Charles Kersey's office most days, 'clamouring to become a lady detective. I suppose the idea of meeting plenty of thrills attracts them.' *The Graphic* published photos of the 'Woman 'Tecs of Baker Street' learning 'the copper's clinch'. The tone of the report was admiring, but as always with female detectives, it was also humorous. One photo showed two trainees in character as men, ready to 'shadow any crook whose eyesight is not good'.

Charles Kersey, meanwhile, didn't seem too interested in staying on the right side of the law himself. He would later be sentenced to three months' imprisonment for fraud, and then jailed for two months for obtaining credit from tradesmen. It also emerged that he'd been the subject of numerous complaints about business transactions ever since his retirement from the police force, and he'd been declared bankrupt in 1929, while running his detective agency and training school.

But private detection was being presented as a serious career option for women in the 1920s. Jobs were available at private agencies and large, busy stores, explained *The Dispatch*, the work was fascinating and the pay substantial. Female detectives were astute, resourceful and just as clever as their male rivals and 'Miss Sherlock Holmes' often proved herself 'more capable in certain cases of criminal detection than male investigators'.

Scotland Yard could only boast 'two or three' women detectives in the mid-1920s, but the private side of detection was booming. A staff detective in a West End store earned an average weekly wage of around £5, but a 'chief' received as much as £500 a year. The private lady detective, engaged by lawyers and litigants, reportedly earned over £1,000 a year – equivalent to around £64,000 today. She was a woman of culture, explained the *Dispatch*, who spoke several languages and was able to adapt herself to 'any society without embarrassment'. She sounded very much like Victorian sleuth Antonia Moser.

The 1920s also witnessed a major change in the divorce laws. The Matrimonial Causes Act of 1923 allowed women to petition for the dissolution of a marriage on the same terms as men – they only needed to prove adultery. Two years after the Act was passed, women made up 63 per cent of all petitioners. Divorce remained costly and complicated and it still carried a sense of moral shame, but the Act led to more work for private detectives.

Charles Kersey might have described himself as the only trainer of women detectives, but Maud West was training her recruits as well. By the mid-1920s, she'd been in the business for over ten years, still operating from her offices on New Oxford Street. Her one-time competitors were no longer on the scene. Antonia Moser had died in 1919 and Kate Easton's adverts for her Warwick Court agency seem to have ended in 1917, when her address for telegrams was 'Inquirendo' – the authority to conduct investigations. The suffrage supporter and ex-actress, who'd boasted of doing a man's work, appears to have retired by the end of the First World War.

Kate did, however, appear in *The International Police and Detective Directory* of 1922. The directory was produced in the States and listed thirty-five detective agencies in London, but only two were headed by women – Miss Kate Easton, who now had a male competitor on the same street, and Miss Maud West. Kate Easton died at St Mary Abbot's Hospital in Kensington on 24 November 1931, following an accidental fall. She was 75 years old, and her profession was recorded as 'spinster. Of independent means.'

But Maud West was still rushing around the world, dressing as a man and relaying true crime stories to the press. Her tales grew ever more hair raising – lady drug takers, car chases and gangsters – she frequently dashed to Holland, Spain and Italy at an hour's notice and tracked her targets all the way to South Africa, the British East Indies and Buenos Aires.

Detective work was 'not sensational,' she warned, 'in spite of the popular cinema representations, and except for criminal work, carries very little danger with it.' But Maud made good use of cinematic representations, which often featured female detectives on dangerous missions. In *There Are No Villains*, a female sleuth was employed by the American secret service to track down opium smugglers, while in the British film *Cocktails*, an undercover maid caught a gang of crooks smuggling cocaine and opium into England.

As for Maud West, in March 1926, the *Sunday Post* reported she was going undercover to a séance, where she would fire a revolver to 'test' whether a ghostly figure was a spirit. Spiritualism had seen a revival in the 1920s, with people desperate for contact with loved ones lost during the war, and Maud's investigations sounded a lot more exciting than the days when Annie Betts and Dorothy Tempest had pretended to have their palms read. Maud would not shoot to kill, she explained, but 'this experience will be the most remarkable in the whole of my career'. The article was accompanied by a photo of Maud, looking remarkably like Charlie Chaplin, with bowler hat and fake moustache, and described as one of the best lady shots in the country.

But where exactly had she got her gun from? The Firearms Act of 1920 had introduced a registration system. A licence cost half a crown and was issued by local police forces, who could refuse any applicant 'unfitted to be trusted with a firearm'. Those who wanted a gun had to prove they had a good reason – which presumably didn't include shooting spirits at séances. But private sleuths like Maud West and Kate Easton had established links with Scotland Yard, and if they did apply for a licence then they knew who to turn to.

Maud was now 'probably London's only woman detective', according to *The Sphere*, and just like Charles Kersey, she too was training her recruits. Maud charged an undisclosed fee, applicants were given a two-week trial, and 'if they are unsuitable or unfitted for the game, I frankly tell them so'. They were then put on probation for three months.

Maud also gave her pupils a test, informing them, 'I shall be at a certain big store at a given time, on a given day'. The trainee detective had to describe 'exactly what I have done and where I have been before arriving there. In other words, to "shadow" me', and then file a full report. Maud trained her staff in observation skills as well, teaching them to recognise mannerisms and facial features and identify people from their descriptions.

The training offered by Charles Kersey and Maud West sounded practical, active and physical. Women learned restraining holds and self-defence, court procedure and evidence giving, and the science of shadowing and observation. But there were still no requirements needed to open a detective agency other than capital. No qualifications were necessary for those who dreamt of private detection, experience was not essential and they definitely didn't need to pass any exams.

16

AN UNDERGROUND JOB

'Congratulations! This is just to let you know that you have successfully passed the above Award.'

A few days after sitting my Level 3 for Professional Investigators in Paddington, I receive a surprise email. Despite being convinced that I'd failed the two exams by answering all the questions in roughly fifteen minutes, I've passed. When I tell our trainer Will Clayton that I can't believe it, he replies, 'Don't underestimate yourself!'

But passing an exam is one thing. If I now wanted to gain some work experience then I'd be unlikely to find it. Most PIs in the UK work for themselves and, according to Bluemoon College, they have 'no interest in sharing their methods or technologies'. Investigations are confidential and sensitive. PIs tend to view newcomers as competition and the general attitude is 'Why should we share our knowledge?' So how does someone become a private eye?

I contact the case officer who sat the exam with me and she agrees to meet on Zoom. It's a Monday evening and she's in her London office, but there's very little in the background except for two small clocks on a white wall.

'How do people get work?' I ask. 'If they've taken a BTEC qualification, for example, who will give them work experience or offer them a job?'

'It's hard,' says the case officer. 'It's really difficult to get first-hand experience, because as an industry it's very anonymous or low profile.' She pauses for a long time. 'It's difficult,' she says again. 'The nature of the job is almost underground.'

'How did you get into the industry?' I ask. 'What was your route into investigation?'

The case officer initially studied psychology, and then worked as an assistant psychologist. One day, she saw a job vacancy for an intelligence analyst, investigating insurance fraud for a company that specialised in using social media. 'I learned the tools and the tricks,' she explains, 'to pull out information about people.' This was followed by a stint at the government's Land Registry, working on property fraud. For the past four years she's worked for a specialist legal intelligence provider, investigating fraud, corruption and money laundering. 'They're high-profile due diligence cases,' she explains, 'like investigating someone who is being hired for an executive role, digging into their lives and background.'

She's also investigated a man who disappeared while travelling in South America, and helped to find a young woman who went missing in the UK. Some of her cases have attracted huge media attention, but she can't go into details, and she doesn't want me to use her real name either.

'What skills do you need,' I ask, 'to be a successful PI?'

'You must be a creative thinker,' says the case officer, 'and think outside the box. You also need tenacity. You spend hours reading and researching, coming to all sorts of dead ends, and you have to stick with it. You also need a level of instinct. And that's why ...', the case officer pauses and drinks from an enormous bottle of water, 'I think women are better at the job than men.'

'You do?' I ask. 'Are we naturally better? Do we have an inherent sense of instinct, or is this something that we learn?'

The case officer considers. 'Women have a higher level of awareness,' she says. 'We need it in order to protect ourselves. But it's also innate because women are more nurturing, and that gives us a certain type of instinct.'

This sounds similar to the Victorian belief that women's intuition had its roots in protecting offspring and was closely linked to the notion of maternal instinct.

'What does instinct tell us?' I ask the case officer. 'Is it a feeling that something's not right, is it knowing, for example, when someone is lying?'

'Not really,' she says. 'It's more that it leads us to conclusions. Clients don't just want research but professional assessment. It's knowing where to start, and which path to go down.'

'Can you give me an example?'

'Well, a couple of weeks ago, we had to find where a businessman was living. He has homes in different countries and links to a lot of places, and we needed to find his current location. I looked at his companies, and I just felt he was in London.'

'And he was?'

'Yes.'

'So that must take quite a lot of confidence in your own instinct?'

'Confidence and nerve. You have to tell your clients what you think.'

'What advice would you give to other women,' I ask, 'who are just starting out as investigators?'

The case officer laughs and takes another swig of water. 'Be aware of your surroundings. Don't ever stop asking questions. Stay curious. And, it sounds so cheesy, but I would say tap into your third eye.'

★ ★ ★

A few days later, my Level 3 certificate arrives, and I put it on my notice-board, along with pictures of the women I've found so far. Victorian sleuths Ellen Lyons and Paulowna Upperley look stern and rather down at heel in their *Lloyds Weekly* pen portraits of 1895 – after Ellen had entrapped young Gertrude Barrett and Paulowna had been accused of blackmail.

Dorothy Tempest, the part-time actress, looks wistful during the Keiro fortune-telling trial of 1904 when she fainted on the stand. Antonia Moser appears businesslike in *Reynolds's Newspaper* in 1909, when she'd broken free from Maurice and started her agency on the Strand. Matilda Mitchell beams with happiness at her marriage in 1914, the day she retired from store detection, while Maud West is dapper in her top hat and tails, working undercover in West End nightclubs.

For many of the women, however, I can't find any images at all – not railway detective Elizabeth Joyes, store detective Annie Betts, nor even London's Leading Woman, Kate Easton. However high profile some of the women were, the nature of the job was still underground, just like the case officer today.

All of them were confident in their powers of intuition, but none took any qualifications or sat any exams, and when Maud West started training her staff, the industry was still a free for all. But by the 1930s, private eyes would begin to police themselves, thanks to the work of the first professional organisation for detectives in Britain.

A CLEAN PROFESSION

In the spring of 1912, a young man in York published an advert in a Sheffield newspaper inviting men to join the British Detective Association. Twenty-six-year-old William Halton received at least thirty-nine replies, to which he responded, 'Sir, – Please note all correspondence must be done in pencil, blotting pads tell too many secrets … I am pleased to inform you that our secretary authorizes me to visit your references.'

One of the association's 'specials' would now give the applicant 'careful attention (unknown to you)', and gather the information required for membership. But this incurred a cost and if the applicant was 'prepared to meet us half-way', by forwarding 5 shillings, then 'we shall at once put our "man" in touch with you'. When the police caught up with William Halton, he confessed to the fraud and was sentenced to three months' hard labour.

The real British Detectives Association (BDA) was formed the following year, when ex-Scotland Yard detective inspector Harry Smale gathered a small group of private detectives in London. He'd retired from the police force in 1908 and set up a private agency on Buckingham Street, just a stone's throw from Antonia Moser's office on the Strand. Harry Smale also handled European cases for the famous American Pinkerton Detective Agency and his most publicised case would come in the 1920s when he tracked down a crooked American stockbroker who'd absconded with £100,000.

The purpose of the BDA was clear: it would reform abuses, improve and 'purify' detective methods and guard against imposition and fraud. From now on, private detection would be 'a clean profession'. But when the First World War broke out, members were recalled into the police or enlisted in the armed services, and the association disbanded. It re-formed in 1919 and continued its mission to clean up the business.

Membership was 4 guineas to join, plus 3 guineas annual fee. This wasn't cheap; the joining fee alone was equal to the weekly wage of a police constable with five years' service. There was another requirement: BDA members had to have been in regular employment as a detective for at least three years. Despite these restrictions, membership grew and by the 1930s the BDA was pressing for official recognition.

In September 1933, 200 MPs reportedly agreed to support a private member's bill to give private detectives the same legal status as doctors, lawyers, accountants, dentists and other professionals. The problem, explained Harry Smale, was that anyone could open a private detective agency and 'fleece the public without fear of any penalty or punishment'. Blackmail had increased since the war, and reputable agencies were suffering from the frauds of their bogus competitors. The BDA wanted detective agencies registered, then they could be struck off if needed. Some agencies began to cite their BDA membership in newspaper adverts to add to their credibility, but the bill failed to materialise. The government argued that licensing wasn't needed anyway because the BDA already had guidelines of conduct for its members.

Private detective agencies appeared to be flourishing in the 1930s. The *Lancashire Daily Post* counted at least fifty firms in London – in 1922 there had been thirty-five. A growing proportion were run by ex-Scotland Yard men, who were obliged to retire at 50 and were looking for a 'suitable outlet for their energies'. Private detective agencies had always been dominated by ex-police, from Victorians Charles Field and Maurice Moser to Charles Kersey in the 1920s. They had led the way in the field of private detection – and they'd also contributed to its dubious image. They had told lies and used underhand methods, offered bribes, invented evidence and broken the law.

The Metropolitan Police Force was now a century old, and there were an increasing number of officers seeking an interesting life after retirement. But these were men of honour, insisted the *Lancashire Post*, and if they did anything improper then they'd lose their police pensions.

Most of their work consisted of humdrum inquiries and shadowing to get divorce evidence. In 1919, when the BDA was re-formed, divorce made up at least 85 per cent of a private detective's caseload. The new Matrimonial Causes Act of 1937 increased the potential client base even further by introducing additional grounds for divorce: cruelty, three years' desertion, habitual drunkenness and 'incurable insanity'.

Opposition from the Church was fierce. The Act would 'lower the whole tone of matrimony', according to one bishop. There were also fears about collusion, spouses who wanted a divorce needed evidence – even when no 'offence' had been committed. One popular method was the 'hotel bill case'. A husband would hire a woman to spend a weekend in a hotel and her job was to be seen – usually by a chambermaid – in bed with him just before breakfast. The man then sent the hotel bill to his wife, which along with the maid's testimony provided adequate evidence for divorce. But this could be risky; those caught colluding would be guilty of fraud.

The dangers of rogue detectives continued to make headlines in the 1930s. Crooked agents were charging for inquiries they were unwilling – or unable – to make, and as investigations were carried out in secrecy, a client had no idea of the truth. Some detectives accepted bribes for stolen property, used confidential information about private lives for blackmail and sold information obtained during surveillance.

The BDA's Harry Smale described meeting a man he'd arrested while still a detective inspector, 'and he told me he was now my rival in business'. Another man, a solicitor who'd been struck off, started an agency as soon as he came out of jail. It was high time, Harry argued, to end the 'scandal of the crook agent' and 'purge the country of these charlatans'.

The BDA sounded like quite a macho organisation, set up by a group of ex-policemen keen to 'fight the crooks'. There don't seem to have been any references to female detectives during debates over legal recognition, and it's unclear if BDA membership was even open to women.

But it wasn't just men who were busy opening agencies. During a walk through the West End, one journalist noted the nameplates of eleven women. Female detectives were also still very much in the press and a 1931 feature in *Britannia and Eve*, 'The Woman in Blue', showed the variety of detective work open to women. It was lavishly illustrated with photographs of London policewomen and store detectives, as well as a private detective dressed in full evening dress with top hat and gold-topped cane. 'These modern days,' the paper noted, 'the actual hand of the law can be, and increasingly often is, a woman.'

Most female sleuths were still employed as store detectives, and the job could be hazardous. Marks & Spencer detective Violet Molock once chased two young women out of the Oxford Street shop, down the street and into a teashop. One jumped up and gave Violet a hard blow on the breast, the other struck the store detective in the face and tried to stick her fingers in her eye. 'I put my arms round her neck,' Violet calmly told the court, 'and held on to her.'

Violet was in her early 30s, born Violet Emily Williams in Surrey around 1896, and she'd already been a store detective for nearly a decade. Her most dramatic confrontation came in 1933 when she caught Bessie Evans instructing her 12-year-old daughter to steal a watch, a packet of chocolate and an ice cream. Bessie fought all the way to the manager's office, struck Violet in the face and breast, and accused her of planting evidence. According to Bessie, the store detective had flown at her and called her 'a cow and a shoplifter'. But Violet said that, 'so far as she knew', she had not struck Bessie on the mouth; she'd simply acted in self-defence during the struggle for some stolen frocks.

The following year, Violet was complimented 'for the nth time' for her wonderful memory, after giving evidence in yet another shoplifting case. She explained she'd never needed to make notes because she remembered everything. As a test, she was asked to repeat long witness statements that had been recorded the week before. The prosecuting counsel compared her statements to the notes he'd made, and as she concluded, he exclaimed, 'Why that is absolutely word for word! It is most extraordinary. It is phenomenal!'

The *Daily Mirror* was intrigued and sent a journalist to Marks & Spencer to ask further questions of the 'chic little woman', who was 'a quick-change artist and a memory expert'. Violet never carried a notebook, she explained, 'I just tell the magistrate the facts, and that is all that interests him'. When asked if she disguised herself, she laughed, 'Well, I don't exactly wear a false nose, or a wig, but I do keep a fairly extensive wardrobe, so that I can change my clothes, if necessary.' Violet declined to give her photograph: 'That would never do, then I should have to disguise myself.'

Violet Molock sounded practical, down to earth and brave. She worked in an environment where she was repeatedly exposed to assault, was proud of her skills and continued her career into the mid-1950s. But there was no mention of this line of work from the BDA, whose focus was closing ranks against bogus male detectives. 'Women are the most frequent victims of these sharks,' declared Harry Smale. They consulted a detective about their love life and 'lifelong blackmail follows'.

The BDA was apparently saving female clients from exploitation. However, store detection was big business in Britain and most of the workers were women. Many female sleuths who started off in shopwork were soon investigating far more dangerous cases and one, in particular, was intent on saving young women from white slavery.

MAY STOREY: A GREAT CAREER FOR A GIRL

One spring morning in the Midlands, a cautious young woman set off for a job interview, desperate to find work in the middle of the Great Depression. She had answered an advert in a local paper – a married couple were looking for a maid and she was invited to a splendid mansion in the suburbs. There she was introduced to two men and a lady and pressed to take tea with the 'family'.

The young woman was hesitant, she felt something was not quite right. As the lady stood up to pour the tea, she noticed a man's cuff protruding from beneath the sleeve of her dress – and instantly knew she was in the house of white slavers.

The young woman accepted the tea, flung the hot liquid in the man's face, dashed down the stairs three at a time, and ran out the front door. Out on the street she tried in vain to find a policeman, then once she got home, she contacted the one person who could help: private detective May Storey.

May Storey ran an agency which provided detectives for major shops in Manchester, Birmingham and London. Her all-women staff were ju-jutsu experts, many had learnt boxing and they were skilled mechanics who operated their own fleet of motorcycles. 'Sleuthing,' according to May Storey, 'was a great career for a girl.'

Her agency also handled private cases and she knew all about 'white slavers', for she was often asked to find missing girls. The term 'white slavery' had been around since at least the 1860s, referring to the employment of children and the evils of long hours and low wages. Towards the end of the nineteenth century, following scandalous reports of British girls exploited on the Continent, white slavery came to mean an international traffic in women and girls.

By 1912, England had reportedly become a clearing house for the white slave trade. Suffragette and campaigner Teresa Billington-Greig, however, challenged the rising hysteria about dangerous foreign men abducting innocent white women, who were forcibly trapped, drugged and transported abroad. This 'epidemic of terrible rumours' had led to a 'frenzy for legislation measures', and so Teresa decided to investigate.

She approached the topic like a detective: where was the evidence, the eyewitnesses, the first-hand signed statements, the proof? She contacted numerous vigilance societies that had been formed to combat vice and immorality, as well as women's organisations, police chiefs, magistrates, unions and newspaper editors, who all confirmed there was no hard evidence at all. It was a 'campaign of sedulously cultivated sexual hysterics', Teresa concluded, and in reality, more men and boys were going missing than women and girls. Why, she asked, had none of these kidnapping traffickers been 'brained with fenders' or injured with chairs? Women were not 'imbecilic weaklings' incapable of resisting, there was no truth to the press tales and legislation had achieved nothing for the victims of prostitution.

By the time private detective May Storey came to prominence twenty years later, white slavery was in the news again, thanks in part to the rise of the tabloid press, with its reliance on sensation, scandal and sexual content. Towards the end of 1933, a League of Nations committee reported on a ten-year investigation into trafficking. They'd visited the low quarters of London and Liverpool, explained the *Sunday Dispatch*, going undercover at dance halls, cafes and houses of ill repute, where they discovered girls were being trapped by sham offers of marriage or employment – just like the young woman in the Midlands.

May Storey played on these fears about white slavery, offering 'disturbing disclosures' and 'firsthand experience'. While she didn't find the white slavers in the Midlands – they had gone by the time she got to the suburban mansion – she did have success in similar cases. During one investigation, she disguised herself as a man, travelled to London, caught the boat train to Paris, infiltrated an evil-smelling opium den, caught a gang of white slavers and rescued nine drugged girls. She also investigated dope peddling among the Ultra-Smart Set, attending a 'cracker party' in London's Mayfair. May accepted a cone of 'snow', pretended to sniff cocaine and left before the party got too 'disgusting'.

May Storey's articles featured in several Midlands papers in the early 1930s, as well as publications in Liverpool and Lancashire. She often wrote about women as victims of crime – and as perpetrators – and was seen as an expert on topics of the day, such as whether the British police should be armed. May was outspoken and opinionated, much as Antonia Moser had been, condemning British divorce laws as ridiculous and obsolete.

She was keen to correct assumptions about female sleuths, but unlike Antonia Moser, she felt no need to defend her morals. Instead, she wanted to prove that women had the nerve and courage to tackle big cases. A woman 'in a tight corner was no weakling', she declared, and was perfectly capable of self-defence. Some of May's girls had caught armed criminals, chasing motor bandits and bringing their cars to a standstill.

She was tired of being told, 'but a woman a detective – really I can scarcely believe it'. The world had changed, women's place was no longer by the fireside and in the nursery, it was time to 'give the woman sleuth a chance'.

May was annoyed that female detectives still operated in a limited field, mainly preventing shoplifting, keeping an eye on guests and gifts at weddings, and discreet inquiries in divorce cases. Tracking down dangerous criminals was 'regarded as a man's job, and men, I might add, have taken good care to see that such work remains in their own hands'. But women had many advantages, especially when faced with male criminals with 'swollen heads', who laughed contemptuously 'at the very idea of a woman having sufficient ingenuity to lay him by the heels'.

Women possessed a much sharper sense of intuition – 'she can, as it were, feel the presence of the wrong doer' – and some girls could enter a crowded room and pick out the would-be thief in a few moments. But a woman's most valuable asset, according to May, was her insatiable curiosity. She wouldn't stop until a riddle was solved.

May wanted to see women working alongside men at CID, and she also suggested a separate Scotland Yard unit of women, whose 'business would involve the bringing of the male criminal to justice'. These were radical words, and like her forebears Antonia Moser and Kate Easton, she wasn't afraid to speak up or to take on a man's job.

Women police officers had become more involved in covert surveillance by the 1930s, undertaking observations on suspected brothels, illegal gambling, betting and drinking dens. But their numbers remained small, and by the end of the decade only around a quarter of the 183 police forces in England and Wales employed women. As for female detectives, their job was still largely restricted to women and children, although the press admitted 'their usefulness in inquiry work where more serious crime is involved'.

In the summer of 1933, three Metropolitan women police officers were appointed as full members of CID, assigned to plain clothes duty in the West End. They'd been on probation for a year and had undergone 'almost the same tests as the men'. The press anticipated 'thrilling days were ahead' for the new CID officers – catching shoplifters and drug smugglers, working undercover at shady nightclubs and acting as 'decoys'. Their identity was to be kept in strictest secrecy, explained the *Sunderland Daily Echo*, 'two of them are dark, the third is blonde. All are young and good-looking and their ages are between 20 and 30. That is all that can be said about them.'

May Storey's identity wasn't exactly crystal clear either. The press provided very little information on this remarkable woman, not even her age, noting simply that she was from the north of England and ran the International Detective Agency. May implied that she had an office in London, not far from the Old Bailey, and she also referred to 'my office in Liverpool'. But there doesn't seem to be any documentary evidence of her detective agency, and she is an extremely difficult woman to track down.

There is a clue, however, in a 1932 article in the *Birmingham Gazette*. It described her as a 'jolly woman', who sometimes went up north to Tynemouth, near Newcastle upon Tyne, to 'give her mother a hug'. Mrs Harry Storey, it added, was a keen worker for charity, with a silver medal for her services.

Storey was a very common name in the area, but there was a Harry Storey, who in 1901 lived with his family in the coastal town of Tynemouth. He was a coal miner from Yorkshire, while his wife Mary was from Northumberland. In 1911, the family were living at Burradon Colliery, in the mining village of Dudley, a few miles north of Newcastle upon Tyne. The couple had six children, aged between 7 and 20, and lived in a two-room house.

The eldest of the four daughters, Helena, was a dressmaker, followed by Mary Ellen (or Eleanor), Margaret Amelia and Florence Elizabeth. So which one was May? Was she Mary Ellen, born 18 May 1895, in the village of Camperdown, Northumberland, and whose birth was registered in Tynemouth? If she was, then there are no references to her work as a private detective, although a Mary Ellen Storey did appear in the *York Trade Directory* for 1932. There are no details about what her business might have been, however, and York was a long way from the family home.

How had May got into private detection in the first place? How had a coal miner's daughter from England's north-east, an area hard hit by poverty, pit closures and soaring unemployment, become a leading sleuth?

Her press tales often featured young women who left 'teeming Northern towns' and headed to London in search of work, ran out of money, fell into bad company and joined the 'legions of the lost'. Had May, too, travelled down to the capital and perhaps found work as a store detective?

In 1934, she told radio listeners a bizarre story about the roots of her career. Many years earlier, she'd been returning home from a party down a dark country lane in Cumberland when some youths jumped out from behind a hedge dressed in sheets. The shock was so great that May lost her power of speech. A year later, it came back when a young nephew bathing in the sea got into difficulties and she managed to yell out. But during that year of silence, she studied law, languages and chemistry, and turned herself into a private detective. By the time of her radio interview, however, May's all-woman agency seemed to be no more, and now she was accompanied by male assistants.

While I can't be certain of May Storey's identity, the press did provide photographs. In 1933, the *Birmingham Gazette* carried an advert featuring 'Miss Sherlock Holmes!' with a photo that is frustratingly grainy. But there is a clearer one in the *Nottingham Journal*, which advertised a series of sensational chapters from May's casebook. She is decidedly 'mannish', by 1930s standards, with close-cropped hair, wearing an open-neck shirt and jacket. The *Sunday Mercury* used the same photo, but this time May was sitting with 'her secretary' – although it looks suspiciously like the paper simply put two separate photos side by side.

There is an even clearer image in a collection of cigarette cards produced by W.A. & A.C Churchman, a cigarette manufacturer based in Ipswich, whose collectible cards were usually sports related and often featured football stars. In 1938, May Storey was part of a series entitled 'In Town To-Night', presumably referring to the popular Saturday night radio show of the same name, which had started on the BBC Home Service a few years earlier. May Storey looks like the archetypal male sleuth, wearing a brown overcoat and peering out from beneath the rim of a large fedora hat. She could almost be Dick Tracy, the fictional American police detective who'd started life as a comic strip in 1931, and who frequently sported a trench coat and fedora. Today, May's image is part of a collection at the National Portrait Gallery, which identifies her only as 'a detective who was active in the 1930s'.

The 'In Town To-Night' series contained fifty portraits, often of people in unusual jobs – a stunt rider, tattooist, swordsmith, rat catcher and magician. The women covered quite a range from Mrs Nelson, an acrobat and chimney sweep, Florence Bell, head nurse at the Royal Veterinary College, Christina Foyle, the managing director of Foyles, and aviator Pauline Gower, who'd just published a book about her adventures, *Women with Wings*. The text on the back of May Storey's card explained she had 'one of the most exciting jobs possible'. Not only was she engaged in detecting shoplifters, but she had to 'shadow people of every type, from dope pedlars to confidence tricksters, and from blackmailers to missing heirs'. Her work carried her all over the world and she was required to act various parts, including stewardess on a liner, housemaid and charlady. 'Of course Miss Storey frequently adopts masculine roles,' explained the card, 'which suit her particularly well as she has a deep voice and very short hair.'

Short hair – and trousers – were in fashion for women in the interwar years. Clothing had become more practical, with broad shoulders and 'masculine' fabrics of woollens and flannels. By the late 1920s, masculine clothing was also seen as an expression of lesbian identity. However, aside from the reference to May's 'deep voice', there didn't seem to be any insinuations about her sexuality from the press.

Shopbreaker Elsie Carey, on the other hand, who operated in the same period, drew a lot of negative attention for her masculine attire. She was arrested while wearing an overcoat, trilby hat and flannel trousers. The press dubbed her 'Lady Jack' and made repeated hints about her relationships with other women. But May Storey – whoever she really was

– seems to have been a celebrated figure, perhaps because she was a detective and therefore 'in disguise'.

Despite her appearance on a mass-produced cigarette card, she then disappears. By 1939, Mary Ellen Storey's father had died and her mother was living near Newcastle upon Tyne with her two sons, both coal miners, and her daughter Margaret. I can't find any more traces of May – or Mary Ellen – Storey. The woman who had argued that sleuthing was a great career for girls, urged for a Scotland Yard unit of women and allegedly tracked down white slavers had suddenly gone very quiet. But while May's days of publicity were over, her contemporary Maud West was still filling up newspaper columns, and making headlines both home and abroad.

A MODEST WOMAN

When Maud West, the sharp-shooting lady detective, was invited to give a talk to the Soroptimist Club in Ilford in 1932, she knew exactly how to get her audience's attention. The club was an east London branch of a volunteer organisation founded in the 1920s to improve the lives of women and girls, and Maud was an inspirational figure.

One day, she explained, she'd been called in to solve a brutal murder in an unnamed countryside inn. An elderly woman had been found dead at the foot of the stairs in a dark passage, and a considerable amount of money had been stolen. So Maud disguised herself as a male newspaper reporter, pushed her way past the real journalists gathered outside the inn and, to everyone's relief, the murderer was caught. This was 'an actual incident', explained *The Recorder*, although no details were given as to how Maud had solved the crime – and the real murder seems to have happened ten years earlier in Berkshire, when she hadn't played much of a role at all. But members of the Soroptimist Club found the tale absorbing, and the British press continued to lap up Maud's tales. When the *Sunday Dispatch* published a series of 'startling disclosures' on her wartime investigations and capture of enemy spies, it too insisted this was a 'true and thrilling record'.

Maud also gave a talk to the Efficiency Club in London, a networking organisation for professional women. But when the *Daily Mirror* asked for more details, she was not forthcoming. 'No, I can't tell you any of my experiences,' she retorted. 'I am a *private* detective, and, anyway, if I once began, I should never be finished!'

But Maud had never been a very private detective. Her face, even in disguise, had been in the newspapers for years, and her opinions were widely reported. In 1931, she gave evidence in the trial of a 'ring of girl burglars', when she was asked her views on criminal women. The modern girl who took to crime preferred to run crooked, she explained, because of the 'kick' she got out of it. Her thoughts fitted perfectly with the times, the 1930s was witnessing a supposed 'feminine crime wave', blamed on immoral young women intent on flouting the law.

Maud West also handled investigations of a more domestic nature. In 1933, she was involved in a high-profile divorce case, when Lord Inverclyde accused his wife, June Tripp, of adultery. Six detectives were employed on the case, and the couple were watched for nearly two months. Cecil Elliott, James Black and a Mrs Langford gave evidence, as did Maud herself.

By now, her detective agency had become a family affair, just like Antonia Moser's. Biographer Susannah Stapleton explains that Mrs Langford was, in fact, Maud's daughter Vera, who'd been assisting her mother since the early 1920s. Cecil, meanwhile, was Maud's son. Another daughter, Evelyn, carried out secretarial work and was later reported to have taken over her mother's agency, while a niece, Pat, also worked briefly for Maud, as did her father Geoff.

In 1938, the same year that May Storey appeared on the Churchman cigarette card, the *Sunday Pictorial* launched yet another series of Maud's 'exclusive' adventures. This time, she was chased through the streets by an armed gang, posed as a man to trap a master crook and disguised herself in a leopard skin to secure vital evidence. There was only the occasional hint that her tales might be too far-fetched to be true. This demure, modest, middle-aged woman, noted the *Adelaide News*, could 'tell you stories that would make you doubt their authenticity'. But she was doing well – with a staff of ten, a London flat and a 'lovely country property'.

By now, another mature – and far more modest – woman had made her debut as a detective: Agatha Christie's Miss Jane Marple. She first appeared in a novel in 1930, *The Murder at the Vicarage*, as a gentle 'spinster lady', who sets out to solve the murder of Colonel Protheroe.

Miss Marple used the scientific approach once favoured by Sherlock Holmes. She drew 'amazingly neat and apposite deductions from the facts that come under her notice', noted the vicar, and her conclusions had a 'logical certainty'. She also drew on the 'natural' instinct of a woman. Women liked shortcuts, according to Agatha Christie, and preferred an 'inspired guess' to the 'more laborious process of solid reasoning'. Many of the novel's male characters display a dim view of women, but the gossipy spinster – 'a noticing kind of person' – turns out to be the best detective of all.

This was the 'Golden Age' of detective fiction, which had begun in the 1920s and achieved a mass audience in the 1930s. The detective, whether professional or amateur, gathered together clues in order to prove 'who-dunnit', with the action often taking place among landed gentry at a secluded English country house. The murder mystery model offered a reassuring world, explains crime writer and critic Julian Symons, in which those who tried to disturb the established order were discovered and punished. But the detective was supposed to take a logical approach, and members of the Detection Club, formed by a group of mystery authors in 1930, were asked to swear an oath that their detectives would 'well and truly detect' their crimes without reliance on 'Feminine Intuition' or 'Mumbo Jumbo, Jiggery-Pokery, Coincidence, or Act of God'.

Maud West and Jane Marple offered very different images of private detection in the 1930s. One was a professional, who hunted down crooks in the underworld and jetted around on the trail of drug dealers and spies. The other was an amateur, who tended to solve mysteries on her doorstep, and whose previous cases involved the disappearance of some pickled shrimps.

The real Maud West was a working-class, married woman with six children. The fictional Miss Marple was a genteel single lady, who'd never worked for a living, had attended an Italian finishing school and was apt to quote Shakespeare. But real female detectives had something in common with their fictional counterpart. They too relied on their instinct, and they all had to prove their skills in the face of male opposition.

By the late 1930s, private detection had become 'one of the highest paid careers a girl can take up', according to journalist Sheila O'Callaghan, considering how little training and qualifications were required. She interviewed two unnamed women for the *Aberdeen Press and Journal*, and both saw the job as a vocation. 'I simply love the work!' declared 'Miss Detective No.1', who worked for a London agency. 'Anything else to me now – a job with regular routine, for instance – would be intolerably monotonous. I drive a car – some of us fly, even pilot a plane if necessary – and I've had some 'fun' chasing people, I can tell you!'

Nancy Drew, the fictional American sleuth, also enjoyed the fun of private detection, dashing around in a new blue convertible, solving mysteries and helping people in trouble. In *The Secret of the Old Clock*, published in 1930 and the first in the *Nancy Drew Mystery Stories* series, she tracks down a missing will, pits her wits against a local wealthy family and catches a gang of burglars. Nancy is a twinkly-eyed teenager, resourceful and resolute, able to change a car tyre, handle a motorboat and smash her way out of a locked closet. But it is her intuition and 'those hunches of mine' that are equally important.

Despite the huge interest in private detection, in both fiction and real life, the number of female professionals in Britain appeared to be shrinking. In the 1939 Register, taken at the onset of the Second World War, only eleven women were listed as private detectives in England and Wales – one of whom was a cloakroom attendant. In comparison, there were seventy-six men. Four years earlier, the *Lancashire Daily Post* had counted the nameplates of eleven women in London's West End alone, and each of them would have employed female agents. By now, some detectives were calling themselves 'private investigators', with eighteen men and three women listed in the Register. But they must have kept a low profile – I can't find any reports about them in the press.

Maud West, meanwhile, had moved into local politics. In 1934, she was elected a councillor for Holborn Borough Council, standing for the Municipal Reform Party, which fiercely opposed the 'spread' of socialism. Maud sat on several committees, including maternity and child welfare and public health. But she still presented herself as a working sleuth, with her adventures serialised in the *Sunday Pictorial* and interviews with the press.

'You must have something of the primitive hunting instincts to enjoy being a detective,' she told the *News Chronicle* in November 1938, and when she arrived at her office in New Oxford Street each morning, she never knew where she'd end up that day. A telephone call could come from a client and off she would go to Paris, New York or Vienna. Maud often received letters from girls who wanted to be detectives, and when they came for an interview, she started her training right away. What kind of lift had brought them upstairs? How many typewriters had they seen in the outside office?

But shortly after this interview, Maud West closed her detective agency, and in the 1939 Register, she appeared under her real name, Edith Elliott, as a 'secretary'. Maud spent her last years in Bexhill-on-Sea in East Sussex, where she died on 13 March 1964. She had led an astonishing life, even if a lot of her detective tales were made up. She'd made the job of private investigation hugely visible, even more so than Antonia Moser, and unlike her Victorian predecessor, she'd also managed to keep her personal life very private. I ask her biographer Susannah Stapleton what motivated Maud – was it fame?

'No,' she says at once. 'Maud wanted success. She wanted financial security, a nice suburban home, and respect. And she did have those things. Family was really important to her; she had a very poor childhood, and she didn't want that for future generations.'

'Did she come to believe in her thrilling detective case stories?' I ask. 'The ones she told to the press?'

'I don't think she ever believed her own tales,' says Susannah. 'It was not a game, it was business, and she was an extremely talented businesswoman.' But Susannah found her subject frustrating, 'I'd never researched anyone who I changed my mind about every 2 seconds. I had to accept that I would probably never find the answers I wanted.'

'What would you ask Maud, if she knocked on your door right now?'

Susannah laughs, 'I would dive for cover! She was pretty terrifying, but I would like to hide in a cupboard and watch her. I would like to know the truth about how she started as a detective, and if she enjoyed her work. She spoke a lot about the drudgery, so which part did she enjoy? Was it creating a persona? Sitting in a car watching a house? Or was it earning respect? I think I'd have to spend a few days having a chat with Maud.'

I've wondered if Maud West actually wrote her own stories, and Susannah believes she did write the early ones, which were then polished up by journalists. She also believes that someone in Maud's circle may have written the later case stories, possibly her brother-in-law, Geoff, and her husband Harry. 'He was her supporter,' she explains. 'He adored her, and he didn't really have a job of his own.'

By the late 1930s, Maud had finished with the fabulous character she'd invented. Her detective days were behind her, and the Maud West persona was consigned to the archives, for Susannah to rediscover a century later. Maud often stressed that private detection was 'a very arduous life', it could be dull and temper-trying, involving long hours and hard work. But, as she once told an interviewer, 'Always I have had the action, excitement, and adventure which I craved'.

When Maud closed her agency at the beginning of the Second World War, many other private detectives followed suit. Ex-police officers were recalled to service, conscription forced both men and women into the armed forces, civil defence and munitions work, and the British Detectives Association saw a marked drop in membership. But once peace returned, things quickly went back to normal, and by now, another remarkable woman was waiting in the wings to take on the mantle of England's most famous lady detective – and she would take self-publicity to a whole new level.

ANNETTE KERNER: THE MAYFAIR DETECTIVE AGENCY

In September 1946, a new detective agency opened in London and at its helm was former opera singer Annette Kerner, the self-styled Mrs Sherlock Holmes. The Mayfair Detective Agency was situated at No. 231 Baker Street, an address whose connections she was keen to promote. 'Whenever I step into […] my consulting room in Baker Street, London,' she wrote, 'only five doors away from the chambers made fictionally famous by Conan Doyle's Sherlock Holmes, my spine tingles with excitement.'

Baker Street had suffered bomb damage during the war, and Annette appeared to share the address with the British Friendship Society, but her clients were wealthy and came from 'the magic square mile of Mayfair'. Her earliest newspaper adverts were reasonably modest – a few lines in the personal column of the *Harrow Observer*, 'Divorce, private enquiries, consult Mayfair Detective Agency'. It was only in 1947 that she added her own name, 'Private Enquiries in Strictest Confidence. ANNETTE KERNER.'

When Annette opened the doors to her Baker Street agency, she already possessed 'over 20 years' experience, and her journey into detective work had been an extraordinary one. She was born Annette Symons in London in 1902, according to her own account, and her background was 'rather unusual'. Her family had been big property owners 'for one or two generations', holding the freehold of most of what became Wardour Street – a major West End route running from Leicester Square to Oxford

Street. The Symons family sold most of their property during the era of Victorian development, but her father kept hold of several sites around Soho and the family did not lack for money.

As a child, Annette lived at No. 120 Wardour Street, once a noble town house. She wasn't expected to work for a living, instead her 'career' was mapped out for her – a French governess, finishing school and then an introduction to an eligible young man with good prospects. But Annette feared she would wither away into a social career and a staid marriage, and she dreamt of a more adventurous life. As the only girl in a family of boys, she was pet-lambed and cossetted – and she was also a rebel. One afternoon, she ran away, eager to explore London, and her eldest brother Ben caught her as she was boarding a bus. Annette was soundly walloped; it was improper for a young lady to be out alone. But she resisted 'this masculine prison', and while a Symons girl wasn't even allowed to attend the theatre, Annette set her heart on the stage.

Her father agreed she could take singing lessons with Madame Clara Novello Davies, the well-known singer, teacher and conductor, whose son Ivor Novello would soon be one of Britain's most popular actors and composers. Annette was a specially favoured pupil and was invited to the family home for weekends. In May 1918, she sang in public during Clara Butt's great 'Pageant of Freedom' at the Queen's Hall, the capital's leading concert venue. Clara Butt was a celebrated contralto concert singer and the show, which featured actresses, musicians and society ladies, was held to raise funds for the Red Cross. Annette was such a success that Ivor Novello urged her to pursue a singing career, and when she received an offer from a Swiss impresario to appear in Geneva, she agreed. Annette lied to her parents, arranged a false chaperone, and at the age of 17 she set off to seek adventure in war-torn Europe.

On the boat to France, Annette was approached by an unnamed man – Mr X – who was on his way to Zurich on a 'special job'. He explained there was a man on board who had some papers he wanted to see, did Annette think she could help? So she sauntered along A deck, found the man's briefcase in a cabin by a bulkhead, and brought it back to Mr X. He flicked through the papers, and three minutes later, the briefcase was back in the cabin. A delighted Mr X revealed he was a security officer with a warrant to arrest a German espionage agent, and Annette was thrilled with her first taste of undercover work.

She continued her journey to Geneva, where she sang nightly to a packed house at the Omnia Theatre. The '*chanteuse d'opéra anglais*' was top of the bill, followed by gymnasts Fred et Julot and an American step dancer. The programme also included Les Padus, who performed '*poses plastiques et visions d'art*', in which semi-naked women posed as living statues. 'I was seeing Continental life on a G-string for the first time,' wrote Annette excitedly.

Then Mr X reappeared. The German espionage agent had been apprehended and was being taken back to England to stand trial. Would Annette consider heading to Basle and Zurich to work for British espionage for three months? Annette leapt at the chance; it would mean 'doing a job for England', and it was also an opportunity to hone her acting skills. 'I was to tread the boards,' she wrote, '– not of the theatrical stage, but the flesh-and-blood stage of real life.'

Annette was booked to sing at a smoky, orange-lit salon, known to be a meeting place for political extremists and 'sexual perverts'. She sang with the orchestra and watched the customers, relaying information 'through official channels set up for me'.

After three months, Annette returned to England, where she discovered her father had known what she was up to all along. A Special Branch officer had invited him to a round of golf, and he'd given permission for his daughter's involvement.

Annette Kerner's life so far sounded like the stuff of fiction – and it may well have been, for official records tell a very different story. According to the 1901 census, she was born Annie Symons on 21 October 1893 – ten years earlier than the date she gave for her birth. Her father Jacob (also known as John Simons) was not a wealthy property owner, but a self-employed ladies' tailor. He worked from home, assisted by his wife Betsy (or Bella) Nicols. The family did indeed live at No. 120 Wardour Street – where their neighbours included a pawnbroker's assistant, plumber, tailor and bootmaker – but there's no sign they owned the street. And rather than having lived around Soho for one or two generations, Annette's parents were immigrants from Poland – where she herself had been born. Her three older brothers, named on the 1901 census as Barnett, Sullivan and Abraham, were also born in Poland, while her younger brothers, Ceasman and Isaac, were born in London. The final member of the household was her maternal Polish grandmother.

The Symons were Jewish, and they appear to have moved to England around 1894, fleeing persecution in Eastern Europe. In 1890, the Russian Empire had barred Jews from owning land, attending school or university, or holding professional or governmental jobs. 'These edicts will affect about one million Jews,' reported one British paper, 'many of whom will be reduced to absolute beggary.' Like Jacob and Betsy Symons, many of those who settled in London worked as tailors. The job could be done from home with minimum capital and did not require working on the Sabbath. In Soho, there was soon a thriving Jewish neighbourhood centred around Berwick Street Market, just round the corner from Annette's family home.

In June 1910, her father became a naturalised British subject – five years after the Aliens Act was passed, a piece of legislation that was directed against Jewish immigrants from Eastern Europe and which allowed immigration officers to bar 'undesirables'. The family lived at No. 23 Noel Street, Soho. It was a less classy address, but they now had a nine-room house.

Jacob ran a ladies' tailoring business at No. 52 Oxford Street, although a few years later he was on the verge of bankruptcy after making a series of rash speculations on a wholesale business, a shop in Westbourne Grove and the purchase of leasehold and freehold property. His son Abraham was also working as a tailor, while 17-year-old Annie was a clerk – and not, presumably, on the way to Switzerland being recruited for the security services. And far from being a single young woman, in March 1915, at the age of 22, Annette had married a tailor, Maurice Feigenbaum, at the Western Synagogue in St Pancras.

But these biographical facts would be hidden from public knowledge, and Annette always portrayed herself as rich and well connected. Her father was a golf-playing landowner with solicitor friends, and she was a young lady with a French governess.

But it is true that she sang on the stage – and she did have at least some connection to the famous Novellos. In August 1918, *Tatler* published a photo of Miss Annie Symons, looking cheeky in a fashionable fur-collared coat and embroidered hat. She was 'doing good work' for Madame Clara Novello Davies' Musical Instruments Fund for soldiers and sailors, which was opening a depot at Eastbourne. 'Help is badly needed,' explained *Tatler*, 'and we hope the public will note this fact.' The same photograph appeared in *The Sketch*, where Annette was described as an 'assiduous worker for a war fund', as well as in the *Sunday Mirror*. Her lifelong skills at PR had begun.

By 1921, she had changed her name from Annie to Annette, and was appearing at the Willesden Hippodrome with violinist Anne Godfrey and a pianist, in what *The Era* described as 'a capital vocal and musical show'. Three years later, Annette took part in the Music Hall Ladies Guild annual fundraising matinee, at the 800-seater Garrick Theatre. The guild was a beneficent society, supplying baby clothes, medical aid, food and coal to those who were out of work, ill or pregnant. It was based at Albion House, New Oxford Street, in the same building as Maud West's detective agency.

In September 1924, Annette's portrait appeared in *The Stage*. She was a 'bright little lady', appearing during the cabaret interlude at the Queens Hotel, Leicester Square. She'd had 'a dazzling success' in her four songs, including 'Just One More Night in Your Arms' and 'I Want 'Em While Weak, Warm and Willing'. The following year she appeared in a musical comedy, *The Dairymaids*.

But her stage career never seemed to take off, and soon Annette was the mother of two children. Her son, Jack Gerald, was born in April 1922, and her daughter, Ruth, in November 1925. However, according to Annette, she'd already moved into more exciting work, that of private detection.

The idea seems to have come while singing at Bournemouth at a 'rather important social event', when she was introduced to Field Marshal Sir Douglas Haig, who congratulated her on her counter-espionage work in Zurich. Her adventures had helped to build the foundations of European peace, and she was keen to play an important role again. She couldn't join the police, because at less than 5ft tall she was too short, and while she admired pioneers like Lilian Wyles, she disliked the police's unimaginative uniform, which made them a target of ridicule. Annette also resented the fact that women officers weren't usually allowed in the witness box, and so their work was 'read out in court by men!'

Then Annette had a stroke of luck. Her father's solicitor friends heard what she'd been doing abroad and asked her to make some private inquiries. Senior police officials gave her work, too, and soon she was dealing with racecourse pickpockets, missing persons and company fraud.

She also took on more delicate inquiries. When an acquaintance of her mother's discovered a friend was stealing from handbags during games of bridge, Annette was hired to catch the thief and prevent a scandal. Then, a friend in hunting circles wanted a divorce without publicity. Annette was shocked by 'the shame and degradation of it all', and more divorce cases followed.

Then life turned even more exciting: she was hired by Scotland Yard to track down the international mastermind behind a booming traffic in cocaine, morphine and opium. Cocaine had been largely acceptable during Sherlock Holmes' day, and Annette's fictional hero had taken it himself to escape 'the dull routine of existence'. Cocaine, heroin and opium remained legal until 1916, when there were reports of foreign troops buying cocaine from British prostitutes.

Drugs were now a threat to the armed forces, and a wartime regulation criminalised the possession and sale of opium and cocaine, except by licensed chemists. After the war, concerns about drug taking switched to modern young women, apparently hell bent on gratification in West End nightclubs.

In March 1922, Freda Kempton, a 'dance instructress', died after a cocaine overdose. She'd been a regular at a Regent Street restaurant run by Brilliant 'Billy' Chang, a Chinese entrepreneur who reportedly arrived in England as a chemistry student in 1913 and whose real name was said to be Chan Nan. He denied giving Freda any 'dope', but the press employed every racist trope imaginable to whip up fears of 'white slavery'.

He was portrayed as a real-life Dr Fu Manchu, the fictional master criminal who, just like Brilliant Chang, lived in Limehouse on the northern bank of the Thames. The area had been home to small numbers of Chinese sailors and shopkeepers since the nineteenth century. By the early 1920s, Limehouse was depicted as a dangerous place where white women were lured by 'aliens'. 'Yellow' men held a fascination for white women, warned the *Evening News*. They could easily be caught in their spell. Freda's death was ruled to be suicide while temporarily insane, and Brilliant Chang walked free, but Annette Kerner was not about to let him off and, shortly afterwards, she went undercover for the police.

Annette was 'barely 20 years old' when off she went to Leman Street, one of the 'foulest' in the East End, along with a policewoman, Joan Knight. The women posed as drug addicts, hung around dirty cafes and pubs, begged for drugs, played 'the coquette', and didn't change their clothes or wash for four months. Then they moved further east to Limehouse, where Annette whiled away her time playing fan-tan, a Chinese gambling game, in the back room of a cafe.

One day, an 'elegantly dressed dope pedlar' in a Savile Row jacket walked in, and Annette knew she'd found her man. She told a waiter she had a rich friend who needed drugs, and at 4 a.m. she returned, dressed in a mink stole with jewellery glinting round her neck. She was led upstairs, where a man began to prepare an opium pipe. When a loud crash came from below, he shouted, 'You damn bitch!', pulled out a razor, aimed it at Annette's throat and thrust it twice into her arm. As blood poured from the wound, the police burst in and hit the dealer over the head with a truncheon.

In February 1924, Brilliant Chang stood trial for possession and supplying drugs to actress Violet Payne, and the police produced a single bag of cocaine, found beneath a loose board in his house. He was sentenced to fourteen months, followed by deportation. 'It is you and people like you who are corrupting the womanhood of this country,' declared the Old Bailey judge. 'Girls must be protected from this drug.'

Headlines screamed, 'Chinaman dope fiend' and 'Chinese pest'. But was he really the international drug king the police and press made him out to be, or just a businessman whose staff were involved in small-time drug deals? And had Annette Kerner *really* been involved in his capture?

News reports show that she'd been singing on the stage between 1921 and 1924, the period in which Brilliant Chang was operating restaurants in London. She could have combined performing with undercover work, as Dorothy Tempest had done in the early 1900s, but it would have been unusual for a married woman who, at the time of Freda Kempton's inquest, had only just given birth to her son Jack. Policewoman Joan Knight, meanwhile, doesn't seem to exist, unless this was not her real name.

But Annette's tale of undercover drug investigations did have a basis of truth. Women Patrol Volunteers had investigated the sale of cocaine to soldiers before the war, while Lilian Wyles described one unnamed police constable who spent weeks as 'a pseudo-prostitute', tracking down cocaine pedlars and distributors in the West End. Female police officers also worked with CID in Limehouse, where Annette allegedly caught Brilliant Chang and survived a razor attack, although Lilian Wyles described the area very differently. The Chinese population ran their businesses with decorum and respect for law and order, and the many small cafes were neat, tidy and 'the acme of cleanliness'.

But as far as Annette Kerner was concerned, she'd successfully put an end to the drugs trade, and now she returned to her wealthy clients. If Brilliant Chang was corrupting English womanhood, then Mrs Sherlock Holmes was going to save it.

TRUTH AND LIES

Annette Kerner had the uncanny ability to be linked to all sorts of celebrity cases in the 1930s, often rescuing her clients from tragedy and scandal. One day, she had a surprise call from a baronet who was anxious about his son. He'd fallen in with a bad crowd at Cambridge and absconded with a gun.

Annette tracked the boy down to the West End, where he'd moved in with a 'lady of the town'. She persuaded him to return to university just as 'the Petts drama' was unfolding, when a Cambridge undergraduate shot his tutor, a detective and then himself. Annette's client was eternally grateful, he might have lost his son as well, and he gave her a cheque for ten times her fee.

Not long afterwards, she received a call from 'the Hon Mrs Peters', who had naively bought a painting from a 'butler'. Annette returned it to its rightful owner, an unnamed lord. Then she read that a Van Dyck painting had been stolen from Lord Clarendon's home in Hampstead. Annette approached 'a West End girl', who confessed she was living with a well-known receiver, and an hour later, police had searched a north London flat and found the missing Van Dyck.

As with the story of Brilliant Chang, both the Cambridge shooting and the stolen painting were based on true events. They'd taken place in 1930 and had been well covered in the press – although the university student was Douglas Potts rather than Petts. There was no mention of any private detectives in either case, but once again that doesn't mean they weren't involved. Like her predecessor, Maud West, Annette was exploiting the fact few people could really prove what she did and didn't do.

She also 'provided security' for department stores, such as a new Littlewoods branch in south London, which opened in 1938. Annette became well versed at dealing with professional male 'lifters'. Some used an unpleasant ruse known as the fly pocket, altering their trousers to create a deep pocket with an opening parallel with the fly. A woman's natural instinct was to drop her gaze when she saw a man's hand near his fly, and if a store detective did try to 'whisk' a suspect by tapping his thighs and loins, she wasn't likely to tap in that region. But Annette had no trouble bringing such offenders to justice. The 'only way to counter this trick', she explained, was 'to stare, and stare!'

But shop work had none of the 'romance' of detection, and for a woman who'd caught foreign spies and international cocaine dealers, store work was far too routine. So, in 1946, she launched the Mayfair Detective Agency.

It had only been open for two months when *Pathé News* made a one-minute film about 'two women's private battle against Britain's crime wave'. The clip began with senior detective Annette Kerner sitting in her rather sparse Baker Street office, wearing a sharply cut suit and fur-trimmed hat, along with 'good looking sleuth Trixie Etheridge'. Reporter John Parsons then set off to watch the female sleuths at work.

Annette, standing by a tree reading a newspaper, stops him as he's walking down a leafy residential street. 'Oh, excuse me,' she says, in rather plummy tones. 'I'm a private detective, do you mind talking to me. I'm just watching that house over there.'

The reporter is intrigued. 'How long have you been doing this sort of work?'

'Oh,' says Annette, 'quite a long time.'

When asked if she's on her own, she replies, 'No, I have a colleague, she's just come out of the police. Here she comes to relieve me, I've been on all night.'

Then Trixie Etheridge appears, looking remarkably glamorous.

'Do you enjoy this kind of work?' asks the reporter.

'Rather!' says Trixie. 'Yes, it's most exciting.'

Trixie's real name was Beatrix Etheredge, and she was indeed a former police officer. She'd served four years in the Metropolitan Police in C Division and left the force in August 1946, when her 'Nature of Certificate' was marked 'Very Good'. A few months later, Annette and

Trixie were pictured together for the *Melbourne Argus*, using a magnifying glass to examine a pair of gloves in a divorce case. Trixie was also photographed studying a pile of files and disguised as a 'woman of few morals' in a crowded pub. But her involvement in the Baker Street agency appears to have been short-lived, and after her starring role in the *Pathé* film and her photographs in the *Melbourne Argus*, she was never mentioned again.

The Mayfair Detective Agency expanded rapidly. By the early 1950s, it reportedly had twenty-two male operatives, mainly ex-police officers, and five women. Annette's 'male counterpart', bodyguard and 'Dr Watson' was Eddie Parsons, who had trained as a boxer before joining the police. In May 1941, he'd been presented with the George Medal for bravery after dragging people to safety after a bombing raid in Brixton, along with PC Jackson. Eddie then joined the Corps of Military Police, before becoming a full-time member of the Mayfair Detective Agency. But I can't find any Edward Parsons among those who received the George Medal, although a PC Jackson was recognised for his bravery during a bombing campaign, but that was in Birmingham.

When it came to female agents, Annette boasted that many women in private detection 'learned their job with me'. But the loss rate was high, because the qualities that made a good private detective also made a very good wife – tact, patience, sympathy and being a good listener. Annette often trained a woman and then off she went and found herself a husband who didn't want her risking her neck.

'Of all the girls,' she wrote, 'Audrey Howes remained with me the longest.' She'd been recommended 'through official channels' and went on to establish herself as a store security officer. Audrey Howes was indeed a store detective, who'd started her career in the mid-1930s and was known to the police as 'little Audrey'. She worked for various shops in London up until the 1970s, including Whiteleys, Woolworths and Safeway's, and was often praised for her diligence and first-class observation. One civil servant, found guilty of stealing a packet of figs, insisted 'she was like a wild cat'.

Annette's detectives were also trained in the latest gadgets. Sleuths no longer had to bore holes in walls or rely on a change of disguise; their techniques were far more advanced. When a young woman was blackmailed over photographs taken by a 'peeping tom', Annette installed a second phone at her client's home, with the 'cooperation' of the Post

Office. The phone was fitted with a tape recorder, the client was given a script and when the blackmailer called again, one of Annette's operators listened in and he was caught.

Mrs Sherlock Holmes was a great believer in the mechanical tricks of modern detection, which she used to 'support my feminine intuition'. When she'd first started out, 'Nobody could be spied upon and conversation recorded unawares'. But then she began using a Recordon dictating machine, a 'modern miracle' and no bigger than an attaché case, which recorded sound magnetically onto a disc. The Mayfair Agency also collaborated with the research laboratory of a 'famous industrial concern', rushing across specimens for ultraviolet ray analysis and chemical tests.

The late 1940s was a prime time for spy gadgets, often developed during the war – including a covert camera designed to fit inside a matchbox – as well as new crime-fighting equipment, police laboratories and office technology. Annette's Recordon offered users special 'Codit' discs to provide 'complete secrecy where desired', which sounded perfect for a private detective.

Annette used less-scientific methods as well, and she was quite happy to enact a 'harmless bluff in the interests of justice'. She helped a 'distressed working-class husband' watch his wife by entering the house through a cellar trap, tiptoeing up the stairs and catching the wife in the lodger's bedroom. She also paid porters at blocks of flats to 'loan' her passkeys and offered the 'usual fee' to office watchmen on Park Lane. Private detectives, she admitted, sometimes had to 'sail rather close to the law'.

Matrimonial investigations remained a central part of the job, and Annette's Baker Street office became 'a Mecca of men and women seeking dissolution of marriage'. Unhappy wives were more likely to bare their souls to a woman detective, and she became something of a counsellor and therapist. One tearful client gave 'signs of sex repression' or 'sex-hunger' – she chain-smoked and her jaw quivered nervously. Annette spent an hour discussing the intimate aspects of married life, then referred the woman to an expert at the Tavistock Clinic in north London. By the end of 'the treatment', her client had abandoned the idea of divorce, and the couple became 'among my greatest friends'.

Annette Kerner was scathing on the absurdities of British divorce laws, just as Antonia Moser and May Storey had been. They might make profitable work for solicitors and private detectives, but they caused private agony and grief. 'When it comes to divorce,' she wrote, 'the law is certainly an ass.' But what Annette didn't mention was that back in 1936, after twenty-one years of marriage, she herself had petitioned for divorce from Maurice Feigenbaum.

'Most of us have only very frail skeletons in the cupboard,' she later wrote, but Mrs Sherlock Holmes seemed to have a cupboard full. Annette had accused her husband of having 'frequently committed adultery', initially with a woman 'whose name and identity are unknown'. A few months later, however, she had established the woman's name, and it was added to the divorce papers – Florence Instone, whom her husband was living with in Maida Vale. Annette was granted a divorce in September 1937 and given custody of the two children.

That same month, she married again, to Henry Isidore Kerner, a 58-year-old widower. He was a skin merchant and furrier, as was his father, and in the early 1950s he ran a business on Great Portland Street. Annette's age was correctly given as 45 on the marriage certificate, and she was described as 'formerly the wife of Maurice Feigenbaum otherwise Finberg from whom she obtained a Divorce'. Her first husband appears to have started using the name Finberg in the early 1920s, and their two children adopted the name as well. But Annette didn't seem to have a job, for the occupation box on the marriage certificate was left blank.

Annette Kerner had allegedly started working as a private detective in the 1920s, when she went undercover to catch Brilliant Chang. But there's no hard evidence of her career until the establishment of the Mayfair Detective Agency in 1946. So could her sleuthing skills have actually started during her divorce? Did Annette carry out her own inquiries in 1936 – or hire a private detective – in order to identify her first husband's lover? Perhaps it was this that had given her a taste for the job, before she eventually set up shop on her own.

In September 1949, Annette followed in the footsteps of her predecessors by opening her casebooks to the press. *The People* ran a series of six tales, ghost-written by a journalist and revealing 'the sensational details of some of her greatest case secrets involving world-famous celebrities' – including murder, blackmail, poison pen letters, forgery and fraud. *The People* billed itself as 'The Paper that finds out the Facts'. 'Remember,' it told its readers, 'This is fact, not … – … fiction'. The stories were accompanied with photographs of Annette, disguised as a man outside a luxury block of flats, 'working the telephone trap' to catch a blackmailer, and in her Baker Street office with 'one of her assistants', ex-detective inspector Wilson of Scotland Yard.

In 'How I Trapped the Rogues Who Prey on Film-Struck Girls with Flattery', Annette explained how she'd disguised herself as an out-of-work actress to get evidence against fraudulent film and theatrical agencies. She warned of the 'grave moral temptation' faced by young women in show business. It had been her privilege to 'help and protect these girls, tortured and helpless' from greedy, vicious, illicit agents.

Once again, Mrs Sherlock Holmes was saving British womanhood. But London County Council was not amused by the story. It reflected badly on the licensing work of their Public Control Committee and made people believe the industry was full of frauds. It was not based on fact and the names cited were not real. *The People* was unconcerned. This was an attack on press freedom – of course newspapers used pseudonyms in 'cases of this kind' and 'the facts were none the less accurate'.

Annette also told the story of 'Case No. 408', when she'd trapped handsome fraudster Howard Robinson, moving into Claridge's and entreating him to sell her bogus oil shares. *The People* photographed her at the door of the West End bank where she'd persuaded him to hand over a transfer form before her undercover operatives pounced. As with many of Annette's tales, this too was based on a real crime, only the confidence trickster was William Frederick Robinson and he'd been jailed nearly twenty years earlier, in January 1930.

By the end of the 1940s, Mrs Sherlock Holmes was virtually a household name, and so was her Baker Street agency. She'd been filmed by *Pathé News*, acclaimed as 'Britain's most famous woman detective', and her casebooks in *The People* had netted her £540 – the equivalent of around £20,000 today. But then, quite suddenly, it all went wrong.

THE CASE OF THE DISAPPEARING WHISKY

In October 1951, Annette Kerner found herself on the wrong side of criminal proceedings when she appeared at Marylebone Magistrates' Court, smartly dressed in a fur coat, to face charges of fraud. It was a strange case, involving large amounts of confiscated whisky, and when the trial came to court, the allegations and counter allegations were hard to follow.

Annette and her husband were living in St John's Wood and the dispute centred on their downstairs neighbour, company secretary Hyman Williams. According to Hyman, Annette told him she owned a West End club, her brother was well known in the film business and her son was a scenario writer. Then she told him she could 'legitimately' buy whisky from the confiscation branch of Customs & Excise – she knew the superintendent, a Mr Skip.

In the autumn of 1951, Annette told her neighbour she had secured ninety-eight cases of whisky and hoped to make £3 on each bottle. So Hyman gave her £1,250 to finance the deal – roughly £40,000 today.

But then he became suspicious and demanded his money back. Annette returned a few hundred pounds. Then she appeared at his flat, crying and in great distress, and said she was in serious trouble. She'd been on a lorry delivering the whisky to a club in Curzon Street when a 'Chinese boy', also on the lorry, spotted the police. Annette jumped off and watched as the police spoke to the driver. The vehicle was confiscated, the whisky was returned to Customs and so Hyman Williams had lost his money.

But why was Annette on the lorry in the first place? And why did a Chinese boy feature in the tale? According to the prosecution, there was no Confiscation Department of Customs, no Mr Skip, no sale of any whisky and no involvement by the police. She'd simply run off with Hyman's money.

Annette vehemently denied this. The money had been a loan to be repaid in six months, she had an IOU and the allegations were 'all nonsense'. Hyman Williams had told her he was a genius; he had a scheme to make lots of money and he'd shown her a large tureen full of envelopes stuffed with cash. But then he'd come up to her flat looking 'like a fiend' and shouting, 'I know who you are now. You are a dirty copper's nark and you are the one who has closed all the places around here.'

Hyman, it emerged, had been running gambling parties. A porter had seen a roulette wheel in his flat, groups of men in their shirtsleeves gathered late at night to play cards and a peephole had been made in his front door.

So had Annette been gambling in her neighbour's flat, borrowed money and then when he demanded it back, threatened to tell the police about the illegal sessions? Or had Hyman learned about her relationship with the police and, as the defence argued, decided to 'get in first' and prosecute her for false pretences?

When the prosecutor asked why Annette hadn't reported the gaming parties to the police, she responded, 'You are trying to make me out an informer. You don't know what harm you are doing to me ... you are giving my enemies loopholes to do the same as Mr. Williams has done.' She'd given the police assistance with gambling parties, that was all, and when they had information then she was asked to investigate. She was not a copper's nark; she simply confirmed the information already received. According to the *Marylebone Mercury*, Annette then broke down and sobbed. Hyman Williams had destroyed her, she had a book coming out and a television programme arranged, 'but it has all gone because of the publicity over this case'.

Annette did, however, have backing from the police. Superintendent William Wilson of X Division was asked whether Mrs Kerner was a police informer, and he replied, 'She was not an informer in the sense that she volunteered information. She was a person to whom I would go to check information I had already got, including information about gaming parties.' Inspector I.S. Davies added that Annette had been 'of considerable assistance to the Metropolitan Police'. Their testimony confirmed that Mrs Sherlock Holmes did indeed have police connections, and two senior officers were willing to publicly support her. But what exactly was their relationship?

Annette later wrote about an Inspector William Wilson, a striking 6ft-tall figure with blue eyes and pale red hair, who'd called on her help during the Second World War. He'd asked her to find the 'chief pimp' behind West End prostitution, so she'd settled into a club in Beak Street, where she'd stayed for days, drinking gin and befriending prostitutes. Annette identified the chief pimp – although she didn't name him or explain how – and, thanks to her, Inspector Wilson had cleaned up the West End.

But strangely enough, when Annette had opened her casebooks for *The People* in September 1949, it had provided a photograph with 'one of her assistants', ex-detective inspector Wilson of Scotland Yard. William Arthur Wilson had joined the Met Police in 1924, been promoted to inspector in the 1930s and then to superintendent after the war, but he hadn't retired from the force until April 1954. So had *The People* got the caption wrong? Was this another man, or had the inspector been moonlighting as Mrs Sherlock Holmes' 'assistant'?

It took the jury just seven minutes to acquit Annette Kerner of obtaining money under false pretences and on 10 March 1952, as she left the dock she was greeted by her husband and friends. 'We were never in doubt about the result,' Henry Kerner told a reporter, in a rare public appearance, 'but it has been a worrying time.' 'I know I am free,' said Annette, 'but this case has done me a lot of harm and it will please my enemies.'

Her trial was certainly well covered in the press. The *Daily Express* described her as the silver-haired sleuth of Baker Street, who'd sent a woman operative out on a missing persons inquiry the moment she was acquitted. It provided photos of 'the many disguises of 'Mrs Sherlock': Annette in nightclub land with a glass of wine in her hand, disguised as a barrow-girl in a shawl and pretending to be a railway porter in a cap and coat. But other papers described her as a 'former sleuth', and during the trial she gave her occupation as private secretary and retired detective.

Annette now used the press to put the record straight. 'I am not a copper's nark,' she told the *Daily Mirror*, which ran the story on its front page with a photo of 'the woman they used to call The Little Chief'. She was nearing 60 now and looked rather frail, dressed in a fur coat and holding a cup of tea. 'Now I know how the law looks to the criminal,' she explained, 'I don't think I shall ever have the heart to arrest anyone again.'

Apart from the fact Annette had never had the authority to arrest anyone, she then relayed the usual story of how she'd become a private detective. This time, it was a policeman on a cross-Channel boat who'd asked her to look at some papers in a suspect's cabin. 'I have done the work because I love it,' she told the *Mirror*, and the police had paid her 'small fees and expenses' ever since. She'd been to opium dens to investigate a drug-dealing murderer and 'he did this to me', then she pulled up her sleeve to show the 'scars of razor slashes'.

Her only weakness, she confessed, had been gambling. Her father had left her £20,000 in his will and 'I lost the lot. That was the cause of this recent trouble. I got into debt.'

Her father Jacob had died in 1927. Having recovered from his earlier bankruptcy, he'd been operating from No. 72 New Oxford Street as a costume maker. But while he'd left a huge sum of £1,400 – equivalent to around £90,000 today – this was far short of the figure cited by Annette.

She insisted her gambling days were over, 'What is worrying me now is that the underworld will think I'm a nark. I am really afraid.' Two men had followed her after she left court. 'I dodged them with an old trick at Oxford Circus tube station. But I shall have to move.'

Was Annette Kerner becoming paranoid? Did she really feel threatened? Or was she just sticking to her persona as a woman who moved in the dangerous underworld?

Her history of gambling, however, was true. Nearly twenty years earlier, she had been sued under the name Annette Finberg – the surname adopted by her first husband, Maurice Feigenbaum. Annette had lost £500 in one sitting, written a dud cheque to cover her losses and was described in court as a woman whose 'principal occupation' was playing bridge, poker and chemin de fer.

Not long after her acquittal in the whisky case – and having still not repaid her neighbour Hyman Williams – she was in court again, now owing gambling debts of £1,245. On 15 October 1952, she appeared at the High Court of Justice to be publicly examined by the Official Receiver. He reminded her that she'd previously given the court an assurance she would not gamble again.

'Yes, Sir,' she replied. 'I must have done – I do. I should not gamble.'
The whisky case had been a malicious prosecution, she explained, and
'they are threatening me now'.

The Receiver seemed sympathetic, 'Do not distress yourself, Mrs Kerner.'

It then emerged that Annette had already been declared bankrupt in
July 1946 – when she owed £999 in gambling debts – the very same month
she'd opened the Mayfair Detective Agency on Baker Street. Between
1945 and 1946, meanwhile, she'd been working as a store detective in a
'large multiple firm' – so she hadn't been employed to provide security at
the 1938 opening of Littlewoods after all. There don't seem to be any press
reports on this stage of her career, so either it wasn't true or she'd never
been required to give evidence in a shoplifting trial.

But it was clear that the Mayfair Detective Agency had been a short-
lived financial disaster. Not only had she opened it while bankrupt, but
it had made a loss of £136 during the whole period of trading – and that
covered just two years and three months. She had closed the agency in
September 1948, 'My health began to break down and I decided to enter a
less exacting occupation'. Annette agreed she'd put more into the business
than she ever took out, 'I never charged enough the accountant said'. And
far from being inundated with clientele from the magic square mile of
Mayfair, 'poor people came to me. I never charged them.'

But the Receiver was puzzled. In July 1949, Annette had become a
director of the Film Studios Club on Oxford Street – so when she'd told
Hyman Williams she owned a West End club, it was true. The club had
been set up by one of her brothers, who'd also provided the capital for her
detective agency. It lay at Nos 37–39 Oxford Street, opposite Frascati's,
one of the West End's most famous restaurants, and just near where Jacob
Symons had once run his ladies' tailoring business. The club catered for
'all sections of the theatrical profession,' explained the press, 'under the
direction of Mrs Annette Kerner'. It had rehearsal and audition rooms, a
lounge and library, and a restaurant serving lunch, dinner and supper. 'A
rendezvous for variety folk has been a need for some time now,' remarked
The Stage. 'One could not help thinking of the previous frugal meeting-
places of "pros" and comparing them with the sumptuous surroundings
of the new club.'

In February 1951, Annette sold her £50 shares in the club and made an
impressive profit of £450. The Official Receiver pointed out this could

have wiped out her detective agency debts. 'I am not good at figures,' she replied. 'I do not quite get what you mean.' Was she genuinely confused – or was she playing the ignorant woman? Her 'casebook' stories had often illustrated her knowledge of financial affairs. She knew all about clumsy forgeries and dud cheques – she'd single-handedly trapped an international bonds fraudster in a West End bank – yet now she couldn't follow a simple profit and loss.

Annette confirmed that her husband had 'always maintained me' and gave her a comfortable living. In which case, said the Receiver, there was no reason for her to borrow money at all.

'I apologise,' said Annette. 'I have been naughty in this gambling. I have done a lot of it.'

Most of her losses came from greyhound racetracks. She owed the bookmakers and 'they kept ringing me up and threatening me, and Mr. Kerner has been ill, and I did not know what to do … I caused him such a lot of worry'. Annette appeared very concerned about the impact of her gambling on her 'darling husband', who had been 'an honest man all his life'.

The Receiver asked if it was true that a Mr Eve owed her £120 for film extra work. Annette corrected him, 'The film made about my work.'

In the summer of 1950, she'd struck a deal with the New Realm Film Company, based in Leicester Square, but she hadn't seen Mr Eve since the film had been made. It's not clear if this film was ever completed or shown, but in 1951 the New Realm Film Company made a ninety-minute film about the Festival of Britain and six years later, it released *Rock You Sinners*, starring Jackie Collins and often described as the first British rock-and-roll film.

Annette Kerner cut a pitiful figure during her cross-examination at the High Court of Justice. She was distressed, addicted to gambling, heavily in debt, worried and guilty about her husband. Now she appeared to be pinning her hopes on her literary endeavours, and she'd received an advance of £100 from literary agents.

'There is a prospect that something will be realised from the publication of her book *Woman Detective*,' noted the Official Receiver, and any profits would go towards her debts. Just a week earlier, Annette had signed a contract with publishers Werner Laurie, who produced a range of gripping yarns in the early 1950s, including *Guns, Drugs and Deserters* and *Spycatcher*. Her agent was Ursula Winant of Richmond Towers & Benson Ltd, who went on to represent best-selling adventure writer Wilbur Smith in the 1960s.

It had been 100 years since the British press had first started writing about female detectives and, since then, countless readers had been treated to the thrilling stories of Antonia Moser, Kate Easton, Maud West and May Storey. But now a woman sleuth was finally publishing her memoirs and she must have been hoping it would pay off.

23

A WOMAN PRIVATE DICK

When Annette Kerner published her memoir *Woman Detective* in 1954, she estimated there were 200 private inquiry agencies in Britain – but hers was unique as the only one run by a woman. She presented herself as a motherly figure, who frequently found herself at the heart of family life, rescuing missing children and reuniting warring couples. Too many people got married and then strove to get divorced, Annette complained, 'without any sincere understanding of what Holy Matrimony means'. There was no mention, of course, of her own divorce. She was simply 'a happy woman with a nice home and career'.

Annette's memoir was ghost-written by the same unnamed journalist who'd penned the case stories for *The People*, and it played on several concerns of the 1950s, especially the break-up of family and the post-war position of women. The divorce rate remained low in the 1950s, but the idea of 'marriage for life' was in danger and the Royal Commission on Marriage and Divorce wanted more marriage guidance and conciliation so couples were 'saved' before they broke up. Mrs Sherlock Holmes might have an unusual job, but she was still portrayed as a traditionally feminine figure, a 'detective with a heart', whose ultimate goal was to uphold family life.

Woman Detective was a rollicking read. It opened with Annette's recruitment by the Secret Service in 1919, her wealthy family background and how she first became a 'private eye'. This was a relatively new term in Britain, at least in a popular sense. The expression 'for the private eye' had been used since the early 1800s, to indicate a document was confidential and not to be made public.

In terms of detection, 'private eye' doesn't appear to have emerged until the late 1930s, although some credit Allan Pinkerton with coining the term when he launched his American detective agency in the 1850s. By the time of Annette's memoir, it had become a common cinematic term. Groucho Marx played a 'near-sighted private eye' in the Marx Brothers' *Love Happy*, while Benny Hill set himself up as a private eye in the Ealing Studios slapstick comedy, *Who Done It*. It's doubtful that any self-respecting private detective would have used the term; it had the sort of crude connotations that had always surrounded the profession, ever since the days of ex-inspector Field and the peephole servants.

Annette Kerner was also, according to one crook in the book, 'a woman private dick'. The phrase was common slang in the 1950s, apparently a shortened version of 'detective'. Some suggest it came from the Romany word '*dik*' meaning 'to see' or 'to watch', others attribute it to Dick Donovan, a fictional nineteenth-century Scottish detective, or to American author Raymond Chandler, who used the term in his 1939 novel *The Big Sleep*.

By 1950, there were 2,400 'private dicks' in Britain, according to *Britannia and Eve*. Their main clients were women aged between 45 and 55, who were 'overwrought' or 'feeling the pangs of lost appeal' and rushed to private dicks to 'have their husbands' spare time activities checked'.

The press was more than happy to publicise Annette Kerner's memoir, even though some of the stories had appeared in newspapers several years earlier. The public appetite for 'great true crime' tales was insatiable, whether sensational press reports, *Secrets of Scotland Yard* on the radio, or memoirs of famous detectives, including Lilian Wyles' autobiography, published in 1952.

Robert Fabian, an ex-Scotland Yard detective, became a household name after his memoirs were turned into the BBC TV series *Fabian of the Yard*, while *Dick Barton – Special Agent*, the BBC's first daily radio serial, drew audiences of up to 20 million. The *Sunday Dispatch* reported that business was booming for private sleuths, with a 'flood of would-be Dick Bartons'.

Annette's book couldn't have come at a better time, and reviewers seemed impressed with her tales of stolen paintings, Cambridge shootings, Park Lane divorces, blackmail and poisoning. 'Sherlock Holmes should have had reality, lived a little later and married Annette Kerner,' commented the *Liverpool Echo*. 'Together they would have scared most criminals into honesty.'

'What does a woman detective look like?' asked the *Sydney Morning Herald*. 'If you think you know, then try meeting one for the first time in a crowded London restaurant.' The *Herald*'s journalist mistook Annette for 'a tall, well-built woman in a severe black suit and mannish hat', when suddenly there was a tap on her arm. 'Here I am, dear,' said Annette. 'I never mistake a newspaperwoman.' She looked like an average London housewife, in a no-longer-new coat of brown fur fabric, her silver-grey hair pinned into a bun and pushed under a nondescript black straw hat. 'If I were following you, you wouldn't even notice me, would you?' Annette asked. 'Insignificant. That's how a detective should look.'

But Annette Kerner had not made a career out of being insignificant. She'd been filmed for *Pathé News* in her Baker Street office and, just like Maud West, her face – even in 'disguise' – had been in the pages of the press for years. 'See this,' she told the *Herald*, revealing two scars on her wrist and another on her forearm from when she'd helped the police break a big dope gang and 'a Chinese' had attacked her with a razor. The journalist must have shown some concern, for Annette told her, 'Afraid? No, dear. I've never been afraid of crooks.' Sometimes, she'd worried 'they might turn nasty and take it out on my family', but she'd never been scared of them.

Where *had* Annette got these scars? She had talked about them for years, and shown them to several journalists, none of whom had implied they weren't real. Perhaps she had once had an accident, or received the wounds during a bombing raid in the war. Or could she have been attacked over unpaid gambling debts? It's impossible to untangle, just like so much of her life and career.

Not long after her memoir was published, Annette appeared at the Crime Writers' Association's (CWA) first exhibition. The CWA had been formed in 1953 and now it put together a display of original manuscripts, Scotland Yard exhibits, thousands of crime books and the authors themselves. It was opened by actor Boris Karloff, famed for playing Frankenstein's monster.

'One of the most interesting members I met was not a crime-writer at all,' wrote one reporter, 'although her book is very much on crime ... No one would suspect that this tiny, plump, matronly little woman, mother of two children, had investigated some of the most notorious scandals of the last thirty years.' Not only that, she still 'bore the marks of razor slashes to this day'. However, there doesn't seem to be any evidence that Annette Kerner was ever a CWA member, and she certainly wasn't present at the association's founding meeting, which included novelists Elizabeth Ferrars and Josephine Bell.

Annette also took part in a series of lectures at the Regent Street Polytechnic, treating her audience to three cases from her dossier: an MP who'd been blackmailed by a young girl, a married Yorkshire woman who became romantically attached to a drug-peddling cloakroom attendant, and a woman from Somerset who received a poison pen card which read, 'How dare you marry. You are mad.'

Annette's publicity tour must have gone well, for in 1955 she published another book, *Further Adventures of a Woman Detective*. Her reputation hadn't been ruined by the whisky case after all. People still wanted to hear her 'true-life' tales.

The second memoir was even racier, and the contents more thriller than casebook style, beginning with Brilliant Chang and the razor attack of the 1920s. It also had a foreword by Lady Docker, who described Annette Kerner as 'my friend', praised her courage and sagacity 'in the cause of good', and found a 'breath of excitement' on every page.

Norah Royce Docker was an English socialite, known for her extravagant lifestyle with her third husband, the industrialist Sir Bernard Docker. The year before, she'd invited Yorkshire miners to a champagne party on the couple's yacht, where she'd danced the hornpipe, and she'd recently won the 'first women's marbles contest ever held', while wearing a peacock blue satin dress and diamonds.

Lady Docker was 'Britain's most fabulous society hostess', according to the press. She drove a gold-plated Daimler and was nicknamed 'the last of Mayfair's red-hot mommas'. She didn't seem to be the most obvious person to lend gravitas to a detective memoir, but she was certainly famous – and Annette Kerner had always been an avid name dropper. Her list of apparent friends and colleagues was long and impressive, including the lawyer Sir Russell Vick, Flying Squad driver George 'Jack' Frost, nightclub queen Kate Meyrick, Harley Street psychiatrist Dr Laurence J. Bendit, Durham's longest-serving Chief Constable Alec Muir, and Claud

Mullins, one of London's best-known magistrates and a founder of the Marriage Guidance Council.

Annette's second memoir also had photographs – an undated playbill from the Theatre Cinema Omnia in Switzerland, an undated photo of 'the authoress as a singer' in an off-the-shoulder evening dress, and a newspaper photo of Miss Annette Symons 'doing good work' for Madame Clara Novello Davies' Musical Instrument Fund. There was also, oddly, a photo of the Queen Mother walking down a street during an official visit, 'snapped' by the authoress.

The Mayfair Detective Agency now had new staff, including two male operatives, Fred Stokes and Johnny Green. Annette didn't explain what had happened to her Dr Watson, ex-cop and strongman Eddie Parsons. Had he objected to being in her first volume of memoirs? Or had she tired of the character and invented a new one? But Fred Stokes proved equally useful, working undercover at hotels or appearing at an open French window just in time to hear a blackmailer confess.

Annette's cases were becoming increasingly melodramatic. She dressed as a nurse to eavesdrop on a blackmailer's conversation in a park, armed with her trusty tape recorder. At the crucial moment, she whipped off the pram's leather cover and declared, 'My name's Annette Kerner ... and this – is my baby.'

The stories were also more salacious. A teenage girl at a boarding school received poison pen letters containing 'filthy language ... accusation of lesbianism', while an unnamed psychiatrist was accused of an affair with his patient. When an 18-year-old called Violet was reported missing, Annette went to extreme lengths to rescue her. She tracked Violet to a Soho flat and sent in Fred Stokes, dressed in a blue drape suit, to threaten Violet with a razor. At that point, Annette burst in, fired her gun twice, and Violet fled back home, having 'had enough of Soho to last her the rest of her life'. It sounded like a replay of the Brilliant Chang story – Soho, a razor, a rapid escape. Only now it was Annette doing the saving rather than the police – and for the first time, she was armed with a gun.

Mrs Sherlock Holmes was at the top of her game, a moral law enforcer who saved women from 'sordid tragedies' and unsavoury men. She was not bankrupt and addicted to greyhound racing, with an agency that had lasted two years before closing down in 1948. Instead, she received daily referrals from bank managers, Bond Street jewellers, titled ladies and insurance companies. Her investigations also involved major amounts of money. When Lady Windermere's £6,000 diamond necklace was stolen, the insurance company was straight on the phone to Annette.

In 1957, when the Crime Writers' Association met for their annual conference, *Daily Herald* journalist Victor Thompson found himself chatting with 'a comely woman' who handed him her card. It was none other than Annette Kerner, 'gay and chic' and one of the 'most successful private eyes of our time'.

But she was still in trouble financially and still in debt. The year after her second memoir was published, she briefly worked as an Employment Agency interviewer on £6 a week, when her creditors included her son Jack, Dickins & Jones and the Gas Board.

Annette Kerner disappeared from the press after this; I'm not sure what happened to her in the years after 1957. Her memoirs were out of print by the early 1960s – when she owed her agent for unpaid books – while her husband Henry died in 1967. She didn't become an avid letter writer, like Antonia Moser, or stand for council election like Maud West. I'm left wondering what she did do in the years after her memoirs came out. There is so little concrete evidence of her sleuthing career, aside from a Mayfair Detective Agency letterhead in her bankruptcy file – 'over 20 years' experience in every branch of detection' – with the famous address: 231 Baker Street.

Sherlock Holmes, the famous consulting detective, possessed a scientific, inquiring mind – traits that were seen as distinctly masculine. (New York Public Library)

Charles Field enjoyed a long career as a high-profile police detective, before opening a Private Inquiry Office in Westminster 'to make inquiries and detect frauds'. His methods came under close scrutiny during the scandalous Bryanston Street divorce case of 1854. (Wikimedia Commons)

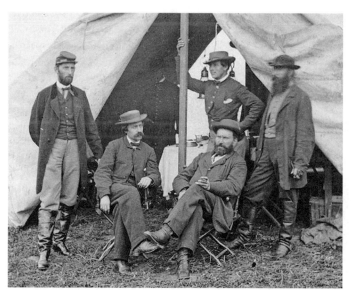

In 1856, Kate Warne became the first female agent employed by the Pinkerton National Detective Agency. Little is known about her identity, although some have claimed she's pictured here during the American Civil War, standing behind her employer Allan Pinkerton (seated on the right). (US Library of Congress, Wikimedia Commons)

ELLEN LYONS.

'I only go where a stylishly-dressed person is required.' Ellen Lyons, whose portrait appeared in *Lloyd's Weekly* in January 1895, when she stood trial for perverting the course of justice. (© The British Library Board. All rights reserved. With thanks to The British Newspaper Archive)

Loveday Brooke, who worked for a detective agency in Fleet Street, was one of several fictional female detectives to emerge at the end of the nineteenth century. The above illustration appeared in the *Ludgate Monthly* in 1893. (Wikimedia Commons)

Moser's Detective Agency, run by ex-CID Inspector Maurice Moser, was situated at 31 Southampton Street. It was here, in the autumn of 1888, that Charlotte Antonia Williamson arrived to ask for a job. The couple were soon lovers and business partners, and she adopted the name Antonia Moser. (Author's own)

Antonia Moser opened her own agency on the Strand in 1905 and became the first female private detective in Britain to publish 'true-life' crime stories. She's pictured here in *Reynolds's Newspaper* in 1909.
(© The British Library Board. All rights reserved. With thanks to The British Newspaper Archive)

Antonia kept hold of Maurice Moser's surname until the end, even though there's no evidence they ever married. When she died in 1919, her occupation was given as 'Private Enquiry Agent. Widow of Maurice Moser.' (Author's own/Crown Copyright)

Registration District ST. GEORGE, HANOVER SQUARE.								
1919. DEATHS in the Sub-District of BELGRAVE in the County of LONDON.								
Columns:— 1.	2.	3.	4.	5.	6.	7.	8.	9.
No.	When and Where Died	Name and Surname.	Sex.	Age.	Rank or Profession.	Cause of Death.	Signature, Description, and Residence of Informant.	When Registered.	Signature of Registrar.
361	Nineteenth September 1919. St. George's Hospital	Charlotte Antonia Moser	Female	63 Years	Of 55 Addison Gardens, West Kensington Private Enquiry Agent Widow of Maurice Moser a Private Enquiry Agent	"Cerebral Thrombosis No P.M. Certified by W.E. Waller M.B.	M.W. Williamson Daughter, present at the death 55 Addison Gardens West Kensington	Nineteenth September 1919.	P. Hemitoph Registrar.

In 1910, Antonia was living at 317 High Holborn, where she ran an advisory service for women. She also supported the suffrage campaign, through a stream of letters to the national press. (Author's own)

'Blackmail, divorce, evidence, robbery. I undertake it all.' In 1905, Kate Easton opened an agency at 241 Shaftesbury Avenue. (Author's own)

Kate then moved her agency to Warwick Court, just a minute's walk from Antonia Moser's advisory service for women on High Holborn. (Author's own)

Kate advertised her services in the *American Register*, a weekly publication aimed at wealthy Americans. (© The British Library Board. All rights reserved. With thanks to The British Newspaper Archive)

London's top three female sleuths placed adverts next to each other in the *Daily Telegraph & Courier* in 1909. Yet while they publicly competed for clients, each behaved as if she was the only woman to work as a private detective in the capital. (© The British Library Board. All rights reserved. With thanks to The British Newspaper Archive)

In 1912, store detective Matilda Mitchell became head of Selfridges secret service. Two years later, she married cricketer Tom Hayward and *The Sketch* provided a photo of the happy couple leaving the register office. (© The British Library Board. All rights reserved. With thanks to The British Newspaper Archive)

Private detective and part-time actress Dorothy Tempest, depicted in the *Penny Illustrated Paper*, fainted on the stand during the 1904 trial of two West End fortune tellers. (© The British Library Board. All rights reserved. With thanks to The British Newspaper Archive)

MRS DOROTHY TEMPEST A LADY-DETECTIVE

Registration District HAMPSTEAD.								
192**8**.	DEATHS in the Sub-District of HAMPSTEAD in the County of LONDON.							
Columns :— 1.	2.	3.	4.	5.	6.	7.	8.	9.
2a. When and Where Died.	Name and Surname.	Sex.	Age.	Rank or Profession.	Cause of Death.	Signature, Description, and Residence of Informant.	When Registered.	Signature of Registrar.
23. Tenth June 1928. 45 Eton Avenue.	Dorothy Tempest	Female	About 55 years	of 28 King Henry's Road Spinster. Solicitors Process server.	Fatty and medical disease of heart. Bronchitis and congestion of lungs. Head failure. Certified by Walter Schroder Coroner for London. 24th P.M. without Inquest.	C. Muggeridge Caused the body to be buried Merton House St. Brides Avenue. E.C.4.	Thirteenth June 192 8	A. Griffiths Registrar.

Dorothy Tempest had become a solicitor's process server by the time of her death in 1928. Process serving had formed an important part of private detective work ever since the nineteenth century. (Author's own/Crown Copyright)

'One of the last strongholds held exclusively by men had been stormed.' In 1918, Lilian Wyles joined the newly formed Metropolitan Police Women Patrols. But while she was eventually given the power of arrest, she had far less freedom than her counterparts in private detection. (Wikipedia)

WOMAN 'TECS OF BAKER STREET

A College for Feminine Undergraduates of Crime Investigation

"YOU KNOW MY METHODS, WATSON": MR. KERSEY DEMONSTRATES

Mr. G. H. Kersey, the private detective, gives a lesson to his class of girls on how to render an assailant helpless by using "the copper's clinch"—having, of course, caught the criminal in a suitable attitude. There are twenty lady pupils in his School for Women Detectives

THE USE OF MAKE-UP

One of the students putting finishing touches to a masculine disguise. The principles that govern stage make-up, or even those of the more discreet boudoir-table, have to be modified for this grim work, which will have neither the aid of artificial light nor the enchantment lent by distance

MAKING A MAN OF HER: FIRST LESSONS IN THE ART OF DISGUISE

On the left are two women detectives in the making about to practise their craftmanship in disguise. The second picture shows them in "character," ready to shadow any crook whose eyesight is not good

A DESPERATE CHARACTER: THE FINISHING TOUCHES

One of the pupils hides a tell-tale strand of hair, while making-up for this "problem picture" of criminal investigation

A CLASS IN ANTI-SHOPLIFTING METHODS

Part of the training consists in studying the various forms of "shoplifting," and general detective work connected with the big departmental stores, where there are many openings for women detectives

A NEW profession for women—that of the trained detective —has been made possible by the enormous increase of shop-lifting and the need for skilled shadowing in divorces. Baker Street, famous as the fictional home of Sherlock Holmes, now has a school for lady sleuths, which is run by Mr. G. H. Kersey, himself a successful private detective. More than twenty pupils in the organization are going through a course of criminal investigation and the artifices of disguise

Students at the College for Feminine Undergraduates of Crime Investigation on Baker Street, which opened in 1927, learned shadowing, disguise, ju-jutsu and the 'death grip', as seen here in *The Graphic*. (Mary Evans Picture Library)

Maud West became Britain's leading female sleuth in the 1920s, famed for her skills at disguise, including impersonating a Salvation Army worker. (Wikimedia Commons)

CHURCHMAN'S CIGARETTES

ALBUMS FOR CHURCHMAN'S PICTURE CARDS CAN BE OBTAINED FROM TOBACCONISTS AT ONE PENNY EACH

"IN TOWN TO-NIGHT"

A SERIES OF 50

42

MISS MAY STOREY
Woman Detective

A woman detective, Miss May Storey has one of the most exciting jobs possible, for not only is she engaged in detecting shop-lifters, but has to shadow people of every type, from dope pedlers to confidence tricksters, and from blackmailers to missing heirs. Her work carries her all over the world and, in order to gain her objective, she has to act various parts, such as stewardess on a liner, house-maid, and charlady. Of course, Miss Storey frequently adopts masculine roles, which suit her particularly well as she has a deep voice and very short hair. In the picture she is in one of her masculine disguises.

W.A.& A.C. CHURCHMAN

ISSUED BY THE IMPERIAL TOBACCO CO. (OF GREAT BRITAIN & IRELAND), LTD.

MISS MAY STOREY

'Sleuthing is a great career for a girl.' May Storey reportedly ran an all-female detective agency and was famed for catching 'white slavers' in the 1930s. (The New York Library Digital Collections)

Lady Marye Violet Isolde Rous, the daughter of the 4th Earl of Stradbroke, apparently worked for a Soho detective agency and was said to be its 'top woman operative' in the mid-1950s. (Mary Evans Picture Library)

Annette Kerner, the 'Little Chief', after she was found not guilty of fraud in 1952. (Mirrorpix)

'It's a grand job is sleuthing. I wouldn't give it up for the world.' May Greenhalgh, pictured with her advertising poster in 1955, ran an agency from her home in east London. (Getty Images)

Zena Scott-Archer with her mother Marion and father Sydney, an ex-Flying Squad officer who launched Scott's Detective Bureau in Liverpool in the 1930s. (Zena Scott-Archer family collection)

Before and after: Zena (centre) with two 'assistants' at Scott's Detective Bureau: close friend Win Hobson (left) and private detective Barbara Macy who later bought the agency. Zena preferred to work with women, who were far more observant than male agents. (*Sunday People*)

In 1960, Yvonne Colborne-Malpas, a partner in a West End firm of investigators, was attacked while attempting to hand a court summons to 'man about town' Dominic Elwes. The day after he was fined, she was pictured at home with her dachshunds Bunty and Coco. (Alamy)

'But I couldn't do that!' The mysterious Anne Summer, commentating at a fashion show in 1967, the year before her detective memoir was published. (*Daily Mirror*)

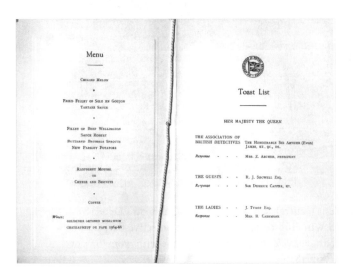

The Association of British Detectives' annual banquet of 1969, when 'Mrs. Z. Archer' was president. She was one of only twelve women among its 500 members. (Zena Scott-Archer family collection)

By the 1960s, Zena had moved offices to Princes Building, 81 Dale Street, Liverpool, where her agency handled 300 matrimonial cases a year. (Alan Stephenson)

Zena Scott-Archer received more than her fair share of publicity in the 1970s – and was delighted when no one recognised her on the cover of the *Sunday Telegraph* magazine. She also showed off some of her other disguises, which the magazine described as 'efficient secretary', 'hard-bitten but prissy blonde' and 'frowzy lady'. (© Martyn Goddard)

In 1981, Zena Scott-Archer was the leading British detective on the world stage – elected president of both the Association of British Investigators and the World Association of Detectives. (Association of British Investigators)

'Zena was an inspiration; it was a dream to follow in her path.' Siti Subaidah Naidu, pictured with Zena in 2011, the year she became the second woman to head the World Association of Detectives. (Siti Subaidah Naidu)

The Sherlock Holmes pub in London boasts a recreation of Sherlock's Baker Street flat, put together by the Sherlock Holmes Society for the Festival of Britain in 1951. (Author's own)

Jen Jarvie, death investigator and winner of the 2022 Zena Scott-Archer Award for Investigator of the Year, pictured with her business partner Jaz Khan, a former detective superintendent at West Yorkshire Police. (Jen Jarvie)

'I would say I can justify sitting in a car much better than a man.' Sam Cooper, professional investigator and founder of Rogue Daters, which helps people being scammed by romance fraudsters online. (Sam Cooper)

Charlotte Notley in the offices of Taylor Investigations, situated on a busy street in Norwich. Her aim is to take away the air of mystery that's always been associated with private investigators. (Charlotte Notley)

DO YOU WANT TO KNOW A SECRET?

It's the autumn of 2021 and I'm back on Baker Street, looking for the address that once belonged to Annette Kerner's detective agency. When I first came to the Sherlock Holmes Museum, several months ago, I had no idea how difficult it would be to try to trace her career. Annette did leave a trail of documentary evidence: her bankruptcy files at the National Archives are as hefty as an old-fashioned phone book, and I've seen and heard her on *Pathé News*. But she remains frustratingly elusive, and her references to real people and real criminal cases make it even harder to unravel the truth. There are too many gaps to be filled, and her change of name, age and birthplace don't make matters any easier, nor does her habit of telling lies.

I pass No. 130 Baker Street, where Charles Henry Kersey, the trainer of lady detectives, once taught his students the death grip in the 1920s, and which is now a branch of Snappy Snaps. I cross the Marylebone Road, walk past a bank and donut shop, a block of flats and a tourist gift shop, then stop at a handsome blue door with faint lettering, No. 231. The door is closed so I move to the window, where there's a huge drum embossed with the words 'Sgt Pepper's Lonely Hearts Club Band'. Then I see another door and walk in. 'Is this number 231?' I ask a young assistant, standing at a counter by the window.

The man nods.

'Great,' I say. 'Did you know there used to be a detective agency here, run by a woman?'

'Oh?' he says, 'I didn't know,' and he hands me a flyer for the London Beatles Store.

This ground floor of Nos 231–233 Baker Street has been a Beatles shop for the past ten years, and it sells the 'world's largest range' of Fab Four merchandise. 'Can I have a look round?' I ask, squeezing past Beatles sweatshirts, Monopoly boards, yellow submarine lamps, waste bins, travel mugs and umbrellas. It's even more crowded than the Sherlock Holmes Museum gift shop. A TV screen on the wall shows the Beatles performing on stage in shiny 1960s suits and the words of 'Do You Want to Know a Secret' reverberate round the shop. In the second room, there's another assistant, standing at a photocopier, so I tell her I'm writing a book about female private detectives. Did she know there was once a detective agency here?

'Yes,' she says.

'Really?' I'm surprised. 'How do you know?'

'A customer told me that in ancient times there was a detective here, this was the location.'

'Who was the customer?' I ask, intrigued. What did they mean by 'ancient times', were they referring to Annette Kerner? It seems strange that someone else might be looking for her, when hardly anything has been written about Mrs Sherlock Holmes, either in print or online. I hope they're not on her trail; she feels like she's mine now.

'The customer was a boy,' says the shop assistant. 'He said this used to be a detective agency. But,' she adds, 'he didn't say it was run by a woman.'

'Oh,' I say, feeling strangely relieved. 'Do you get a lot of customers?'

'Yes,' says the woman. 'People often come here after they've been to the Sherlock Holmes Museum. They are both famous, the Beatles and the detective. They were super, super geniuses. People go to the museum then this shop, it's a kind of tour.'

'Do you know who lives upstairs?' I ask.

'No,' says the assistant. 'It is privately rented.'

Annette Kerner's office was reportedly on the third floor, up a set of rickety stairs and behind a door with a thick glass window. But although it featured briefly in the 1946 *Pathé* film, I've been wondering if she just used the address as a selling point and perhaps a place to receive post, sharing it as she did with the British Friendship Society. There would hardly have been room for 'twenty-two operatives' to pop in to receive instructions or deliver reports to the Little Chief. What would Annette have thought of the fact that No. 231 Baker Street is now a Beatles store? She may well have liked the idea that her address is part of a tourist trail of super-geniuses, for she did love celebrity. If she were alive today, she'd probably have claimed a connection to the Beatles.

I squeeze back past the Fab Four merchandise and leave the shop, crossing the road where Annette once narrowly missed being hit by a mobster's car and ended up in hospital with broken ribs. I pass the exit to Baker Street tube station, where she was followed by two razor-wielding hoodlums, and eventually come to the massive statue of Sherlock Holmes on the Marylebone Road. There is nothing to remember Annette Kerner, of course.

She may have once been Britain's most famous female private eye, but her tales were as much fiction as fact. Yet she certainly made her mark on the world of private detection, acclaimed by the press and posing as a member of the Crime Writers' Association when she hadn't actually written any books. The very few crime historians who do mention her tend to take her memoirs at face value. Aileen A. Rivers, in *A Brief History of the Private Detective*, describes Annette as 'one of the earliest female detectives in England'. Graham Nown's *Watching the Detectives* dubs her the 'Queen of disguise', who was born into a family of wealthy property owners before opening a detective agency in the early 1920s.

Annette's full story has still not been told, aside from the work of Professor Louise Jackson, over twenty years ago, when she examined the colourful narrative of 'Mrs Sherlock Holmes'. In recent years, at least two authors have been tempted by the famous detective's story. Writer Naomi Clifford came across one of Annette's memoirs in a second-hand bookshop in Arundel, West Sussex. 'I was drawn to Annette because of the North London Jewish element,' she explains. 'I am 50 per cent Jewish, or 51 per cent, according to my late father, and from North London, and was curious to know why Jews felt compelled to hide their Jewishness.' Naomi tried to identify one or two of Annette's cases, 'but I got nowhere. I think she was keeping a lot back. I'm not sure I believe all the stuff about the family being so well off, nor about her life as a spy.'

The Swedish writer, Mattias Boström, author of *From Holmes to Sherlock: The Story of the Men and Women Who Created an Icon*, also considered writing a book about Annette and her detective agency. 'But the more I read,' he explains, 'the more complicated she seemed. And the less I believed in her. I got the feeling that a lot of her doings were exaggerated. Annette Kerner was great at PR, and really got people to believe in her. But I think the truth was far from what was told.'

Maud West's biographer Susannah Stapleton also decided to give Annette 'a wide berth', when she realised her stories 'were as crazy as Maud's' and that she'd been declared bankrupt just before she wrote her memoirs.

Professor Louise Jackson, however, was more interested in what Annette Kerner was saying about 'self, identity, appearance and persona', and less in whether specific case stories were true. 'Was she really parachuted into France as a spy?' she writes. 'Did she really go undercover for the police? Maybe it doesn't matter; perhaps the significance lies in the dream that it could happen.'

Louise first stumbled on female private detectives while working on a history of women in policing in the late 1990s. She read snippets in the *Policewoman's Review*, mainly on Maud West, and thought, 'Hello, that's interesting.' She also went through private collections of press clippings at the Metropolitan Women Police Association archives. Then she came across Annette's first memoir, *Woman Detective*, in a bookshop, Murder and Mayhem, in Hay-on-Wye. She found Annette a far more subversive figure than the elderly spinster model of Miss Marple, especially in terms of gender and class.

Did her image of Annette change, the more she researched?

'I was intrigued by her,' Louise says carefully. 'I was aware of a certain sort of dubious social status associated with being a female private detective. They were hard to pin down and categorise anyway.'

Did she find her case stories plausible?

'Well,' Louise laughs, 'is anyone going to surface and say, "it's not true?" Her claims are impossible to test.' Louise believes that Annette used the press 'as much as they were using her'; she was keen to promote herself as heroic, and so were they.

★ ★ ★

Annette Kerner wasn't the only family member with a flair for publicity and a love of the theatrical. When she told her gambling neighbour Hyman Williams, during the whisky fraud case of 1952, that her brother was well known in the film business, it was true. Annette's five brothers are not easy to find, with a habit of changing their first names and using variations of Symons. But at least two went into the film industry.

She seems to have been closest to Jules, who provided the capital for the Mayfair Detective Agency, first as a loan and then as a gift, and who also funded the Film Studios Club on Oxford Street. Jules' birth name appears to have been Ceasman, but by his teenage years he was registered as Julius. When he married Jeanette Berman in 1925, he used the name Julian J. Symons, but a few years later, when he'd entered the film business, he was now Jules Simmons. In the late 1920s, he joined 20th Century Fox in Manchester as a salesman, and according to *Kinematograph Weekly*, he was already well known in local film circles. The trade paper, popularly known as *Kine Weekly*, frequently updated its readers on Jules Simmons' career. It would also publish adverts for his sister's Mayfair Detective Agency, 'recommended by many executives of the Film Trade'.

Jules Simmons worked for Allied Artists and then moved to RKO Radio Pictures, one of the big five Hollywood studios, famed for the 1941 film *Citizen Kane*. He was praised for his 'widespread knowledge of the film industry' and his picture often appeared in *Kine Weekly*, attending RKO annual sales conventions and gala shows. By 1939, he'd joined British Grand National Pictures, which produced films that sounded like stories from his mother's detective case files – *Cipher Bureau*, *I Met a Murderer* and *Shadows Over Shanghai*.

In 1941, Jules was employed by Anglo-American, based at No. 123 Wardour Street – right by the Symons' old family home. This was Hollywood's golden age and Wardour Street, where Annette and Jules had spent their childhood, was now the heart of the film industry in Britain. Film Row – or the High Street of Film – housed around 100 film companies by the late 1940s and so perhaps it was Jules who interested *Pathé News* in making a film about his sister's detective agency. In 1954, the year Annette's first memoir was published, he was photographed with hugely popular actress Phyllis Calvert, started work on a film about the Red Cross, and announced plans to make 'a skit on emigration' called *There is a Happy Land*.

His brother Ben – presumably Barnett – who Annette mentioned in her memoirs, also worked in the film industry. In 1930, he was district manager for Paramount in Leeds and Liverpool. A later advert from the

1950s for B.J. Simmons & Co. Ltd in Covent Garden suggests he set up a business supplying costumes to the theatrical and film industries and had 'dressed many notable TV productions for the BBC'.

Jules Simmons died in 1968, and his wife Jeanette ten years later. They left two sons, Michael James and John Raymond. Michael was an optician in Shepherd's Bush, described by friends as 'very focused and quietly successful'. His wife, Shirin Simmons, is an author and cookery writer and her book *A Feast of My Persian Heritage* was written in memory of her husband.

John Simmons, meanwhile, went into the entertainment industry, like his father. In 1955, he was appointed television and film executive at Gordon & Gotch Advertising. He was also film critic to the Inns of Court magazine, *GLIM*, and a member of the British Film Institute's lecture panel. John was frequently described as 'son of pioneer film man, Jules Simmons', although there was never any mention of his detective aunt. He became head of TV production at Hobson, Bates & Partners, then head of production at Soundrama Ltd, where he was credited with introducing electronic music to British feature films.

In 1958, John married Cecilia Green, a trained ballerina, painter and the favourite model of the watercolour artist Sir William Russell Flint. John opened an advertising company, Simmons Consultancy, on Bateman Street, a couple of minutes' walk from his aunt's old home in Soho. He wrote and directed commercials for Bosch and Marks & Spencer, ran an art gallery in Chelsea, and organised the first public art to be displayed in the House of Commons. While Annette felt forced to hide her Jewish identity, both her nephews left money to Jewish charities, the Jewish Blind Society and Jewish Care.

Annette Kerner's career as a private detective doesn't seem to have been spoken about within the family, and few were aware of her Mrs Sherlock Holmes persona. When Maud West retired in the late 1930s, she turned her back on the character she'd created, and Annette seems to have done the same. 'I've never heard of Annette Kerner,' says Susanna Fyson, whose parents were beneficiaries in John Simmons' will. 'I knew John since I was 13, his mother was Jewish and had a nightclub in Soho.' Susanna, who is a prop maker, remembers John as 'very much larger than life, and he loved an audience. He was very charismatic and flamboyant; he wore Liberty shirts and always had a silk handkerchief in his breast pocket.' John and

Cecilia travelled a lot, she explains, especially to Italy. 'They were real opera lovers and loved musical theatre' – just like John's detective aunt, who'd started out dreaming of a career as an opera singer.

Gillian Harrison, who lived opposite John from the 1960s, also hadn't heard of his aunt. 'He was quite a character,' she says, 'and a bit of a name-dropper. He dressed like a film producer, was a great raconteur, and had lots of contacts.'

Anthony Cassin-Scott, an executor of John's will, never met Annette Kerner – but he does remember that his parents often mentioned an 'eccentric' aunt. 'One evening,' he explains, 'sometime in the mid 1970s, my parents accompanied John and Cecilia to visit his aunt and they didn't return until the small hours. Apparently, she was convinced that she was being spied upon and there were "people hiding behind the curtains". She would ring and say someone was there, and that they needed to come round.' Perhaps Annette's fears that she was being followed, after the 1952 whisky case, had intensified.

During her subsequent bankruptcy hearing, she told the Official Receiver she'd 'received numerous threats', and a few months earlier, 'an attack was made on me in a quiet street, necessitating hospital treatment'. She had lived in fear of further attacks ever since, staying in hotels and not revealing her address to anyone. Annette didn't explain the reason behind the attack, but she seems to have believed she was being persecuted as a 'police nark'. Perhaps by the 1970s, her years as a private detective, however short-lived, had taken their toll on her mental health.

Helen Varma, who worked with John Simmons for years, says he rarely spoke about his family, 'other than to entertain me with stories about the club his mother ran in Soho. It was very glamorous, Hollywood film stars came, possibly Bogart and Bacall. The women in the Simmons family seemed to have quite a pioneering spirit!' Helen describes John as 'flamboyant, charming, loveable, fearless and very witty. He had quite a robust ego, and he never let the truth get in the way of a good story.'

He sounds a lot like his aunt, the famous sleuth who entertained British readers with her wonderful tales in the 1940s and '50s. Helen believes that if Annette did have mental health problems, issues with gambling and allegations of fraud, then her nephew may have seen this as shameful and wouldn't have talked about her. 'He was very keen to present his family as very successful,' she says, 'and glamorous.'

As for Annette's own children, her son Jack, using the name Finberg, was a director at the Film Studios Club. He then became a court reporter, combining his interest in the legal world with that of entertainment by writing scripts for production companies. When his mother stood trial for the whisky case in 1952, the court shorthand writer was none other than 'Jack Fineberg [*sic*] – Mrs Kerner's son by a former marriage'. How would it have felt to be the court shorthand reporter when your own mother was on trial? Did he send her a sympathetic glance as she stood in the dock, or keep his head down and focus on transcribing her words?

That same year, Jack opened an office, Temple Bar Court Reporters, and became official shorthand writer to the Old Bailey. His mother had detected crime, while he recorded it, and he remained at Britain's most famous criminal court until at least the mid-1960s.

Jack's work often took him abroad. He toured the Russian Courts of Justice, gave a lecture to legal authorities, attended a trial in Leningrad and visited a film studio which was shooting Tolstoy's *War and Peace*. He also went to Hollywood, where he wrote a film script.

In 1964, his photo appeared in the *Daily Mirror* after he'd been a victim of assault while returning home one night. It gave his age as 35 – he was nearer 42 – but perhaps he was following in his mother's footsteps and knocking a few years off his age.

Annette's daughter Ruth, meanwhile, who used the surnames Finberg and Kerner, stayed close to her mother. In August 1952, she was living with Annette and Henry, and according to a report submitted to the Official Receiver she was 'of independent means, being employed'. However, at the same time, Annette declared that Ruth was a dependent, 'I have to contribute to the support and medical treatment of my daughter by my first marriage, who is mentally retarded'.

'Mentally retarded' applied to all levels of learning or intellectual disability in the 1950s, replacing older derogatory terms like 'idiot' and 'imbecile', and many children were institutionalised. By the 1970s, Ruth was a poet, and her work was often published in local London papers, with her poems focusing on the misery and suffering of the homeless in Fulham and Chelsea. 'Ruth Finberg is a lady of many talents,' commented the *Fulham Chronicle*. 'She is a poetess, a writer of children's stories, and she even finds time to work at a local cinema.' She was also a member of the Chelsea Labour Party.

Had her mother been telling the truth when she said Ruth needed medical treatment, or had she been trying to come up with a reason for her debts? Annette dedicated her second detective memoir to 'darling Jack and Ruth' – and she would have been proud of her children, both were highly creative with interests in storytelling, law, politics and social justice.

★ ★ ★

Annette Kerner died on 25 July 1978, at No. 4 King Charles House, Wandon Road, Chelsea. She was aged 84, and her birth date was correctly given as 21 October 1893. But her birthplace was given as London, and her stated occupation was 'widow of Kerner'. Annette left everything – £601.25 – to her daughter, apparently because her son was financially secure. 'I hope my well-beloved son Jack will understand,' she wrote. 'He is more able to manage than she is.' Annette's will was signed by 'B. Simmons', perhaps her brother Ben, and an ex-police constable S. Stephens, both residing at King Charles House.

Female private detectives rarely mentioned each other – Kate Easton, Maud West and May Storey behaved as if they were the only women in Britain doing the job. But Annette Kerner did acknowledge the tradition she came from, and at the end of her second memoir, she wrote of her pride in following 'in the footsteps of the great Maud West, first of Britain's women detectives'. Maud had not been Britain's first female detective, of course, but the two women did have a lot in common. They both took on a man's job and combined it with their 'feminine artifices'. Being a private detective allowed them to live different lives – even if those lives were often made up. Did Annette come to believe the stories she told, or did she, like Maud, simply tell the tales in order to promote herself? Had they ever crossed paths in real life?

Annette could well have read about Maud West in the 1920s, devoured her casebook tales in the 1930s and been inspired to become a private detective herself. Annette Kerner was a worthy successor, even if in a business sense she wasn't a success. The idea that she was 'unique', however, as the only British woman to run a detective agency in the mid-1950s, was a lie. For, by 1953, there was another woman operating a highly successful detective business, and unlike Annette, the crime tales she told were true.

ZENA SCOTT-ARCHER: SCOTT'S DETECTIVE BUREAU

Some 200 miles north-west of London, in a small office not far from the Liverpool Docks, another female detective was hard at work in the 1950s – and her agency was flourishing. 'Merseyside's Mrs Sherlock Holmes' began her career the same year that Annette launched the Mayfair Detective Agency on Baker Street. She would become the most famous female private eye on the world stage, known for her skills at shadowing, surveillance and disguise, as well as her oyster shell nail varnish and passion for hats.

Zena Philippa Scott was born on 29 June 1921. Her parents, Marion and Sydney James Scott, lived in Kingston, Surrey, and she was the eldest of two daughters. Her paternal grandmother was Jewish, but her father Sydney had been brought up in the Anglican faith. He followed his father's footsteps into the police force, spending six years in the Northwest Mounted Police in Canada, before joining the Metropolitan Police. Sydney served in the Royal Navy, Royal Flying Corps and RAF during the First World War, and then became a member of the Flying Squad.

This 'corps of ace detectives', formed in 1919, were regarded as tough and tenacious men and they were known for their fast cars. In 1927, Detective Sergeant Scott had an 'adventure with a motor car', when he chased a gang of burglars across some of the densest areas of London, beginning in Hammersmith and ending near Clapham Junction, where three of the gang were arrested. His vehicle was one of the new 'speed' cars that had been recently supplied to Scotland Yard, explained the press, and capable of 80mph.

Sydney Scott was medically discharged from the force in the early 1930s and lost his retirement payment when he invested in a friend's disastrous butcher's shop in Epsom. Then he took a job with Littlewoods Pools, the football betting company, investigating fraudulent prize claims, and the family relocated to Wallasey, then part of Cheshire, on the banks of the River Mersey.

One day, while on a train, Sydney spotted a briefcase that a passenger had left behind. He tracked down its owner, a local solicitor, who was so impressed that he urged him to set up office as a private investigator. Sydney returned home, laid all the money he had – £3.15 – on the table and asked his wife, 'How long can you make that last?'

When she replied, 'Three weeks', he resigned his post with Littlewoods and rented a small office at No. 3 Cook Street in Liverpool, in the Bank of England Chambers. The street was half a mile from the docks, and home to property auctioneers, estate agents, solicitors and the Law Association rooms. The ex-Flying Squad detective placed an advertisement for Scott's Detective Bureau in the *Liverpool Echo* and sat down to wait for his first clients.

His eldest daughter, meanwhile, had finished her schooling at the age of 14, and her reports had not been encouraging, 'Zena should try harder, Zena is a daydreamer'. She worked as a counter assistant at the chemists Timothy White & Taylor, where she met her future husband, David Humphrey Archer, an apprentice pharmacist. They married in May 1941, and he was soon drafted to India.

When Zena was called up for war work, she was assigned to the US Army, which had a base east of Liverpool at Burtonwood. She was employed as a secretary, initially on £5 a week – more than double her father's pay at Littlewoods – and she also received luxury items like nylon stockings and chocolates.

Zena must have been proud of the posting. She kept her ID – 'Civilian Employee serving the United States Armed Forces' – for the rest of her life.

The Scott family – Zena, her sister Marion, their parents and maternal grandmother – lived at No. 34 Ripon Rd, Wallasey, where Zena would remain for the next sixty years. Her husband, Dave, joined the household when he came back from the war to find Liverpool devastated. At the end of 1940, the city had been hit by 250 tonnes of high-explosive bombs, and the docks were a prime target. The following spring, Merseyside was bombed almost continuously for eight days and 70,000 people were made homeless. Long queues for basic supplies were part of everyday life, food and clothing were rationed, and the Ministry of Information urged citizens to 'Make Do and Mend'. Zena became an expert at designing her own clothes, remaining both frugal and stylish.

In 1946, she was working in the office of the Kardomah Cafe, a chain of coffee shops, and not enjoying it. Then one day, her father said, 'Would you come to work for me in the office?'

Zena was a self-confessed lousy typist, despite her secretarial work during the war, but as soon as she started doing the filing, typing and reports, she realised the potential in private investigation. 'My father was a very good detective,' she later explained, 'but he wasn't a good business-man, and I was.'

Scott's Detective Bureau had around five male investigators at the time, and while they were 'good fellows', they had no talent for report writing. Zena was frustrated by the lack of detail; the men were produc-ing five-line case reports 'that really warranted a lot more explanation and background'. When a man was sent out to case a joint, she had to cross-examine him to get the necessary information: Was the house terraced or semi-detached? Were the windows clean? How much was it worth? But, as Zena later discovered, if a woman was sent out, she would report back on everything from the state of the wall in the front garden to the number of unwashed milk bottles on the step and whether the doorknocker was polished.

Zena complained repeatedly about the men's reports. 'I really used to go off at the deep end to my father, and he said: "Well if you don't like it, why don't you go off and do it yourself." And I did, and the rest is history.'

Zena's first sole assignment, at the age of 25, was to serve papers on a Mrs Williams, a chief stewardess on a ship docked in Liverpool. Zena wasn't sure what the documents were – either matrimonial or debt related – but her father's detectives had failed to locate Mrs Williams and now the stewardess was evading them. Zena knew she was 'on a sticky case', and she hated going on ships. 'I used to wear high-heeled shoes and short tight skirts – and going up the gang plank was an anathema to me,

I never did get used to it.' But once she got on board, she saw a group of women in a corner. She knew that if she asked for 'Mrs Williams', the women would clam up to protect their boss, so instead she called out, 'Elsie!' and the stewardess immediately turned round. 'It was a guts thing,' Zena explained. She'd instinctively known how to succeed where the man had failed.

When she returned to the office, her father said, 'Well, that's the end of you just being a secretary, you're going to get out there.'

Zena enjoyed retelling this story, and while some of the details changed over the years, it was her first real taste of detective work. She'd already gained knowledge from typing case reports, and was given some instructions from her father, but there was no formal training. In the early years, she remembered only ever meeting one other female sleuth.

Her parents were impressed by her new career, and so was her husband, Dave. He was 'a very loyal man,' Zena explained. 'He had nothing to do with the business, but he was very supportive.'

In 1951, a journalist from the *Liverpool Echo* went to visit Scott's Detective Bureau on Cook Street and seemed disappointed to find it resembled a solicitor's office rather than a detective's den. There were no false wigs or magnifying glasses, just Sydney Scott sitting in a black leather armchair, cigarette ash rolling over his coat lapels and settling in the folds of his suit. 'Quite often people ring our office when they really want the police,' Sydney explained. 'We don't like turning business away, but we never interfere with the police.'

Matrimonial investigations occupied about 55 per cent of his time, and he regaled the journalist with the story of an erring wife who, after being traced to a Cheshire hotel, ran outside and threw herself in the river. 'The river was dry,' said Sydney. 'It was only a bit of showmanship on her part. But we had to pull her out of the mud. That job cost us a new suit.'

Sydney was affectionately known as 'Scott of Scotland Yard' and was often described as a 'man's man'. He smoked, played snooker, wore a jemmy mark on his chin from his policing days and shunned the company of women. But he was intensely proud of his detective daughter.

In the coming years, Zena took on a wide variety of cases. She investigated a large restaurant accused of lying about the number of rationed meals it was serving and went undercover to observe the management of a bingo hall, which meant she had to play bingo twice a day for a week. She also spent a week with a circus in Paris, seeking evidence on an Englishman who trained horses for the Circus Medrano. His wife suspected he was having an affair with the trapeze artist. It turned out he was, and she divorced him.

Zena became highly skilled at disguise. She posed as a sales assistant at Blacklers department store, which had been bombed during the war but rebuilt in the 1950s and was known for its lavish displays. Her mission was to find out which staff member was stealing, and she worked in the crockery department in the basement, where she became renowned for persuading customers to buy things they didn't really want. The manager offered her a permanent position, but she declined.

Zena also disguised herself as a nurse to find out who was robbing a 'wealthy hypochondriac widow', stealing valuable paintings and objets d'art from her home. Zena bought herself a white coat and moved into the widow's gloomy old house, but when a doctor asked her to prepare a hypodermic syringe, 'I just stood there, the syringe in my hand, staring at it helplessly. I hadn't the faintest idea what to do with it.' But she still successfully solved the case.

Zena once tracked a couple to a hotel, 'slipped' the housemaid some money, knocked on the bedroom door and pretended she was the maid with the tea. She then identified herself and announced she'd just witnessed the couple 'in compromising circumstances'. She also went undercover for the Dental Council, after reports that a local dental mechanic was illegally making teeth.

Zena became such an expert at the role of the 'ordinary woman' – restaurant customer, bingo player, sales assistant, nurse, housemaid – that she was once outside her home in disguise when a neighbour failed to recognise her. When they later met, the neighbour said there'd been a strange-looking woman looking for her. Zena's main tip for disguise was to 'change your walk and change your laugh', and her favourite outfit was a headscarf and flat-heeled shoes: 'You look nondescript and it changes your height.'

Sydney Scott and his daughter became members of the British Detectives Association (BDA), which was once again pushing for licensing. Hundreds of private inquiry agents had sprung up all over Britain since the end of the war, although exact figures were hard to come by. Journalist Charles Graves estimated there were 'a couple of hundred' and he 'wouldn't recommend more than half a dozen'. The *Sunday Dispatch* put the figure nearer 2,300, and Britain's 'unofficial police force' was now the 'highest ever known'.

Many cases were business related: factory thefts, timber stolen from barges, a chemical firm whose rival took their formula. Some firms also used private detectives to shadow their pay clerks to foil armed hold-ups.

But finding a reputable investigator was difficult because, as the *Dispatch* pointed out, 'Anyone with a stock of printed business cards and the price of a sixpenny noticeboard advertisement can set up in business'.

In 1952, the BDA began a 'witch hunt', according to the *Daily Mail*, to 'crush the growing number of swindlers in Sherlock Holmes guise'. The BDA appealed to people who'd been defrauded to come forward, particularly female clients who had been exploited by rogues. 'Former jail birds, crooks of all types and no-goods are entering this profession now to cash in, they must be stopped,' declared Sydney Scott.

The BDA wanted a Royal Charter of Incorporation, which would give the organisation legal recognition and ensure that 'the right sort of man joins the detective ranks'. Female investigators, noted one journalist, were outnumbered by men 300 to one at the BDA, and 'the association could do with more of them'. Zena Scott-Archer was the only woman in an organisation entirely populated by men.

In 1953, when the BDA gathered for its biannual meeting, Sydney Scott was elected president. He had achieved a long-held ambition, but tragically died just nine days later. Zena was devastated by her father's death but was determined to keep Scott's Detective Bureau going. She took over the business and 'I took over his motto too – I always get my man'.

MERSEYSIDE'S MRS SHERLOCK HOLMES

When Zena Scott-Archer took over Scott's Detective Bureau in 1953, she had a battle to be taken seriously. One day, she received a phone call from a client who wanted to speak to the principal, and she replied, 'I am the principal.' The client was confused; he'd already spoken to one of Zena's detectives, who'd told him he was the principal. Zena soon put him right. 'He is not the principal, I am. If you would like to continue you continue with me.' When she confronted the detective on his return to the office, he was unperturbed. 'Well, it is for the good of the business,' he said. 'Male clients are not going to want to put their trust in an agency that's run by a woman, are they?' Not surprisingly, this private eye didn't last long at Scott's Detective Bureau.

Zena established new ways of doing business. A solicitor who worked in the office above had been in the habit of asking for favours – 'Ah Sid, could you get your girl to type this invoice for me?' But when he appeared in the doorway and asked, 'I wonder if you would mind typing this up for me?' Zena replied, 'Certainly, 10 shillings a letter.'

'I might have known,' said the solicitor. 'Mercenary bloody Mary.'

She also developed a new relationship with the press, who imaginatively dubbed her 'Merseyside's Mrs Sherlock Holmes'. Her father's newspaper advertisements had been minimal, just a line or two in the local paper giving the address and phone numbers, although one did promise 'Investigations of all kinds throughout the Kingdom'. But after Zena took over, Scott's Detective Bureau began to specialise, offering

'Surveillance Investigations Car Shadowing' as well as 'Maintenance Divorce Observation Tracing'.

When journalist George Eglin from the *Liverpool Echo* paid a visit, he assumed the glamorous woman who greeted him was the secretary. Then he realised she was the boss, and the two male operatives in the back room were her employees. The article referred to her as 'Mrs. Archer' through-out and provided a photo of her briefing a male assistant – much as Annette Kerner had been photographed with her 'assistant', ex-detective inspector Wilson of Scotland Yard.

Female private detectives who ran their own businesses were a rarity in the 1950s, and those who did receive coverage tended to be portrayed as housewives or society ladies. Melodie Walsh worked with her husband John, and the couple were often hired by fur and jewellery firms to attend society functions. She could 'borrow all the diamonds and furs that she wants', explained the *Weekly Dispatch*, 'lucky woman'. In 1953, the *Daily Mirror* provided a photo of Melodie cooking at a stove, with a tea towel over one arm. She led a 'double life', explained the paper, part of the day she was a suburban housewife and the rest she was out with her ex-Flying Squad husband, delivering mink coats and enjoying fabulous parties. By the 1960s the couple's Walsh Agency was one of the largest in England, providing personal protection to screen stars like Sophia Loren.

Lady Marye Violet Isolde Rous, the daughter of the 4th Earl of Stradbroke, apparently worked for a Soho agency and was said to be its 'top woman operative'. She seemed to be very publicly trying out her hand at several jobs – actress, waitress, factory hand, housemaid, govern-ess, chocolate seller, air hostess, cattle hand on a ranch – and now private eye. A press photo showed her lurking on a street corner while 'on a tail-ing job' in the West End. She was slim, blue-eyed and 'lovely', with a taste for the bizarre and 'the nerve to indulge it'.

May Greenhalgh, however, had a much longer career, which seems to have started in the 1930s. Like Maud West, she was a mother of six and she ran an agency from her home in Walthamstow, east London. May was reportedly the daughter of a Lancashire schoolmaster, she'd trained as an artist before working as a telephone operator and insurance clerk. Then she joined an agency run by a former Scotland Yard officer, before starting her own business. 'It's a grand job is sleuthing,' May declared. 'I wouldn't give it up for the world.'

In 1954, she appeared on BBC TV's afternoon show *For Women: Leisure and Pleasure*, relating some of her adventures as a private eye. The following year, at the age of 70, she was photographed holding a poster advertising her business. 'You must have evidence,' read the text, above a picture of a judge in a wig. 'Why not consult M. Greenhalgh, private enquiry agent.'

But most women in the 1950s seem to have reverted to helping their detective husbands, as they had a century before, and now private inquiry agents often worked from home rather than an office. The 'normal attitude was that women did the clerical work,' explained Janet Finlay, who joined her husband's agency, Finlay's Bureau of Investigation, in south-west London after her marriage in 1954. She kept a low profile but acted 'as the control officer with agents out in the field'.

Zena Scott-Archer, on the other hand, had a very public persona and she regarded presentation and image as vitally important. Female investigators needed to look respectable, and she was known for her fashionable dress sense and a large selection of hats. When she once served a writ in a Liverpool council estate, a little girl rushed up and asked, 'Are you the queen?'

'No, I'm not,' said Zena. But she was wearing a similar hat to the queen, who was then on an official visit to the city, and the little girl was insistent, 'You are the queen, aren't you?'

Zena was happy to share some of her investigations with the press. She was particularly proud of the time a colleague in the Isle of Man asked her to find a man at the Grand National in Aintree. Zena knew the target, having met him before, but trying to find anyone in such a crowd seemed impossible. She was told he'd be at the county stand, along with hundreds of others and, as luck would have it, she spotted the man, walking in the pouring rain with 'a girl on his arm'. Zena started to follow, worried that at any moment the couple might jump in a car and drive off. Then she saw a 'walking photographer', who took photos at race meetings, and when he took her picture, she realised he'd probably snapped her target, just a few yards in front of her. So she requested several photos and got the evidence she needed. The trick, she explained, was to think on your feet and use any opportunity that presented itself.

In June 1954, the *Daily Herald* described Zena as Britain's most glamorous private eye. 'My success as a detective,' she explained, 'is due to the fact that I don't look like one.' Indeed, she didn't. She was smartly dressed in a leopard-print grosgrain coat and a yellow Bangkok straw hat.

The following year, the *Daily Dispatch* published a photo of Zena marching down a Liverpool street wearing a 'Paris model' hat, one of thirty in her wardrobe. She had just been appointed editor of the *Private Investigator*, the official magazine of a newly formed organisation, the Association of British Detectives (ABD). It was launched in 1953, the result of a merger between the BDA and another organisation, the Federation of British Detectives. Like its predecessor, the ABD was dominated by ex-policemen and, as one paper explained, it resembled 'a club organised by Scotland Yard's Big Five'.

The ABD tightened membership rules. Applicants had to prove themselves 'a man of integrity', with two years' permanent employment experience and two character references. Membership was open to 'principals' of agencies, but not their employees, although former policemen with 'exemplary records' were admitted. According to the press, members were issued with a distinctive badge 'so they can recognise one another'.

In 1956, *Reynolds's News* sent a journalist to the ABD conference at the Waldorf Hotel in London, where he admired Zena's flashing hazel eyes, dainty feet, white straw hat and black figure-fitting costume. 'I could not imagine anything nicer following me around,' he leered, she was 'a private eyeful'. He must have asked Zena what her pharmacist husband thought of her job, for she explained he 'doesn't mind when I'm out of town … Frequently he helps me by providing fuchsine, which we sprinkle over money. Catches thieves, you know – stains their fingers red.'

A journalist from *Woman's Magazine* also paid a visit to Zena's Liverpool office and noted her hobbies – making all her own clothes and hats, studying criminology and unsolved local murders, and devouring detective stories, especially Raymond Chandler. The *Mirror* was similarly interested in her hobbies – she baked cakes and bottled homemade wines – but this 'elegant brunette with a model girl figure is not a typical housewife'; instead, she provided evidence in 200 divorce cases a year.

Zena Scott-Archer was a far cry from Raymond Chandler's fictional investigator, Philip Marlowe. The old mystery murders of the Golden Age had evolved into the crime novel, a hardboiled action genre where private eyes dealt with corrupt cops and organised crime. Philip Marlowe was a lone wolf, a wise-cracking, hard-drinking misanthrope, who was usually a few seconds away from being slugged by a cop or a hoodlum. Unlike British private detectives, however, he did have a licence – regulation had been introduced in California as early as 1915. Novels like *The Long Good-Bye*, published the year Zena took over Scott's Detective Bureau, provided escapism. She enjoyed the 'tough American pistol-packing detectives. I've never met one like that myself. The only weapon I carry is a hat pin.'

Zena rarely found herself in dangerous situations, and rather than being antagonistic, she found 'the best way is to be disarming'. Her work was 'really rather gentle. I'm not sent into terrible dens of iniquity or any-thing'. She did not emphasise danger like her predecessors Kate Easton, Maud West, May Storey or Annette Kerner, or feed a press appetite for near-death encounters. Instead, she described being a private detective as 'rather provincial ... you're usually trying to help people who are in trouble with misdemeanours, not out and out crime. They go to the police for that.'

During one case in 1957, however, she did become frightened. Zena was hired by Silverman Livermore, a well-known firm of Liverpool solicitors, to serve papers on a man who'd failed to pay his divorce costs. He'd now fallen out with his new 'lady love' and was doing everything he could to avoid paying.

Zena went to his shop, where he sold fireplaces, and discreetly handed over the documents when no customers were around. But the man denied knowing anything about a divorce and insisted she'd 'got the wrong chap'. Zena was certain of his identity; she'd taken a signed confession statement from him during the divorce, when he'd provided his driving licence as ID. So she left the documents in his shop and walked out.

But as she was driving off, there was a terrific thump on the window. The man was trying to thrust the documents back. The window was closed, and so Zena drove off. Then she realised he'd leapt into his massive truck, used for delivering fireplaces, and was chasing her, his hand con-stantly on the horn. Zena tore through red lights and went down one-way streets, until finally she decided she had better face him.

She stopped her car, the man stopped his truck, and they both got out and walked towards each another like a scene from *High Noon*. As they came face to face, the man suddenly shoved the documents down the front of her clothing, 'which was very demoralising: it was stiff paper that they were on and they were sticking out of my dress'. Overcome with fury, Zena slapped his face.

By now, a group of people had gathered to watch, and the man implored them to call the police. When a constable arrived, Zena gave him her business card, 'I'm serving documents on this chap and he won't take them.' The constable turned to the man and asked his name, 'and he stood there, he didn't speak for a long time and you could positively hear the little cogs in his brain squeaking'. At last, the man gave up, confessed his real name and paid his costs. The anecdote was one of Zena's favourites; she'd ultimately gained the upper hand in her determination to do her job.

★ ★ ★

Document serving had always been an important part of a private detective's work, ever since the nineteenth-century Bow Street Runners, like Henry Goddard, who had carried court documents inside their tipstaffs. But Zena Scott-Archer wasn't the only female private detective to be faced with an uncooperative man or the threat of assault.

Dorothy Tempest, the part-time actress who'd investigated fortune tellers, had become a solicitor's process server in the years before the First World War. In 1918, she attempted to serve divorce papers on Samuel Harris, better known as the comedian Gus Barrie. She waited at the door of the Metropole Theatre in Manchester, accompanied by Samuel's wife, and when he came out, she tried to serve the papers. He flew into a temper, knocked her down, kicked and struck her 'many blows' and pushed her into the road. He was found guilty of assault and fined £10, plus costs.

Dorothy worked in the job for at least ten years, and when she died in 1928 her death certificate gave her occupation as solicitor's process server. It must have been lucrative work. Dorothy lived in Hampstead, north London, yet she was willing to travel to Manchester to serve a comedian with divorce papers.

The increase in divorce work after the Second World War meant more demand for process servers. Large solicitors' firms had often used 'office boys', but now they turned to private detectives. Women were seen as particularly good at the job, but they still risked assault.

In 1960, Yvonne Colborne-Malpas, a partner in a West End firm of investigators, attempted to hand a court summons to 'man about town'

Dominic Elwes. He was being called as a witness at the High Court, in a high-profile libel case brought against the Duchess of Argyll by her former social secretary. Yvonne gave him the summons outside his house in Bayswater and, according to Dominic, she then ran towards a car shouting, 'It's all right, I've got him.' He was so 'unnerved' by this that he 'tried to give the subpoena back' – punching her in the back and thrusting the subpoena down the front of her dress.

The magistrate was not amused. 'This was a disgraceful exhibition, you must learn to keep your hands to yourself.' Dominic Elwes was fined £50, while Yvonne Colborne-Malpas was pictured at home after the trial, relaxing on a chaise longue with her dachshunds, Bunty and Coco.

Process serving was integral to Zena Scott-Archer's detective agency; her very first assignment had been to serve papers on a stewardess on a boat. But as the industry wasn't regulated, and as private detectives had no legal authority, how, then, did they have the power to serve court papers?

DULY SERVED

'PIs have absolutely no authority at all … the only exception to this is when you are serving papers.'

It's December 2021 and I've just signed up for a Professional Private Investigation Diploma run by the UK Private Investigators Network (UKPIN). The network was formed in the late 1990s and currently has 828 members. The course contains lots of practical-sounding modules – and in particular, process serving. It's also on sale at a 'special limited offer' of £149 and includes a free lock-picking manual. So I sign up, pay the fee and download the course.

The Level 3 award might have taught me plenty of theory, but now I want to learn more about practice. The course is written by senior investigator Philip Smith, who has around twenty-five years' experience in the field, and the style is down to earth, encouraging and easy to read. The introduction covers the variety of PI work, from the unpleasant job of repossessions – 'you cannot be a PI, and a sensitive moralist!' – to the more exciting area of matrimonial work, which can include 'some pretty hair-raising stunts' in the name of surveillance.

The question of morals is a recurring theme, just as it was in the Level 3 award, but investigators are paid to do a job, not worry about the 'rights' and 'wrongs' of an issue. PIs are advised to take on work that is profitable and realistic, not because they're intrigued by the case. If you're a 'social worker type' with a sympathetic ear for problems, then 'this job is definitely not for you!' It's not our business to put the world to rights.

I don't think the diploma would have appealed to Victorian sleuth Antonia Moser or twentieth-century detective Annette Kerner. They prided themselves on providing a sympathetic ear, rescuing their clients from trouble and generally putting the world to rights. I'm also not sure if I could remain impartial at all times and always be motivated by money rather than being intrigued by a case. Perhaps I'm a social-worker type.

I turn to the first section of the course: process serving. It makes up around 30 per cent of all income at a typical private detective agency, with PIs working on behalf of solicitors, local authorities and financial institutions. Papers can include a summons, injunction, bankruptcy petition, final demand for payment or subpoena to attend court. This is the only time that a private detective has any official power or authority; they're hired because they're independent, and it's in their professional interest to tell the truth.

But how do you actually serve papers? From what I've seen on TV, you sneak up on someone or appear on their doorstep, trick them into taking the papers or thrust them into their hands – and run. But the process is detailed and there is a clear set of rules to follow, covering how, when and where papers can be served and who can accept them.

Ancient laws mean you can't serve papers in the precincts of a court, within a place of worship or in the Houses of Parliament. In the past, you also weren't allowed to serve papers on a Sunday. Investigators are given two copies of the documents in question, with one set to be attached to an affidavit when a PI swears on oath that they delivered the papers. Sometimes the affidavit must be sworn on a Bible in court and the investigator may be cross-examined, so every detail needs to be correct. If it's not, the case could collapse and that might be the end of your career.

If someone refuses to take a document, you can put it on the ground and walk away – then explain this in the affidavit. The same applies if they tear it up. If they do take the papers then you write 'personally served', and if they refuse, then it's 'duly served'. PIs should also briefly explain the contents of the document and suggest the person seeks legal advice.

The end of the module on process serving is upbeat: 'I KNOW you can do this,' writes Philip Smith. 'I did, and so can you.' But I'm not sure that I can because, as the course explains, PIs serve papers 'on people who often would rather you went away and served them on someone else!'

I wonder what it would be like to spend a lot of your time handing strangers official documents that warn or threaten them. Are women still particularly suited to it? Are we less likely to meet with violence on a doorstep?

★ ★ ★

Two days after finishing the module, there's a knock on my front door. It's a stocky white man in his early 60s, wearing a none-too-new grey suit. He flashes a plastic ID, announces he's from 'the court service' and asks for my name. The man is very matter of fact, as if he's on official business and I have to comply. He explains he's here on behalf of a company to serve me with court papers and, without thinking, I take the form.

It looks like the sort of form anyone could type up, and it's from a company I've never heard of. It says I owe them several hundred pounds. They have claimed a PPI – payment protection insurance – refund on my behalf, and now I owe them.

'I don't know anything about this,' I tell the man. 'I don't owe these people any money.'

He looks annoyed. 'What's your address?'

I tell him he already has my address; he's standing outside my house.

'What's your phone number?' he asks.

'Why do I need to give you my phone number?'

The man scowls, he's intensely irritated. 'I'm recording this,' he says, and I look down at the little camera around his neck; it's at the same height as my knees.

Then it suddenly dawns on me. 'Are you a PI?'

The man doesn't answer.

'Are you a private investigator?' I ask again. 'Who hired you?'

The man refuses to answer, and after a few minutes he leaves.

The moment he's gone, I Google the name of the company. A lot of people are complaining that they've applied for a PPI refund and somehow this company has got hold of their details. But was the man a private detective?

He was certainly acting like a process server, and as if he had legal authority, although I can't remember if he had two copies of the papers or if he suggested I get legal advice. A PI serves papers that have legal power because they come from a court, but they must never imply that they've been instructed by a court – and he just did.

I wonder what it feels like when he goes home after spending all day arguing with people on their doorsteps. A year ago, it wouldn't have occurred to me that he might be a private detective. It doesn't go with the image. It might take up a third of the workload of real private eyes, but in film and TV they're far more likely to be busy with high-speed car chases or relaxing with a martini.

★ ★ ★

I finish the diploma a few months later – studying modules on status and credit reports, accident reports, debt collecting, surveillance and tracing. The course includes lots of tips, such as how to use windows to see round corners, sticking reflective tape on the back of a target's car at night and how to spot a two-way mirror. It also provides guidance on setting up an agency, how to market it and the best way to get solicitor clients.

'Our course is the most practical for the real world,' Philip Smith tells me. 'We are all PIs running functioning agencies and can tell you first-hand stories of what not to do in the heat of the moment.' The aim of UKPIN was to provide a network, as well as exchange information, ask for advice and get work. Membership is free, and there appears to be lots of jobs available through the network forum.

Every day, I read up to a dozen requests posted by PIs looking for colleagues to carry out work in their local area – whether a door knock, hand delivering a letter, taking a set of fingerprints or serving divorce papers, non-molestation orders or statutory demands. There are tracing requests all over Europe, as well as in Indonesia, Australia and Saudi Arabia, credit checks in Canada and Mexico, and a repossession order in Las Vegas. A lot of the jobs require serving papers on someone who's in prison, while a few involve serving papers on rough sleepers – because rough sleeping is still considered a criminal offence under the Vagrancy Act of 1824.

Eventually, I'm ready for the exam. It's multiple choice, like the Level 3 award, with 100 questions. There is the occasional humorous question: 'What are the three most vital pieces of equipment required for a private eye? Bug detector, receiver and transmitter; car, computer and camera; or moustache, hat and glasses?' But there are also an awful lot of questions on the rules governing process serving.

A few days later, I'm sent my diploma. I've passed with distinction, and I'm now entitled to use 'Dip PI (UKPIN)' after my name.

I print out the diploma certificate and pin it on my wall, next to the Level 3 award and my collection of female inquiry agents from the past – Antonia Moser, Ellen Lyons, Dorothy Tempest, Matilda Mitchell and Maud West. I have more images of women to add now: May Storey posing in trench coat and fedora for the 1938 Churchman's cigarette card; Annette Kerner, the 'Little Chief', enveloped in a fur coat and holding a cup of tea after her 1952 fraud trial; and Melodie Walsh cooking breakfast before swapping her apron for a mink coat.

I pin up a photo of Lady Marye peering round a West End street corner on a tailing job; 70-year-old May Greenhalgh holding her business poster, 'You must have evidence'; and Zena Scott-Archer striding down a Liverpool street in her Paris fashion hat. Zena was the only woman among 300 men in the BDA in the early 1950s, and as the nation entered the swinging sixties, the popular image of the 'private dick' was about to get even more macho.

A DANGEROUS PROFESSION

In the opening credits of *Dr No*, a man in a suit and trilby hat is viewed down the barrel of a gun. Suddenly, he turns and fires and the screen is washed with blood. As the theme tune starts, the silhouette of a dancing woman appears and there's the promise of more violence and sex to come. *Dr No*, released in 1962, featured an MI6 spy rather than a private eye, but its hero James Bond became synonymous with the image of the PI – tough, suave men who drove fast cars, carried guns and used high-tech gadgets.

The British press was fascinated by private detectives in the 1960s and eager to reveal 'the truth about the private eye'. *Tatler* devoted nine pages to 'The World of the Private Detective', written by Mark Peploe and focusing on a handful of men who seemed to believe they, too, were James Bond.

Peter Merken, who ran the Ace Detective Agency, lived in a villa in Wimbledon, fortified with electronic security, and drove a silver Mark 10 Jaguar. He was photographed wearing a suit and surrounded by the 'tools of the trade': four different-coloured telephones, a radio, a pair of binoculars and a bugging device. He was also photographed framed in the shattered windscreen of his Jaguar, 'Just one of the scars of a dangerous profession in which an adversary can easily become an enemy bent on revenge.'

The private eye of the 1960s was an action hero, not a shady figure who peeped through keyholes or advertised 'secret watchings'. Some had military backgrounds, like Barrie Quartermain, who ran Kingston Detective Agency and could split ashtrays into perfect halves with his index finger. Barrie also liked gadgets, and wore an enormous black steel watch, a Nivada Grenchen, which informed him how many minutes he had left on a parking meter or how long before his oxygen tank ran out.

Private detective agencies were constantly pestered by 19-year-old boys who wanted to become PIs. 'Today everyone is a James Bond,' complained a Mr Leach. 'They actually ring me up and say they only want international work – life and death stuff. Who do they think they are?'

The ABD, meanwhile, was still trying to improve the industry's image. Its members preferred to be called private investigators, explained *The Times*, 'private inquiry agents smacks too much of the bad old days'. But once again, rogue PIs were a major problem. Half of the seventy detective agencies listed in the classified London telephone directory didn't actually exist, according to *Tatler*, and those that did often consisted of one or two men, a telephone and a car. There was 'no guarantee that the agent you contact is trained, qualified, or even honest', and at least one agency was run by a man with a criminal record.

The ABD, on the other hand, had a code of ethics, no ex-crooks would get past the selection board, and 60 per cent of applicants were turned down. It now issued a copperplate certificate for detectives to hang on their walls, as well as 'a warrant card', and took disciplinary action against erring members by expelling them.

But some agents were sceptical. 'It's a collection of retired policemen,' said Peter Merken, and most were 'too old for the job'. Five years after the *Tatler* profile, Peter was found guilty of stealing industrial secrets by trying to obtain details of a million-pound paint process for an unnamed client. He was fined £1,501 but allowed to return to work.

Tatler didn't interview any female PIs, aside from Mrs Merken, who'd once worked as an investigator under her maiden name, Yvonne Clark. The magazine made her sound unusual. She'd been 'one of the few women in England who really was a detective' and 'not just a store detective'.

Yvonne was 'blonde, pretty, and quiet', and had spent six years in the business. Now she was at home with the couple's three children.

Most women in private detection were still working behind the scenes, as were their counterparts in the police force, who were often relegated to a background role. More opportunities had opened up in the 1950s for decoy, observation and undercover work, and Lilian Wyles describes women firmly entrenched in CID with a 'workmanlike' uniform, comfortable pay packet and pleasant police station quarters. Joan Lock recalls being 'often loaned' out to CID for plain-clothes work in West End clubs, brothels and bookies. She sat for hours in steamy cars or found herself 'worn on the left arm by rather small policemen while sauntering through Soho'. By the 1960s, there was still a 'lingering unwillingness to put women in charge of men'.

The only woman *Tatler* did interview in depth was 30-year-old 'Dawn', who worked as a 'woman named'. Divorce still made up around half of all cases of private investigation in the 1960s, and petitioners needed to provide evidence or a voluntary confession. Many couples still used 'collusion', and detective agencies and solicitors provided male clients with a professional co-respondent – a 'woman named'.

Dawn was 'blonde, pretty and well spoken', wore lurex boot stockings of red and gold and her services were in frequent demand. A client arranged to pick her up at home or they met somewhere in town. Sometimes, they went to a film, dinner and dancing or drinks in the country 'at one of those Mr and Mrs Smith hotels, you know the sort'.

The important thing was to make a point of ordering a double bed, 'but this doesn't mean that I sleep with the man ... If they ever got nasty I could threaten them with the collusion business. That would ruin their chances of getting the divorce.' The couple then went to bed and left the door unlocked so the maid could come in in the morning and discover them. 'We don't have to be seen cuddling or anything,' explained Dawn. 'We just sit up and have tea when the maid brings it. We nearly always ask for tea. It's somehow more appropriate.' Then she packed up her luggage, and the client dropped her home.

But those who used collusion still risked being charged with fraud, and in 1973, Peter Merken from Ace Detective Agency was fined £2,000 at the Old Bailey, after offering a female agent £40 to be the 'other woman'. She taped the conversation, reported it to the police and set a trap for Peter Merken at the Regent Palace Hotel in London.

Hiring a private detective remained a luxury in the 1960s, according to Frederick Oughton, and the average divorce inquiry cost a basic retainer of around £10 a day. His book *Ten Guineas a Day: A Portrait of the Private Detective*, published in 1961, portrayed the job as distinctly sleazy.

Mr Rawlinson in Kent, for example, used wall microphones, concealed microphones, lie detectors, two-way mirrors, periscopes, binoculars and movie cameras. Harry Greenhall, in Swansea, once walked into a bedroom where the 'guilty parties' were in bed, 'helped himself to a pair of panties to use as evidence in legal proceedings and shoved them in the pocket of his mackintosh'.

Ten Guineas a Day included a world directory of private detectives, each one apparently checked for reliability and professional membership. England dominated, with 127 agencies, while the United States had fifty-two, France, eleven, and Germany, six. Nearly 250 detective agencies were listed worldwide, but only two investigators identified themselves as women – Miss M.A.K. Melhuish in Bristol and Miss Kathleen Cummings in Bexleyheath.

Kathleen had been a private detective for ten years, beginning as a store detective for John Lewis in London. Her parents had been shocked at her choice of career – objecting that 'women can't do that sort of thing' – but she'd found the danger was rather exaggerated, although she had once been threatened with murder by a 'well-known criminal'.

Figures on female detectives were still hard to come by. By the end of 1962, there were 100 women in the ABD, according to *The Newcastle Journal* – although Professor Louise Jackson has identified just three female members in 1961, out of a total of 115. But there were certainly other women working as private investigators.

Raissa Page, a former journalist and meteorological observer, had been a PI for nearly a decade. She carried out checks for insurance companies, vetted employees, escorted dogs being shipped overseas and once rescued a cat from a deserted mansion. Raissa also tracked down lost jewellery, investigated stamp thefts and watched people at racing tracks. 'Before I've had time for a coffee,' she told the press, in words reminiscent of Maud West in the 1930s, 'I may be off to Switzerland by air or tracing a lost person.'

Raissa sounded less enthusiastic about divorce cases. She spent 'a tremendous amount of time dissuading wives and husbands from having their spouses followed'. She also didn't believe investigation was a career for women, who were too emotional and 'always want to draw a moral from a situation'. She rarely wore disguises, but she did have two props – a briefcase and a shopping basket – which she described as 'the two extremes' of womanhood.

Zena Scott-Archer was not listed by name in the 1961 world directory, but Scott's Detective Bureau appeared twice, once under her home address in Ripon Road, Wallasey, and the other under her new Dale Street address in Liverpool. 'It's busy all right at the moment,' she told the *Echo*. 'I'm in and out of the court giving evidence for petitioners and I'm well known up at Walton Gaol.'

Zena had moved to No. 81 Dale Street sometime in the late 1950s. It was a busy commercial road, home to Liverpool Magistrates' Court and just a five-minute walk to the Cavern Club where Beatles mania was about to take off. Liverpool now had one of the highest numbers of detective agencies of any English city, with four companies listed in the world directory, and Zena had two male competitors on the same road.

Unlike other female sleuths, she remained highly visible, and she continued to handle a wide range of cases, whether checking up on prospective sons-in-law, following commercial travellers who misused company cars or investigating cinema ticket collectors. For relaxation, her favourite TV show was *77 Sunset Strip*, an American series featuring two wisecracking former government secret agents who set up a stylish detective agency on Sunset Boulevard.

Zena enjoyed the macho portrayal of detective work, just as she'd been entertained by the fictional adventures of Philip Marlowe. 'It's just like a fairytale,' she explained. 'The stories are so unlike a real detective's life.'

In reality, the job was hard work, and professionals needed to remain on the right side of the law. Towards the end of the 1960s, however, a new female private eye appeared on the scene, and she was far more like the snooping sleuths of old.

ANNE SUMMER:
'I COULDN'T DO THAT!'

One afternoon in the summer of 1965, private detective Anne Summer received a worried call from an African diplomat. He was working at an embassy in London and had rather a personal problem. The diplomat lived with his wife in an imposing mock-Gothic house in Golders Green, next door to Mr East – 'the son of a Maharajah' – and his wife. The foursome had become friends, enjoying dinners out and visits to the ballet, but then things had turned strange.

The diplomat's wife was pregnant and no longer felt like going out, so he agreed to meet his friends alone, but Mr East repeatedly failed to turn up. The diplomat grew puzzled, until one morning a divorce petition arrived, suing him for damages for adultery with Mrs East.

Desperate to save his marriage and reputation, the diplomat turned to Anne Summer. The very next week, she went to Golders Green in north-west London, noticed a 'For Let' sign outside the Easts' house and arranged a viewing with an estate agent. She met the couple, accepted a sherry and had a good nose around the master bedroom. Then she hatched a plot.

Anne suggested that the diplomat bore three small holes in the wall between his hallway and his neighbour's sitting room. She then placed a powerful microphone up against the holes and connected it to a tape recorder. It was 'rather nasty and snoopy,' she admitted, 'but effective'. At four the next morning, Anne returned with a male friend, took a long ladder from the diplomat's back garden and heaved it over the hedge.

Then she placed it up against the neighbour's house, outside the master bedroom window.

The Easts were supposed to be divorcing, so she wanted to know whether they were sharing a bed 'in connubial bliss'. They were, so Anne took photos with an infrared camera she carried round her neck and whizzed back down the ladder.

But photographic evidence wasn't enough – she needed more. Two days before the divorce case began, the Easts were overheard discussing how much money they'd make from the false adultery claims. Anne had the proof she needed.

The tape was played in court and the diplomat won the case hands down. A century after ex-inspector Charles Field hired Sarah Grocott to spy on her mistress, the world of private detection was once again snooping, peepholes and sex.

It seems incredible that photographs taken of a couple in their bedroom, as well as surreptitiously recorded conversations gathered from boring holes in a wall, were admissible in court, but this was how Anne Summer solved the case. She was an expert in matrimonial subterfuge, according to *The Times* – and she was also a glamorous redhead and 'as pretty as the Avengers' heroine'.

The Avengers was one of Britain's most popular TV series, featuring bowler-hatted gentleman spy Jonathan Steed and his assistant Cathy Gale, who wore leather suits and 'kinky boots' and kept a gun tucked into her garter. Anne Summer seemed happy at the comparison, explaining she was often mistaken for an 'off-screen Cathy Gale'. She saw her detective work as 'almost a social service', although *The Times* felt that 'some would dispute that'. It also pointed out that she was a 31-year-old wife and mother.

But being a woman had its benefits, as it always had. Most people expected a private detective to be 'a greyish man in a mackintosh with a trilby', Anne explained, so she was rarely spotted. If she was, then she'd simply laugh and tell her accuser, 'Of course I'm following you, you have been doing such interesting things.' Her detective equipment consisted of telescopic lenses, a tiny tape recorder tucked in her bra and a target shooter, which sounded 'like the gas mains exploding'. It was a lovely gadget, she told the press, rather like a small sink plunger. If she'd been sitting outside a house for hours and nobody had gone in or out, then she set off the target shooter and soon everyone was 'tumbling out of the French windows to see who's been shot'.

Anne Summer came to prominence in 1968 with the publication of her memoir *But I Couldn't Do That!* It was subtitled, *Well, you're supposed to be the woman detective*, and the pink cover featured her smiling face, upside down in pop-art style. The publishers, Souvenir Press, had already produced several true adventures and showbiz biographies, and in 1965 they'd also published *Modesty Blaise* by Peter O'Donnell. It was originally a comic strip, featuring an ex-criminal turned secret service agent who was often promoted as a female James Bond and a 'sexy secret spy'.

Anne Summer, meanwhile, was a girl about town who wore a no-nonsense little Jackie Kennedy hat. Her tone was jaunty and humorous. She'd fibbed her way into private detection and fibbed while out on the job. The emphasis on sex – and sexual threat – suggests the book was ghost-written by a male tabloid journalist, much like Annette Kerner's memoirs.

Anne's book reflected concerns of the 1960s, as her predecessor's had played on fears of the 1950s. The number of divorces was steadily rising, and there was a new 'permissiveness' in sexual behaviour, which was particularly attributed to women. Anne Summer's escapades sounded like an episode from *Carry On*, the TV comedy series loaded with sexual innuendo. She tracked down wealthy adulterers, investigated brothels and once hid in a client's penthouse wardrobe listening in on two lovers. Her home life was also unusual. She rented out rooms to four flirtatious young men, who made helpful comments like 'I can see through your nightie'.

Unlike her predecessors, Anne also wrote about her personal life. She was 'going through the aftermath of the miseries of an unhappy marriage' and could therefore identify with her female clients.

Anne's first ambition had been to be an actress, just like so many previous female sleuths, but her mother insisted she become a secretary. So Anne enrolled at 'a rather debby and expensive' business training school in the West End, where she learned shorthand typewriting. She then worked for a large market research company before getting married.

By January 1964, Anne was depressed and desperate. Her marriage had broken up six months earlier, she'd left her husband and there had been a 'tussle' over custody of their 3-year-old son. Her husband – who was a lawyer, as was his father – took the boy, hired a nanny and denied her access. Anne had a nervous breakdown and psychiatric treatment.

Now she was living on £5 a week and needed to find work and a home for her child.

Then, one day, a solicitor and old friend, JB, asked for her help. He had a client who wanted his wife followed at short notice. He suggested it would be therapeutic, so Anne agreed. She was told to go to 'a certain street in Paddington and see if a certain woman lived there. It was easy.'

Then she was hired by an agency near Gray's Inn Road, run by 'the Colonel', an ex-army man who didn't ask for references or experience. Anne was told to sign a 'discretion statement'; if she was indiscreet about any client, she would be fined £100 – a significant sum when she was earning £2.10 a day.

Her motivation for detective work appeared to be both financial and to gain custody of her child, but while she did make money, she barely mentioned her son again. Anne's first job for the Colonel involved spending the day sitting in a car park in a borrowed car, waiting for a Mr X to come along and then follow him. 'I took a whole bag of scarves as disguises,' she explained, 'and sat behind a newspaper. I was frightfully enthusiastic.'

Then the cases got harder. 'The boss just said you're a woman so you can do it better than I can.' She stocked up on hats, scarves, hairpieces, sunglasses and different-coloured lipsticks. She also took on new names to suit different personas – Angela Saunders, secretary, Miss Smedley, market researcher, and Anthea Sinclair-Dane when visiting manor houses. Anne's disguise as a market researcher was particularly useful and lengthy questionnaires were an ideal way to elicit information. 'I ask a housewife if she washes her husband's shirts,' she told *The Times*, 'and I find out if she lives with a man.' She also, rather oddly, established 'whether the children eat sweets'.

Anne learned how to write case reports and picked up the detective jargon, which she mocked in her memoir. Private investigators never 'went' anywhere, they always 'proceeded'. They didn't 'watch', instead, they 'observed', and the 'subject' was always known by a number. Anne was given an 'Obbo' car – for observation – and learned how to tell what number someone was dialling in a public phone box, which she declined to disclose as 'a professional secret'.

After a few months, Anne moved to another agency, which specialised in business cases. Its boss, 'The Super', was a former high-ranking police officer who gave her a sherry, looked her up and down, and took her on for hotel work. Her job was to keep an eye on staff – was the chef knocking off early? Had a chambermaid left a dirty bottom sheet on a supposedly clean bed? Was a crafty maid stealing from guests' luggage?

But as a woman on her own in a hotel she was assumed to be 'up to no good', and often mistaken for the 'resident prostitute' or 'a lady looking for a pickup'. Anne fended off commercial travellers with 'primitive hunting urges' and endured a male detective who grabbed her and started kissing her on the tube, ignoring her repeated protests. 'If a woman chooses to do such a damn silly thing for a living,' commented one of her lodgers, 'she just has to put up with whatever comes along.' Anne appeared to accept this, and cheerfully fended off clients who were busy 'making eyes' at her.

After a year of agency work, she started her own business, without any capital, in a borrowed West End office. There was no nameplate outside, as she didn't want people just dropping in, but it appeared to have the rather generic name 'Detective Services'. As work expanded, Anne roped in her father, an ex-army officer, to help, as well as other relatives, friends and 'intelligent amateurs'. She found new talent at cocktail parties, where she met out-of-work TV producers and actresses. She also hired genuine market researchers, housewives, debutantes and playboys. Housewives were generally good at inquiry work, she explained, while struggling writers were useful because 'you can get hold of them in a hurry. They're always sitting by their telephones, waiting for work.'

Her clients – often millionaires and playboys – had expensive tastes, inviting her for lobster and champagne lunches at the Caprice and Fortnum's. At the end of her book, Anne's professional and personal lives collide when she's sent on a job to Paris. A Madame hires her to watch her husband, one of the richest men in Europe, but then Anne's old solicitor friend, JB, turns up and moves into her room. When the client sees two pairs of shoes outside Anne's bedroom door, she guesses the truth, and Anne is on the next plane back to England.

Even before Anne Summer's book was published, she was interviewed on the Eamonn Andrews late night TV talk show, while the *Daily Mirror* published a half-page photo showing her sitting on a swing while acting as commentator at a fashion show. When her memoir did come out, one reviewer was entranced. It was difficult enough to imagine a woman setting up as a private investigator, commented Valeen Marriott in the

Leicester Chronicle, but the idea of a young, attractive redhead was almost impossible to believe. There was something compelling about 'a true story', the dramas, aspirations, disappointments and triumphs were all the more 'poignant and meaningful'.

But others dismissed her career as downright sordid. She was 'playing a squalid game of I-spy', objected John Evans in the *Coventry Evening Telegraph*. She was a nice-looking girl, but she had 'no soul'. She was good at snooping, trailing and persuading unhappy people to tell her their problems, but she regarded her clients in the same way a Soho pornographic bookshop owner saw his customers. John Evans seemed to feel very passionate on the subject; perhaps he'd had a bad experience with a private eye. It was a pity, he wrote, that such a bright, cheerful girl couldn't think of something more helpful to do. It was comforting to know that when the Divorce Reform Bill became law then 'people like Anne Summer will be largely redundant'.

The Divorce Reform Act of 1969 marked another major shift in British divorce laws. The Matrimonial Causes Act of 1937 had added additional grounds for divorce, but now for the first time, people could end a marriage that had 'irretrievably broken down'. The Act was only passed after lengthy negotiation, involving the Archbishop of Canterbury, the Law Commission, a debate in Parliament and a Royal Commission. Its stated purpose was not to make divorce easier, but to 'facilitate reconciliation'. Proof was still required – of adultery, unreasonable behaviour, desertion or that the couple were living apart – but when the new Act became law in 1971 it was a worrying time for private detectives. Divorce had kept inquiry agents busy for well over a century; if the process became easier, would they lose a major part of their income?

Investigators also had to contend with rising concerns about invasion of privacy. 'There has been a great increase in the amount of spying and prying into our personal secrets,' declared MP Tony Gardner, who in April 1969 attempted to introduce a bill for the registration and control of private eyes. Private detectives no longer had to hide under a bed, in the wardrobe or 'in a very damp shrubbery'. Instead, they were using modern electronic devices, telephone tapping and radio transmitters to 'investigate and record what we are doing, often from some distance away'. The MP had seen electronic devices 'that would make Hon. Members' hair stand on end'.

But no one was keeping an eye on the private eye. The bill would mean investigators had to be authorised by a written certificate issued by a county court judge and would be required to take out a £1,000 bond. In the event of misconduct, the court could withdraw the certificate and the bond. But once again, the bill failed to become law.

Anne Summer disappeared from the limelight soon after her book came out, and today – like her 1930s forebear, May Storey – it's hard to find evidence that she even existed. Her memoir was very thin on biographical facts, and she didn't disclose where she was born, only that she'd lived in a convent from the age of 6 to 16. Her family appeared to have strong links to France. Her grandfather was a 'great friend' with the writer and historian Hilaire Belloc, whose daughter Eleanor was Anne's 'godmother'.

She painted a portrait of a privileged family background, as Annette Kerner had done, and her convent education neatly contrasted her innocence with the seedy life of a private eye. But Anne didn't provide much detail: only that she was 5ft 2in tall and was 27 years old in 1964. I can't find any records of an Anne – or Ann or Annie – Summer born between 1920 and 1940, so if her father really was an army officer, perhaps she was born abroad.

As for her marriage, that's a mystery too. At the end of 1967, press reports described her as 'wife and mother' and by early 1969 she was a divorcee, but I can't find any matching records in marriage registers. I also can't find any deaths under the name Anne Summer, so maybe she changed her name in later life – or it was a false name to begin with.

Press interviews didn't give away much either, except that she lived in north London in a small, pretty house. Anne Summer, the expert in matrimonial subterfuge, had succeeded in keeping her real identity a secret.

But many parts of her memoir sound believable: her ambition to be an actress, her training as a secretary, the way she fell into the job via a friendship with a solicitor, the investigator who initially hired her and her familiarity with private detective lingo. Perhaps she'd started off writing up case reports for an agency, just like Zena Scott-Archer, and a journalist or publisher suggested a book and made her an offer she couldn't refuse.

But if Anne Summer's short-lived career as a private eye was apparently over by 1969, Liverpool's Mrs Sherlock Holmes was only just hitting her stride.

A TOOTHSOME SLEUTH

In the autumn of 1968, Zena Scott-Archer was elected president of the ABD, the largest representative body of private detectives in the world at the time. She was the first woman to hold the post – and one of only twelve women among its 500 members.

Zena looked like a senior civil servant or a headmistress, commented *Lancashire Life*, one of many papers to obsess over her appearance. *Competitor's Journal* invited its readers to 'take a look at the picture below, and guess what the lady does for a living'. Zena was photographed at a cafe table, her hair piled high under a turban. Was she a buyer in a dress shop, or a personnel officer? No, she was a 'pleasant faced housewife from Liverpool'.

A stream of journalists found their way up to Scott's Detective Bureau on Dale Street to knock on her glass-plated door. They all agreed on the state of the building – a grimy warren with uneven stone stairs and yellowing walls – but once inside Zena's office, their descriptions differed. Some found the cluster of rooms businesslike and unadorned; others declared the surroundings were distinctly feminine, with potted plants and copies of *Vogue* 'to take your mind off your troubles'. Her desk was crowded, with an adding machine, feather duster, Dictaphone, typewriter, camera, tape recorder, telephone, ashtray, clients' reports and a tiny gilt and mother of pearl 'New Testament', which she used when she popped to the solicitor's downstairs to swear she'd served an affidavit. A large, arched window, with a view down Dale Street, dominated the main room, against which Zena often posed for photographs. She found one photographer from the *Observer* particularly 'coarse' when he demanded she 'put your bum!' on the windowsill and smile for the camera.

The *Guardian Miscellany* described Scott's agency as rundown, with certificates hung askew on partition walls and a mirror 'nibbled by time'. It also presented Zena as a masculine figure, 'well set-up, early fifties, heavy glasses, and a man's watch, takes a drink, likes a joke, gets lucky'. The tone was amused and condescending, as it always had been for female detectives.

Zena tended to be slotted into one of two roles – a gentle, soft-spoken Miss Marple, or 'a toothsome sleuth' who wore 'saucy hats'. *The News* went even further, calling her 'the Modesty Blaise of Wirral'.

Some papers were keen to contrast Zena's 'ultra-femininity' with the criminal underworld. 'She works among some of Liverpool's toughest communities,' explained *Woman's World*, while the *Mail* wanted to know 'how does a lady manage to succeed in a rough tough business in one of the roughest, toughest cities in Britain?'

But Zena had never overplayed the dangers of the job, instead she represented the private eye's bid for respectability, immaculately neat in her pink Marks & Spencer sundress and pearls. She was married, the *Manchester Guardian* noted, but had no children and employed a house-keeper, 'so she doesn't find domestic chores encroaching on her'. Zena was still fielding questions about her marriage and her husband's opinions on her job, as well as whether she had children and who did the housework.

She was also questioned about her male employees. Did they mind working for a woman?

'It's funny you should say that,' Zena responded, 'because until I was asked this very question … they'd never thought about it.'

The only time she sounded really irritated was when it came to the 'completely false image' of private detectives provided by the media. But newspapers couldn't help but compare her to fictional characters. 'She is just as much a detective as James Bond or Cathy Gale,' declared the *Sunday Press* – neither of whom were private detectives.

The *Daily Express*, who photographed her leaning out of a car window with a camera, insisted on portraying her as if she *was* a TV character, 'Zena Scott-Archer, veteran of car chases, secret filming of suspects and foreign assignments'. But Zena repeatedly emphasised the difficulties of the job, just as Maud West had done. 'The work is basically hard grind and rarely exciting,' she explained. 'You can't get hungry or thirsty, and you need an extremely good bladder.' She didn't come into direct contact with the underworld, 'since we deal with mainly civil cases', and none of her agents were judo experts – 'that's pure Hollywood stuff'. Instead, Zena believed the most important skill for a private investigator was diplomacy, just as Maurice Moser had argued in the 1880s, when he described diplomacy as a recognised woman's skill.

Zena appeared to enjoy the press attention, but she wanted to use her year as ABD president to try to finally obtain a royal charter. The ABD might be growing, but it only contained a quarter of the estimated 1,200 private detectives in Britain. Zena was worried about a lack of ethics and anxious to see that private sleuths remained on the right side of the law. 'One man came in the other day wanting me to trace his adopted child,' she told the *Daily Telegraph*. 'He suggested I break into the adoption society and go through the files. I told him it just wasn't possible.'

Zena celebrated her last night as ABD president with a grand ball in Birmingham. 'She will not stop being a detective,' explained the *Manchester Guardian*, 'and she will be thankful to be done with the press and publicity.'

But Zena wasn't quite done with the publicity yet. She continued to provide the press with detective tales and while she didn't break the law, she did use some unusual methods.

One bitterly cold November day, Zena spent several hours lying on the bare floor of an empty house. Her client, a woman whose husband had left her, needed a witness to listen to his threats so she could get a divorce on the grounds of cruelty. The husband normally came round every Sunday, so the woman had a microphone installed in an upstairs room. The wires came up through the ceiling and were fixed to a set of headphones in the middle of the floor, where Zena lay down to listen. When the husband didn't turn up, his wife had a new plan. 'He's bought a bungalow, I'm sure he's got a woman in there. You must give me evidence of adultery.' So Zena sent one of her investigators, who reported that the husband visited the bungalow with a woman three nights a week.

The next time the couple arrived, Zena and the wife were watching. A light went on in one of the rooms and was then turned off. 'I know they're in bed together,' said the wife. 'We must catch them in the act.' Zena explained she couldn't force her way into the house, but 'if you'd like to break in, that's another matter' – for there was nothing illegal about breaking into your own home. 'I'll do anything,' said the wife.

So they crept up to the window, the wife shattered the glass with her torch, shone it into the room, and there was the couple in bed. The wife identified her husband, then Zena put her head through the broken window and said, 'I am acting for your wife, who is going to take divorce proceedings against you on the grounds of your alleged adultery …'

But the couple inside weren't listening. Both were stark naked, and the woman was screaming 'Burglars!!' while the husband was scrambling around the room threatening to call the police. Not long afterwards, Zena's client received her divorce.

Despite initial fears that the new divorce laws would lead to a loss of work, Scott's Detective Bureau dealt with around 300 matrimonial cases a year, and many clients just wanted their partners watched. Men hired her to watch both wives and mistresses, while 'some women just like having their husbands followed, not to do anything about it, but just to know what's going on'.

Attitudes had also changed. When Zena first started out, 'people didn't like being involved in divorce for fear of it damaging their jobs'. But it wasn't looked upon as a scandal any more. 'It doesn't matter a toss these days; you can do what the hell you like.'

Zena became an advisory figure on matrimonial affairs, just like some of her forebears. 'Quite frequently women come to me with problems which have been bottled up for years,' she explained. After a chat and several cups of tea, they'd poured out all their troubles, felt much better and went away no longer needing her services.

Zena also offered advice to suspicious partners. A wife who suspected her husband had 'strayed' should watch his temper. 'Irritability is one of the first signs of infidelity,' she explained, 'and it springs from a guilty conscience.' But it could also just be indigestion, she added, so women shouldn't jump to hasty conclusions.

Unlike some of her predecessors, however, Zena didn't present herself as a crusader for women who'd been wronged. In the early days, she used to 'get very emotional and take the side of the poor downtrodden wife', but now she treated all cases with detachment. This was a theme she returned to a few times. 'You must treat the job clinically,' she told one journalist. 'If you keep thinking about it you get emotionally involved.'

One case sounded particularly disturbing. A well-to-do English farmer suspected his Belgian wife of having an affair. His solicitor hired Zena to visit the couple's farmhouse, confront the wife and get an admission of adultery. While she was doing this, the man's brother went to the wife's car, took her son from the back seat and drove off with her child. 'Despite her infidelity,' remarked Zena, 'I could not help feeling sorry for her.'

But she didn't appear to agonise over cases like this, unusual as they were. Instead, her focus was on doing the job she'd been hired to do. Journalist Harold Brough, however, described Zena as a very sympathetic detective, 'appearing almost troubled at the dilemma of the person she confronts'. So when she repeatedly described herself as clinical and detached, perhaps she was responding to the long-held belief that women were far too emotional to make good sleuths.

Other matrimonial cases were of a more humorous type. Zena was once hired by one of two wives to follow a man everywhere. 'It got so I knew what socks he wore, and what he liked for lunch.' One day, Zena and her target came face to face in the buffet car of a train from London 'and he proposed before we cleared the suburbs. He had me lined up for No.3. I went all flustered and said, "This is so sudden".' Zena managed to 'sidestep' the man, who slipped away to Canada, where he sent for the suspicious wife, who happily joined him.

In another of her favourite cases, a rich married man hired her to watch his mistress on a long Mediterranean cruise, so Zena packed her bag and flew to Naples. When the ship hit a storm in the Bay of Biscay, the mistress fell down a companionway, broke her ribs and was confined to her cabin. 'I just enjoyed myself from then on,' explained Zena. 'Nothing to worry about, no one can make love with broken ribs.' She had a marvellous time visiting Malta and Cyprus and enjoyed 'the holiday of a lifetime'.

Zena Scott-Archer received more than her fair share of publicity in the 1970s – including a bizarre cover photo on the *Sunday Telegraph* magazine, wearing a long wig and dark glasses. Inside the magazine, she was photographed in various disguises, 'efficient secretary … hard-bitten but prissy blonde' and 'frowzy lady'.

But real-life female private eyes were still unusual. Only 3 per cent of private detectives in the world were women, according to the *Seattle Times*, while the British press estimated 5 per cent of PIs were female. However, Zena found the work particularly suited to women, just as her predecessors had. Women knew how to act in an emergency, they were 'more determined, calmer and certainly less easily embarrassed than most men'. She couldn't understand why more women didn't take up the profession. 'They are so observant. Ask a woman for a description of a person and you will get the lot from height and colouring to if they have good teeth or plucked eyebrows. Ask a man and you will probably get "well, average really".'

So why *were* there so few women? What had happened to the days of Antonia Moser, Kate Easton and Maud West, who, in the early 1900s, had run their own agencies in the very same area of London? In the mid-1930s private detection was hailed as 'one of the highest paid careers a girl can take up', and there were at least eleven women running agencies in the West End alone. But, forty years later, there were only a dozen members in the whole of the ABD.

The professionalisation of the industry, which had begun in the 1930s, with its emphasis on fighting male rogues, the relegation of women to background roles in the 1950s, when the job was reserved for men 'of integrity', and the macho image of the private eye in the 1960s had succeeded in keeping women out. In 1970, Zena was one of just two 'girls' among 200 detectives attending the annual conference of the World Association of Detectives, which had been formed in the 1920s and had representatives in thirty-four countries.

In 1972, Zena was again one of only two women attending the Brighton Convention of the Council of International Investigators, an organisation formed in the States in 1955. While Zena wanted more women to join the industry, there seemed to be an issue with recruitment. 'I'd love to have women staff,' she insisted, but when women did respond to her adverts, they never followed up for an interview. Women, she explained, just 'don't see themselves as private detectives'.

In popular culture, the private eye was a man in a grubby trench coat, loitering under a streetlamp, or a tough ex-cop who dealt with murder, hijacking and kidnapping. The female PI was more likely to appear in X-rated films, such as *The Sex Life of a Female Private Eye* in which Linda Marlow played Harriet Zapper. 'If you need the toughest … fastest… deadliest private eye, the best man in town … is a woman!' declared the promotional poster, above a picture of a woman in skimpy clothing, sitting open legged over a burning building.

But there was a new female private eye in literature – Cordelia Gray, the protagonist of P.D. James' *An Unsuitable Job for a Woman*, published in 1972. Cordelia is a former convent girl – like her real-life counterpart, Anne Summer – who starts her career as secretary to ex-CID detective Bernie Pryde, owner of a detective agency in Soho. Twenty-two-year-old Cordelia inherits the agency after his death, when she's hired to find out why a Cambridge student hanged himself. Cordelia deduces that the suicide was murder and sees herself as his avenger. She is not simply an observer but becomes central to the action, and a target for the killer.

Cordelia is impressively efficient and capable, even when attacked and thrown down a well at night by a murderer into a 'vortex of horror'. She's also not averse to breaking the law, covering up a murder and committing perjury at an inquest but getting away with just a fine for illegal possession of a gun. Cordelia Gray is often described as an icon of feminist independence, but she belonged to a tradition that traced back to fictional Victorian sleuths like Miss Gladden and Loveday Brooke, self-sufficient investigators who would stop at nothing to solve a mystery.

When Zena Scott-Archer advertised for staff to join her agency, it was men who replied, often boasting at their skills at karate, handling guns and 'chatting up lovely widows'. 'Domesticity usually interferes with your progress if you're a woman private detective,' Zena explained. 'If you have a home to run, and children to look after and bring up, you just can't do it.'

Those who did try to pursue a detective career often dropped out because of other commitments, and because their husbands didn't want them away from home. By the mid-1970s, Zena employed two full-time male operatives – 'I used to call them "my men" but people misunderstood' – and three part-timers, two of whom were women.

One was Barbara Macy, whose mother, Lyn Naylor, had worked as Zena's secretary since the early 1960s. 'I got into it purely by accident,' Barbara tells me on the phone. 'I had no professional training, and nor did Zena.'

Barbara had attended commercial college and trained as a secretary, then she got married and had two children. In the early 1970s, her mother would bring home bundles of papers from Scott's Detective Bureau and Barbara typed them up, then when her children were a little older, she started to go in on two half-days a week. 'All Zena's agents were men,' she remembers, 'and they only lasted 5 minutes before they went and contacted the solicitors themselves, took the work from Zena and set up on their own. After one left, I offered to do outside work as well.'

Barbara knew she could do the job just as well – and probably better – than the men. 'I didn't view it as a career,' she explains. 'It was convenient; I could do it in the evenings when my husband was home from work.' So Barbara borrowed £85 from her mother, bought an old Wolseley 1500, and started work as a private eye.

Scott's Detective Bureau was still hired for matrimonial surveillance work, but now the job was more about process serving, and Barbara often served applications for injunction orders on men in domestic violence cases. 'They were never violent to me. That was the great advantage about being a woman. People thought I was some sort of social worker, and I didn't enlighten them. I must have that look. I'd be in the house before they realised.'

But Barbara once served an injunction on a man in his 50s who had assaulted his wife. She was invited into the house, and the man told his 6-year-old granddaughter to 'go upstairs and bring that thing down and show this lady what I've got'. When the child came down, she was carrying a rifle. 'He sat with it across his knee,' Barbara remembers. 'He didn't threaten me with it, but it was implicit. He said, "You've no right to be in my house, I'm going to call the police". I said, "Fine". I was hoping he would. I faced him really. He gave in.'

Barbara found some of her jobs fascinating. She was once employed by a firm of stamp dealers who suspected a cartel of stamp collectors of fixing prices, and she investigated a huge factory fire near Preston, taking statements from every employee. But, on the whole, the work was mundane, and it was far more difficult than the fictional image. 'When you see the television programmes,' she explains, 'people think that following people or observation is easy. It isn't. Police have intercoms and surveillance equipment and half a dozen cars following one suspect. When you're one person on your own it's very hard.'

In one case, she followed a woman some 90 miles along pitch-dark country lanes. Occasionally, she took her husband with her. 'If I had to go to a hotel to watch someone, I would ask him to come along so I didn't attract attention on my own.' Barbara laughs, 'He was absolutely useless. He couldn't pretend to save his life. Acting was part of the job, my persona if you like was social worker, and my appearance was perfectly ordinary.'

The only time Zena and Barbara went out on a case together was to serve a writ on a famous American singer performing in Liverpool. 'He'd been staying in various hotels and not paying his bills,' explains Barbara. 'We decided we'd both go, as there was a crush of fans outside the stage door in those days.'

Unfortunately, on the way to the theatre a car crashed into the back of her, and when Zena arrived, she discovered the singer was actually appearing in Manchester. But Zena managed to catch him during a later book signing. She queued up in a long line of fans to ask for an autograph then quietly slipped him the papers, which he immediately handed to his bodyguard.

Barbara would later attempt to serve a writ on a member of an American pop group appearing at the Cavern. 'One of them wasn't paying his maintenance,' she explains. 'I managed to get into the Cavern, and they were on stage performing, and I got to the edge of the stage and these two fellas came one either side of me and escorted me out. They took me across the road to the pub opposite and the manager came across to the pub and said, "He's going to come out and meet with you". But of course he never did.'

Zena sometimes turned her investigations into family affairs, as Antonia Moser and Maud West had done, often taking her mother along on observations, as well as enlisting the services of her close friend Win Hobson. Life did have its glamorous side; she'd been to the Opera House in Vienna while shadowing a target and investigated cases in Denmark and Switzerland. She had also been hired by a client in the States to track down a ship in Nigeria. But sitting for hours in a cold car with her mother and a thermos of tea was hardly the popular image of female private eyes. Zena wasn't amused by the antics of *Charlie's Angels*, the three glamorous Americans with the amazing ability to solve a crime in thirty minutes. 'I hope the public is sensible enough,' she commented, 'to realise things are not like that in real life.'

Real investigations did not always have 'a pat ending where everything resolves happily', and the work was far more 'domestically slanted' than it was on film and TV. Zena handled up to fourteen investigations at a time, and received half a dozen letters every day from new clients. She rarely took breaks, aside from the occasional trip with her husband to the Lake District, where she never divulged what she did for a living. 'When I go on holiday,' she explained, 'I am just the wife of my husband.' But the rest of the time, she was one of the best-known female private detectives – a 'woman James Bond' – on the global stage.

LADY GUMSHOE

In 1980, Zena Scott-Archer became vice president of the Association of British Investigators (ABI), one of only five women among the 2,000 private eyes reportedly operating in England. The ABI had been launched in the early 1970s when the ABD decided to change its name, and it soon had a rival in the form of the Institute of Professional Investigators (IPI), originally established as the ABI's academic arm.

Zena described members trading insults and switching loyalties, but she had colleagues and supporters in both camps. In 1981, she was elected ABI president – but it had been a close call. A few months before Zena's election, there had been moves to change the system, preventing the vice president from automatically becoming president. Zena travelled to a meeting in London and 'said my piece'. The resolution failed, and a few weeks later, when her election was announced, she was 'besieged' by reporters. That evening, it was suggested that 'Madam President should start the dancing', and so she took to the floor, triumphant in a black suit of watered silk.

Then Zena flew to Las Vegas, where she was elected president of the World Association of Detectives, now with 800 members representing forty-six countries. 'Another male bastion has fallen,' reported *The Times*.

But despite the accolades and international recognition, the British press still found Zena Scott-Archer amusing more than anything else. 'We all know what a private dick looks like,' announced *Real Life Story*, '*This* private dick looks like Dame Edna Everage.' Zena can't have appreciated the comparison: Dame Edna was a fictitious female character – played by a man, Barry Humphries. The fact that she was the only 'lady gumshoe' to have been president of the ABD and was now the head of both the ABI and the WAD wasn't treated as a significant achievement. Instead, it was 'not at all bad for a 60-year-old married lady who looks as if the most exciting things she should be hunting are sale bargains'.

Zena dismissed much of the press coverage as 'the usual guff', but she still allowed journalists into her office and sometimes took them along on jobs. An *Echo* reporter accompanied Zena as she set off in her Triumph, wearing a leopard-skin hat and matching coat, to trace a man wanted by private investigators in Surrey. Another reporter joined her as she spent the morning driving around in search of a man who'd defaulted on his overdraft payments.

Zena also showed off her array of disguises and collection of twenty-five wigs, and demonstrated mouth inserts that changed the appearance of her teeth and mouth – much as Maud West had once used orange peel. Merseyside's Mrs Sherlock Holmes now had ten pairs of glasses, six different walking sticks, a pair of crutches and three wardrobes – sports clothes, flamboyant attire and clothes that 'a poor working woman might bemoan as the worst that any woman could possibly own'.

Zena moved into other forms of media, as Annette Kerner had done. She was a guest on *Woman's Hour*, took part in Radio 4's *Women of Mystery* and *The Evening Star* announced the BBC was 'going to make a film about her'. In 1984, Zena joined a TV panel on BBC2's *Saturday Review* to discuss a book about Margaret Thatcher. She seemed to enjoy the trip, she was paid £200 plus expenses, given lunch in the BBC cafeteria – steak, peach crumble and wine – and wore a new candy-striped blouse and question-mark brooch. She even agreed to appear on ITV's *TV AM* to guess who'd killed Bobby Ewing in the American soap *Dallas*.

Zena remained highly visible in the 1980s, and now there was a wider variety of fictional female sleuths on television as well. In the UK, *Jemima Shore Investigates* featured a crime-solving TV presenter, while *C.A.T.S. Eyes* was set in an all-female private detective agency, set up as a front for a Home Office security operation. In the States, the hugely successful *Cagney and Lacey* starred two New York City police detectives, *Moonlighting* featured an ex-model who teamed up with a 'cocky' male PI to run the Blue Moon Detective Agency, while mystery writer and amateur sleuth Jessica Fletcher solved numerous crimes in *Murder She Wrote*.

In literature, the female sleuth was becoming an openly feminist figure. V.I. Warshawski, the protagonist of Sara Paretsky's 1982 novel *Indemnity Only*, had no trouble taking on powerful men in Chicago. 'You are a girl, and things may get heavy,' a client warns her.

'I'm a woman,' she replies, 'and I can look out for myself. If I couldn't, I wouldn't be in this kind of business.'

Vic likes a drink, drives a Chevy Monza, carries a Smith & Wesson .38, and is immune to threats and violence. She is 'full of female-chismo', rescuing and protecting other women in her effort to solve two murders.

That same year, Sue Grafton's *'A' is for Alibi* starred Kinsey Millhone, a PI in southern California who lives in a one room 'bachelorette' and keeps an automatic in her briefcase. 'I've never been good at taking shit,' she declares, 'especially from men.'

This new breed of fictional sleuths caused some concern. Women were 'muscling in' on the world once inhabited by Philip Marlowe, declared the *Reading Evening Post*, and there were more real-life female private eyes 'than ever before'.

The idea that women were only just moving into private detection wasn't new. The press had said the same thing back in the 1920s when it was described as a novel profession for women. It was a convenient way to wipe out a history of female private detectives that went right back to the 1870s. It also reflected fears about the Women's Liberation Movement and feminist campaigns around reproductive rights, equal pay and violence against women.

The 1970s and '80s was a time of protest, marches and strikes, as well as significant legal reform, including the Equal Pay Act and the Sex Discrimination Act. In 1980, the year that Zena became vice president of the ABI, British women were finally allowed to apply for credit cards and loans without needing a man's signature. No wonder women were said to be 'muscling in' on all sorts of areas.

And yet, if there really were more female private eyes than ever before, where were they? They didn't seem to be in the press, aside from reports of a Bristol agency with an all-female staff trained in 'self-defence and fast driving', and Sandra Mara, 'Ireland's only full-time lady private detective', who ran K-Security Private Investigators in Dublin.

It had been formed in 1947 by her father, Bill Kavanagh, an ex-paratrooper hailed as Ireland's first private eye, who provided security for visiting Hollywood stars like Elizabeth Taylor and Bing Crosby. Her father had tried to dissuade Sandra from following in his footsteps, hoping she'd become a barrister. But she got the taste for the job at the age of 9 when she accompanied her father to Limerick, where he was looking for a woman who'd unknowingly inherited a fortune. Sandra slipped out of the hotel and set off to find the woman herself, walking the unfamiliar streets and asking people 'if they knew of a Mrs Ladysmith', until a priest gave her the correct address.

At 19, she persuaded her father to let her prepare case files and by the 1980s, she had a team of twelve detectives employed by government agencies, insurance companies, multinationals and media outlets. Sandra was a founder member and president of the Institute of Irish Investigators, and in 1986, when she was awarded WAD's Investigator of the Year, her father 'finally accepted that I could handle the job'. She also set up a course in professional investigation, the 'first of its kind in the world' outside government agencies, at University College Dublin. But Sandra later left the industry for a career in journalism. 'Perhaps my father had been right after all,' she wrote in her memoir. 'It was no job for a woman, at least not one with a young family!'

★ ★ ★

As for Zena Scott-Archer, her days as a private detective were nearly over. Her husband Dave died in 1982, just three weeks before his much longed for retirement, and Zena now spent most of her time away on official business. When her accountant advised her to close Scott's Detective Bureau or sell it for a nominal sum, her employee Barbara Macy decided to buy it. 'I stopped taking on private clients,' Barbara explains. 'They were a nuisance. I only did solicitors' work, such as witness statements in road accidents.' Eventually, she sold Scott's Detective Bureau, and it was later absorbed into a solicitors' firm.

But while Zena had officially retired, her media career continued. In 1989, she was invited on to the BBC's *Wogan* chat show to be interviewed as England's leading sleuth, along with another senior investigator. Zena travelled down to London, accommodation was booked at an 'all-ladies hotel', and she would be met by taxi from the station and taken to the TV studio.

But the taxi didn't turn up; it had gone to Liverpool Street Station rather than Euston, where trains from Liverpool arrive. By the time Zena had flagged down her own taxi and the driver had found the right studio, she was agitated. Then, instead of the senior investigator she was expecting, she was paired with 17-year-old Ian Beim.

Terry Wogan introduced her as 'a real-life Miss Marple' and the oldest female private investigator in the country. Zena was quick to correct him – she was the oldest woman sleuth in the world. She seemed ill at ease during the interview, as did Ian Beim, both facing insinuations about their chosen career. 'It's not a job that everyone would want to do,' said Terry Wogan. 'It's a pretty dirty job isn't it?'

Afterwards, Zena was driven to her hotel, and the following morning, a chambermaid knocked on her door to deliver a large bouquet from Wogan. Zena was not amused. 'Stick them in the wastepaper basket!' she cried, thrusting the flowers back and closing the door. Merseyside's Mrs Sherlock Holmes seemed to be growing tired after nearly forty years of patronising press attention, insulting assumptions and a general misunderstanding of what the job of private detective was all about.

'SHE-LOCK HOLMES'

In the last decade of the twentieth century, two more women were elected presidents of the ABI, beginning with Patricia Storey in 1990. She'd had no initial ambition to be a detective, believing the job meant 'running around in fast cars getting shot at', until one day she saw an advert in the window of a village shop in Shropshire. Pat applied for a job as personal assistant to a private investigator, and when he retired, she bought the business. But it was difficult to raise the finance and several bank managers turned her down because 'no one could believe a woman could make a go of a private investigation agency'.

Pat found private detection the 'best job in the world ... there's never a dull moment, your brain's always buzzing'. But she also described the pressures for women in the industry, and as a minority, they had to be 'even better' than men.

During her year as president, while still running her own agency, Norstac Inquiry Office in Stoke-on-Trent, there were moments when she 'could have screamed and burst into tears'. But she knew the 440 male members of the ABI would have said, 'Aha! You are a woman, you are menopausal. You can't take the pressure.' It was attitudes like these that meant the few women who were private eyes 'tend to be very good'.

Rosemary Sorrell had been a PI for nearly thirty years when she was elected ABI president in 1998. She was the 'queen of true confessions and special investigations', according to the *Guardian*, a 70-year-old grandmother and – inevitably – a 'Real-Life Miss Marple'. 'I've got a good instinct,' she told a journalist, 'because I like watching people.' Most men, she explained, had such a low opinion of women that no one suspected her of being a private eye; 'as women investigators, we get away with murder, simply because we are women.'

While the ABI's new women presidents did sometimes talk to the press, they didn't receive nearly as much coverage as Zena Scott-Archer. Perhaps being a female private eye was no longer quite as remarkable as it had once been, and now a mainstream TV show had two women running their own agency.

BBC1's *Chandler & Co*, launched in 1994, offered a more realistic image of the job than previous programmes, but it still focused on matrimonial cases and the trailer promised 'sex, lies and videotape'. Affairs of the heart were a 'boom business' in the 1990s, according to the show's consultant, Lindy Grant. She ran an agency in Surrey, S & Elle, with a staff of seven female agents who specialised in tracking down adulterous husbands.

Lindy was a former flight attendant, as was her business partner, Sue Morris, and she'd started her sleuthing career as assistant to an ex-CID officer in Jersey. The press dubbed her 'She-lock Holmes'.

Janet Wilson, who ran Specialised Surveillance, similarly saw two or three women a week who 'think their lover's up to something and want to have it confirmed to prove they're not going mad'. Janet rarely filmed suspects, 'A lot of women don't want to see the video of their husband bonking on the couch, it's too distressing'. Instead, they preferred to read a report of who he met, where and when.

Many clients needed a marriage guidance counsellor rather than a detective, argued Jennifer Sarah Paul, a former teacher who ran Paul Investigations with her husband, near Glasgow. So she had 'a chat and tried to put them off'.

Female private eyes had always served as counsellors, despite being portrayed as hired snoopers who broke up marriages. Annette Kerner's Mayfair agency had become a 'marriage guidance bureau', while Anne Summer counselled couples 'to attempt to make a go of things'. Raissa Page spent 'a tremendous amount of time' dissuading people from having their spouses followed, while Zena Scott-Archer offered her female clients a cup of tea and a listening ear.

Chandler & Co proved to be a popular show and by the end of the first series it had 8 million viewers. It reportedly inspired more women to enter the industry, as did *Anna Lee*, in which a former police officer, who left the force because of bureaucracy and sexism, joins a private security firm. Anna was 'feisty and fun', according to one reviewer, but to another, she was a 'dippy private dick'.

Professional female PIs seemed to be on the increase in the 1990s and one in ten investigators were now women. The percentage had apparently doubled – from 5 per cent in the 1970s – but it was still incredibly low. So who were these real-life female private eyes and what did they do, aside from track down adulterous husbands?

Crime writer Val McDermid decided to find out. She interviewed thirty-four PIs in Britain and the States for her book *A Suitable Job for a Woman*, published in 1995. Three years earlier, Val had written *Dead Beat*, the first in a series of novels featuring PI Kate Brannigan, junior partner at a Manchester agency. Kate is a former law student and a 'bright, streetwise hard case', a fan of interactive computer adventure games and Thai boxing. When she's hired by a pop star to find his ex-music partner Moira Pollock, she successfully tracks down and frames Moira's killer. Kate Brannigan was a tough 'girl gumshoe', according to the *Telegraph*, while *The Times* found her 'a much to be welcomed entrant into the still tiny profession of the female private eye'.

Now Val McDermid wanted to explore the gap between her fictional creation and the day-to-day reality of women in the industry. But while American PIs were relaxed and open and delighted to meet her, British women were more wary, often checking out her credentials with third parties, and some refused point blank to have anything to do with her. The only woman who demanded anonymity in the book was British. Those who did agree to speak tended to downplay their job, stressing that it wasn't glamorous, and appeared nervous that they would contribute to bad publicity.

Val discovered that real-life PIs were much older than their fictional counterparts, half were married and about two-thirds had children. They worked on a wide range of jobs, and they faced the constant possibility of danger, especially when it came to process serving.

Pat Storey, the former ABI president, recalled the day she was sitting in her car when a man drove a JCB at her, then let down a 40ft steel girder inches from her roof. Yvonne Twiby, who ran Twiby, Griffiths & Co. in Solihull, described detection as 'a dangerous job which some men think is no place for a woman. But I've shown I'm not just as good as them – I'm better.' She'd started as an agency secretary before launching her own business, and soon discovered that 'violent criminals ... don't like a woman with court orders turning up at their home'. She'd been 'pushed and shoved and had hot coffee thrown at me. My car's been smashed up and I've lost count of the number of threats I've received. But luckily, I've never been seriously injured.'

Brenda Balmer, an investigator in Sunderland, recalled serving an injunction on an ex-naval officer, who pulled out a machete and then a revolver. She also ended up with a chipped ankle, torn ligaments and a bruised back after serving papers on a man who threw her, literally, out of the house three times. But successfully serving papers 'gives you a buzz in the end', explained Jackie Griffiths, who ran an agency in Wrexham. 'You think, yeah, got him, he's not getting away!'

The women interviewed by Val McDermid all had a strong sense of ethics, 'a universal trait shared by women eyes' – although this wouldn't have applied to some of their sleuthing sisters from the past. Her interviewees actively helped each other, employing other women and assisting on cases. 'With positive support like this,' she concluded, 'it seems likely that there will be more women finding their way into private investigation in the future.'

Zena Scott-Archer also featured in Val McDermid's book. The two women first met on a Merseyside radio chat show, although when Val walked into reception, she didn't pay much attention to the elegant senior citizen who looked 'smart enough to be the captain of the local championship bridge team'. She soon discovered that Zena was a born storyteller, who would have made an excellent actress, and they stayed in touch, with Zena inviting Val to a regional ABI meeting.

Merseyside's Mrs Sherlock Holmes was still appearing on national TV. She was a guest on *Cluedo*, a 'who done it murder' game show, and took part in Channel 4's *Witness: the Lie Detectors*, then in 1999 she became co-presenter on BBC1's *The Crime Squad*, a 'real-life criminal action series'. The show featured barrister Jessica Redford, criminologist Professor David Wilson and 79-year-old Zena Scott-Archer, Britain's 'oldest working private detective'. She was 'a kind of cross between Supergran and Miss Marple,' explained the *Evening Herald*.

Zena told the *News of the World*:

A lot of people are surprised when they find out what I do, because of my age and the way I look and the fact that I'm a woman. But I think all those things act for me. People would never suspect I was up to anything. If people compare me to Miss Marple, I'm very pleased. She was a very clever lady.

In reality, Zena had never liked the comparison with Miss Marple; she much preferred Conan Doyle and Raymond Chandler to Agatha Christie, so perhaps she was just being diplomatic.

When a reporter from the *Daily Post* visited Zena at her modest Edwardian semi in Wallasey, he found her 'like everyone's favourite granny' with silver hair slicked back in a bun and quick to offer a slice of sticky chocolate cake. But Zena hardly sounded as if she'd retired. Her telephone was hooked up to a fax, a photocopier was kept busy in the hallway, and she was devoting her energies to tracing adopted children who'd been shipped to Australia in a post-war colonisation programme.

This would be among one of Zena's last interviews. In 1998 she moved to Cumbria to live with her sister Marion and brother-in-law Bill, telling the press she was 'semi-retired' and still worked on the odd case. Zena was once asked if she would recommend private detection to young people and, with some hesitation, she replied, 'No. It is very hard work with no fixed hours and it is ruinous to any sort of social life.'

So did that mean she would rather have done something else?

'Oh no!' Zena replied, 'It's a fascinating business. I've loved every minute of it.'

★ ★ ★

Zena Scott-Archer died on 6 November 2011, aged 90, in a nursing home. Her obituary in a local paper described her as the 'widow of the late David Archer', with no mention of her own career. However, Zena was widely respected by clients and solicitors and colleagues both at home and abroad.

'I travelled with Zena to overseas meetings on several occasions,' recalls Eric Shelmerdine, former ABI president and Zena's long-time friend, 'and all around the world people who didn't even speak English would come up and ask, "Zena Scott-Archer?"' Shortly before her death, Eric and Ann Shelmerdine arranged a meeting with Siti Subaidah Naidu, from Malaysia, who had just become the second woman elected president of the World Association of Detectives.

Siti had first met Zena many years before at a WAD conference in Singapore in the 1980s when she was working in events. She remembers the meeting vividly. 'Unlike many of the women present, who were partners or spouses of members, Zena stood out as a woman of her own stature, full of confidence. She was an inspiration.' Siti went on to run a detective agency with her husband, Adil Naidu, who became WAD president in 2004, and after his death she took over Corporate Risks Consulting. Siti was elected WAD president at a conference in Hong Kong in 2011, 'but before I took office, my wish was to visit Zena'. She travelled to Cumbria, where 'it was an honour and a blessing to meet the woman whom I admired when I was 23 years old, and it was a dream come true to follow in her path'. Since then, there have only been two other women presidents at WAD: American Christine Vinson in 2013 and Italian Laura Giuliani in 2018.

Zena Scott-Archer had 'always prospered as a woman in a male dominated profession,' explained the *Echo*. She was unusual for her longevity, and her success as a businesswoman. 'We're not all Markers,' Zena once told a journalist, '– slinking around in dirty raincoats and working from tatty offices … we're just businesspeople running our businesses and looking after our clients – like solicitors or accountants.'

Some found her intimidating; she was described as intense, private, unemotional and occasionally as lonely. Zena rarely admitted she was wrong and was not known for apologising. She did not like to lose face, and many saw her as steely and fearsome. But Merseyside's Mrs Sherlock Holmes was a consummate professional. She didn't exaggerate or relish danger like her famous forebears. She didn't cheat, gamble or break the law. She didn't spin tales about travelling for three days on the back of a donkey, shooting spirits at seances, catching white slavers or surviving razor attacks. She didn't pretend to be friends with famous people or work for rich celebrity clients. Most were 'just ordinary working-class people,' she explained. 'I find that the working-class people of England are far more trustworthy and honourable than the wealthy upper class.'

Zena's home life was stable. She had no divorce to hide, and her marital status was always crystal clear. She didn't adopt the role of society lady or glamorous vamp; instead, she dressed down for her disguises, discarding her usual fashionable clothes, make-up and jewellery, and becoming the 'ordinary woman' in a dull brown, patterned dress, carrying a string shopping bag, with grey hair peeping from under a turban.

Despite her fame in Liverpool, she got away with being a private detective for decades because, as a woman, she could still go unnoticed. Disguise was seldom necessary, as *Lancashire Life* explained, 'A headscarf and flat shoes are enough to turn any woman into a faceless nonentity!'

Zena rarely made enemies during her career, although she once made an oblique reference to competitors calling her 'bad names'. Despite her reputation on the international stage, the BBC film announced in the 1980s was never made and Zena tried without luck to find a ghostwriter to write her story. 'You know the way some names have become household words,' she once told the *Liverpool Daily Post*. 'Like Hoover for vacuum cleaner and Thermos for vacuum flasks. Well, I know it sounds big headed, but I would like to hear Zena for private detectives.'

But there have been no biographies, documentaries, novels or films about Zena Scott-Archer, and however many times she was interviewed and written about, she is still difficult to pin down. Her words were usually filtered through the lenses of male journalists and it's sometimes hard to get a feel for the real woman behind the glamorous exterior. Why isn't Zena as famous now as she was in her heyday? How could someone so well established on the world stage be forgotten so fast?

33

PRIVATE LIVES

I'm sitting in the downstairs bar of the Sherlock Holmes pub, just near Trafalgar Square in central London. It's a Thursday lunchtime and the place is beginning to get busy. An American couple are ordering fish and chips, while a man stands by a sign offering customers the chance to win a free bar tab if they dress up as Sherlock Holmes.

I've booked a table in the restaurant upstairs because I've read that there's a detailed recreation of Sherlock's Baker Street flat. It was put together by the Sherlock Holmes Society for the Festival of Britain in 1951, with the BBC providing sound effects: a barrel organ, tin whistle, newsboy's call and the clop-clop-clop of hansom-cab horses. A *Pathé* news clip from a few years later shows diners tucking into plates of food, sitting right next to Sherlock's study. But disappointingly, the pub's restaurant turns out to be closed.

The manager, Vanessa, agrees to let me go up and at least have a look.

'So, who comes here?' I ask, following her through another section of the downstairs bar.

'Lots of Americans,' she says, pushing open a door. '*Lots* of Americans.'

'Do they think Sherlock Holmes is real?'

She laughs, 'Some of them.'

'And do you tell them he's not?'

She laughs again, 'A colleague once told some tourists that Sherlock Holmes used to live here, and they were like, "Wow, really?"'

I can see why they might have thought this. The pub has a beautiful Victorian façade with old-fashioned lanterns, frosted windows and Sherlock's name embossed in gold on the glass. The building was originally a small hotel, which featured in *The Adventure of the Noble Bachelor*. Sherlock sometimes popped into the Turkish Baths next door, while Scotland Yard was just a few minutes' walk away.

Vanessa leads me up a narrow set of stairs, opens another door and we enter the dining area. 'That's his study,' she says, stopping in front of a wooden-framed glass door.

'Can I go in?' I ask, reaching for the handle.

'No,' she says. 'You can't go in. But you can look through the window.'

The room is cluttered with objects, a teapot and cups set out on the table, a skull on a mantelpiece, the Persian slipper in which Sherlock stored his tobacco and a display of chemistry equipment in the corner.

'This all comes from the Sherlock Holmes Society,' says Vanessa. 'They used to come and change the display every few months, but they haven't been for a year because of Covid.'

I go back downstairs and the person I've arranged to meet for lunch has arrived. We've been emailing for a while and have chatted twice over Zoom, but this is the first time we've met in person.

The pub seemed like a good spot in which to meet Lyndsay Bird, a relative of Mrs Sherlock Holmes from Merseyside. She takes off her coat and gives me a hug. She seems like a person who laughs a lot and knows how to make other people feel comfortable. Lyndsay's father is Zena's second cousin, and she remembers her from family parties, where Zena was something of a celebrity. As we sit down and order food and cider, Lyndsay brings out a package of old photos, given to her by Zena's sister, Marion.

'Wow,' I say, as she tips a collection of sepia prints onto the table. I pick up a portrait of Zena as a newly married young woman in the 1940s, then a picture with her beaming father, ex-Flying Squad officer Sydney Scott, and a group shot of her family dressed up for a night at a ballroom in which she's wearing a floor-length, checked evening dress. 'She made that from a parachute,' says Lyndsay. 'She was very good at things like that.'

She hands me a photo of Zena marching along a Liverpool street in the 1950s, wearing a tight-fitting black skirt, a top buttoned in a military style, a pair of white gloves and a white flower in her buttonhole. 'I love this one,' says Lyndsay. 'Zena adored clothes and dressing up, she was so sophisticated and elegant. I remember her in her 60s; she always had her hair up in a bun or a chignon and was always beautifully dressed. This was after her husband Dave had died, and she came to family parties with George Pulley. He ran the Oxford Detective Agency, and he looked like the archetypal private detective in a Panama hat and cravat.'

'What did you think Zena actually did?'

'Well,' Lyndsay smiles, 'I knew it wasn't murder mysteries or that she was a Miss Marple type, but I was too timid to speak to her much.'

I look at more photos: Zena seated at her desk in Scott's Detective Bureau wearing a glittering dress and pearl choker, another with her best friend Win Hobson and Barbara Macy, who later bought the agency.

I pick up a copy of the programme for the Association of British Detectives' annual banquet of 1969 when 'Mrs. Z. Archer' was president and members enjoyed a menu of beef wellington and buttered sprouts.

'What's she doing there?' I ask, pointing to a picture of Zena wearing a white fluffy hat while behind her customers seem to be jostling at a supermarket till.

Lyndsay laughs, 'It looks like she's investigating shoplifting.'

The pub manager comes over and I introduce her to Lyndsay. 'Her relative was a real-life detective,' I say. 'Zena Scott-Archer.'

The manager looks over my shoulder at the pictures, now covering most of the table.

'Aren't they beautiful?' I ask. 'Zena ran a detective agency in Liverpool, and she was president of the World Association of Detectives.' I point behind me at framed prints of famous actors playing Sherlock Holmes on the pub wall. 'Wouldn't it be great if you had some pictures of real-life detectives?'

The manager nods and moves on to another customer.

Lyndsay puts the photos back in the envelope, then she hands me a memory stick that I can look at later.

'What do you think Zena would have been doing now?' I ask, as our food arrives.

'Not adultery.' Lyndsay shakes her head. 'I think she'd probably be doing fraud, maybe blackmail and theft, but now with CCTV that's less likely. She would definitely have stayed up with the times, she was always very up to date with technology.'

'Why do you think no one has heard of Zena these days?'

Lyndsay picks up a chip and considers. 'I'm not sure, but has anyone heard of the real-life detective men? Have they carried on? We obsess over fictional characters, don't we? But not real-life people. There are probably lots of male detectives and we don't know about them.'

'Yes,' I say, because many once-famous male detectives have also been forgotten. But if a male private eye had run an agency from the 1950s to the 1980s, been constantly in the press and on TV, been head of the ABD, the ABI and the World Association of Detectives, wouldn't we have heard of them?

Lyndsay nods. 'You would think they would carry on, that their name would be recognised, that people would still refer to them. But people are more interested in fiction than reality. I know I am, especially when the world is so horrific.'

Zena Scott-Archer is about to become better known, however, because Lyndsay has written a novel based on her relative's detective cases. It's a project she has been thinking about for a while.

Lyndsay is a former primary school teacher, who changed career after volunteering for VSO in Nepal. She then worked for various humanitarian organisations and today she does consultancy work. She remembers one day, in her early 30s, when she'd just come back from Tanzania and she turned on the TV and there was Zena on *Crime Squad*. 'Oh my God,' I thought. 'I'd love to write about her.'

It was another decade or so before Lyndsay plucked up the courage to write to Zena's sister Marion, saying she wanted to write a book. Unfortunately, Zena was too ill to meet, but after her death, Marion gave Lyndsay a large collection of handwritten diaries, newspaper articles, photographs and taped interviews. Lyndsay had taken a year out from work, so she decided to start typing everything out.

The diaries run from 1976 to 1985. Zena made several entries a week, and it took Lyndsay nearly seven months to transcribe them. After being immersed in Zena's world for so long, she considered writing a biography, but then decided to write a novel, *Zena: The Housewives' Detective*, drawing on family stories, archives and real-life cases.

'I wanted her to be recognised,' says Lyndsay. 'For her legacy to be remembered. She was such a strong character. There was a steel about her, a hard-nosed aura. But she could be quite funny, witty, with a sharp sense of humour.'

'Do you think Zena was a mythmaker?' I ask.

'No,' says Lyndsay. 'She was honest and straightforward. Her dad really wanted the industry professionalised. He was very against using tricks, and so was Zena. She didn't use hidden bugs; she wanted proper legwork.'

We finish our pies and chips, and I ask the manager if I can take Lyndsay upstairs to see Sherlock Holmes' study. The dining room is all set out for the evening now, when the restaurant will be open. Outside the windows it's a cold windy day, rain clouds are moving quickly across the sky, but inside it's cosy with yellow wall-papered walls and wine glasses sparkling in a flickering overhead light. We look at a portrait of Conan Doyle hanging above the fireplace, and 'the last Will and Testament' of Sherlock Holmes, dated April 1891. The display reminds me of the Sherlock Holmes Museum, and the enduring desire to pretend the Victorian detective was real.

Then we peer through the plate glass into Sherlock's study. A notice informs us that this is a reconstruction of his rooms, as they were around 1894. We spot the famous Inverness cape and deerstalker hat, and Dr Watson's black overcoat, bowler hat and stethoscope. We see a wax torso at the far end of the study, with a long, mournful, yellowish face – and a bright red bullet hole in the forehead. This is the decoy which fooled Sherlock's enemy Colonel Moran when he shot the detective with a rifle from across the street. It looks alarmingly like Russian President Vladimir Putin.

I wonder what would be in here if it was Zena's room – a Paris fashion hat, perhaps, an array of wigs, a tape recorder, pair of binoculars, feather duster and a Dictaphone?

'Let's take selfies,' says Lyndsay. She holds up her phone and we stand in front of Sherlock's study, but we can't get both our faces in the shot. Then she sees a large wooden cut-out of Sherlock and Watson with holes where their faces should be, propped against a wall. She picks it up and we struggle to hold the board and get our faces behind the holes.

'You be Holmes,' I tell her. 'You're Zena's relative, you have to be Sherlock Holmes.'

'I'm not tall enough!' she protests.

We're about to swap places, when suddenly the door to the restaurant opens and Vanessa, the manager, walks in. We both jump, then look around guiltily.

'Would you take a photo of us?' Lyndsay asks very politely.

The manager obliges. We get our heads in position and I'm Sherlock Holmes and Lyndsay Bird is Dr Watson.

We part a little later at Charing Cross Station, where Lyndsay is getting the train home. 'Do you think you could ever be a private detective?' I ask.

'Quite a few people have asked me that,' she smiles. 'But I wonder if I have that kind of brain. I love the idea of the job, but I have such an appalling memory. I love detective novels, but I never guess who the murderer is. I'm also a bit lazy, I don't pay great attention to detail, I like to do things too quickly. But I do have a no-nonsense approach, just like Zena.'

I say goodbye and walk off along the Strand, thinking of all the female private detectives who once operated in this area of London. I pass No. 37 the Strand, where Detective Expert Antonia Moser opened her agency in 1905 and which is now a Sainsbury's Local. I come to Southampton Street, where Antonia knocked on the door of Maurice Moser's office in 1888 and announced she wanted to be a private detective. I'm just a ten-minute walk from No. 59 New Oxford Street, where Maud West opened her agency in the early 1900s, and less than a mile from Wardour Street, where Annette Kerner grew up, and Warwick Court where Kate Easton set up shop in 1909. The women were so celebrated in their time, the national press wrote endlessly about their thrilling lives and serialised their casebooks, and yet we know so little about most of them now.

When I get home, I put Lyndsay's memory stick into my computer and click on a folder entitled 'Diary'. I read the first line: 'This handsome binder and loose leaves are my diary for 1976. A present from my mama for New Year.'

I feel a little shiver. This is the closest I've come to reading the words of a female sleuth that were not intended for publication. Liverpool's Mrs Sherlock Holmes had been a detective for over two decades by the time she started this diary. I wonder if she will mention any of her cases.

I read quickly, scanning the entries: notes on domestic life, what she ate and what she cooked – often sponge cakes – the health of her family, husband, friends and neighbours, the changeable British weather. There are references to politics and world events, to Cuba and the Angolan Civil War, as well as endless car problems and trouble heating her office. And buried among all of this, in between washing her hair, shopping for bargains and evening French lessons, are casual mentions of her investigations.

One afternoon Zena serves a man with bankruptcy papers at his home in South Birkenhead, 'Such a lovely house. He was charming, gave me a glass of sherry.' She pops in to see a witness in a ransom case, and notes that a client wants a job done on a speculative basis – 'no results no pay 100 pounds double or quits'. One lunchtime, she puts on a long, ginger wig and follows a man as he meets his wife in a park. When she returns to her car, a schoolboy sees her remove her wig and put on her hat and 'his jaw dropped'.

Zena frequently receives 'SOS calls' from panicked solicitors to take a photo of a man with a black eye at a police station, photograph a woman who tripped on a pavement and serve a witness summons for a court hearing the following morning. Sometimes she serves papers on three different people on her way home, handing one injunction to 'a little pip-squeak 5ft nothing, crew cut, 18 years old, pimples and gold earring'.

Zena occasionally carries binoculars and a tape recorder in her handbag, and she notes the satisfaction when things go right, following people until she 'nabs' them. One day, she serves an injunction on a man who insists it's a case of mistaken identity, until she points out he has his name tattooed on his arm.

She also writes about the grind of the job, keeping observation for hours at a time, sustained by fish and chips in a thermos, and nearly freezing to death. She completes 'very depressing jobs in filthy houses', deals with a client who smells of drink at 10.30 a.m., and spends all day trying to serve a subpoena on an orthopaedic surgeon. She also expresses sympathy for her clients, especially market traders faced with debt.

I come to her diary for the early 1980s, when Zena was elected president of the ABI. There seems to have been a lot of intrigue and infighting, and she can be withering about some of the men on the General Council. When she's asked if she'd like to be vice president, she responds, 'I'd do a better job than some lately'. There are endless disagreements and quarrels, and regular phone calls at home from aggrieved members wanting her opinion.

During a conference abroad, one man is accused of trying to sexually assault another member's daughter and Zena decides 'it seems he's a sadist'. But it doesn't look like anything is done to stop him.

Zena doesn't paint a pretty picture of the ABI in the mid-1980s, although publicly she always defended the association. 'I didn't find any hostility towards me as a woman at all,' she once declared. 'They were all rather nice.'

By May 1984, the diary entries are getting shorter, and towards the end of the month, they are often just a sentence. One day, over a meal with her mother, she weeps for her late husband. Three days later, her diary stops, before one final entry, 'my back was very bad but I went to the office'.

I close the folders on my computer and watch as the screen goes dark. Did Zena Scott-Archer keep proper case files and client reports? She must have done – she was a professional – but Lyndsay believes they were destroyed. All that remains is a glimpse of what day-to-day life was like for a female private detective fifty years ago.

Zena once explained that the reality of PI work was more 'domestically slanted' than it appeared on TV. It wasn't all car chases and catching dangerous criminals. Her diaries show how she fitted investigations around her other interests and responsibilities – which is why private detection has always been a suitable job for a woman.

Today, the ABI describes Zena as a 'living legend' and presents an annual award for 'Investigator of the Year', better known as the Zena Scott-Archer Award. In the past thirty-four years, only three women have won it, and the most recent recipient investigates crimes that are far more violent than those of Merseyside's famous sleuth.

DEATH INVESTIGATOR

A few weeks after my visit to the Sherlock Holmes pub, I log on to Zoom to meet Jen Jarvie, a private detective in County Durham, who runs Jarvie Death Investigation Services. Of all the women I've found so far, there have only rarely been mentions of death investigations – and when it came to sleuths like Maud West and Annette Kerner, their murder stories may well have been made up. Fictional PIs like V.I. Warshawski and Kate Brannigan might routinely set off on the trail of a killer, but real-life private eyes have traditionally dealt with civil cases.

Jen's smiling face appears on the screen. She seems to be in an office, which I guess is York St John University, where she's a lecturer in Professional Policing. I can see printouts of maps on a wall, and a very large bookcase with the top shelf entirely filled with white lever-arch files. But then I catch a glimpse of a white greyhound nibbling away on the edge of a bookcase and realise she is at home.

Jen is based near Billingham. She launched her company in 2013 and she's the only member of the ABI who specialises in death investigation. Her work includes analysing forensics at a crime scene, interviewing witnesses, studying motivation, presenting new evidence to the police and liaising with families of cold-case victims.

So, was this something she always wanted to do?

Jen laughs. 'I always wanted to join the police service, that was my goal as a 12-year-old. I had an interest in crime and law and justice, and criminality if you like.' But instead, she did a business degree, got married and had two children, then in 2008 she returned to university to study a BSc in Death Investigation at Teesside University.

'You can do a degree in that?' I ask.

'Not any longer,' says Jen. 'There were ten students and the course only ran for one year. They inadvertently taught us how to commit a crime and how to get away with it!'

Today, she is one of only three people in the UK to hold a first-class honours in Death Investigation. But the degree was 'quite niche' and so she became a lecturer, before deciding to do something more practical.

'I could have joined the police force then, but you have to follow the rank and file, and at that point …' she pauses, 'I had too many opinions.'

Private investigation seemed like the best option, but she had very little knowledge about how to set up as a PI. 'I thought there must be some regulatory body, and I found the ABI through a Google search. I thought, this is going to give me all these lovely detectives and I'll learn from them. At the time I knew nothing about surveillance, or process serving.'

Her very first case was theft in a building company. An employee was making frequent visits to B&Q, ordering brackets and door handles, getting duplicate receipts, then returning the goods and keeping the refund. 'He was pocketing hundreds of pounds each week,' Jen explains. 'I suggested what to do, and he was caught. I was quite proud of myself; I wasn't even doing it properly as a career yet.'

Her first murder case began in 2015, when she decided to investigate the only unsolved homicide in County Durham over the last seventy years. In August 1990, Ann Heron, a 44-year-old nurse, had been killed outside her home near Darlington. Fifteen years later, her husband Peter was charged with the murder, but just before the trial began the charges were 'discontinued'.

Jen was aware of the case, having seen press coverage which included a reconstruction on BBC's *Crimewatch UK*. One day, while on holiday, she vowed to look into it. 'The case was local to me,' she explains. 'It was my chance to be that police officer, to be that detective.'

In 2006 she approached the Heron family, sending a message to Peter's daughter, Debbie Simpson, via Facebook, and offering to investigate further. Debbie had been trying for years to clear her father's name, and she handed the prosecution files to Jen.

Shortly after the murder, a man had been seen speeding down the driveway from Ann Heron's isolated home in a blue car. Jen identified a 'vital suspect', Michael Benson, a Leeds man, who'd been on the run from prison at the time and had died in 2011. Jen used the local press to ask for help: 'If there's anybody who knows him or knew him, even in a sweeping capacity, I would like you to come forward … I'm not the police and I'm not here to judge.'

In 2020, following the publicity surrounding the thirtieth anniversary of Ann Heron's death, Jen was approached by a man who'd been in jail with Michael Benson, and claimed that he'd boasted about the murder. Jen went with Ann's children to meet with Durham Constabulary and handed over her findings, which implicated Michael Benson. 'Basically, what we said to them is, it's thirty years on and we have a viable suspect. We would like to rule him in or rule him out.'

Jen says she'd gathered all the results from her investigation and put everything together in a file, but that the reaction from the police was dismissive. She stresses that she has the 'utmost respect' for senior officers, but this wasn't the first time she'd been treated this way. 'I have been told in meetings, "Could the little girl leave the room please?"'

'What?' I ask.

'Yes,' Jen nods. 'I kid you not. I actually looked around to see if there was a child in the room.'

Seasoned detectives, she says, don't generally like someone who is female, younger and not a police officer, but who has policing knowledge. 'It is a level of threat they dislike. You constantly have to prove your level, but I've never been intimidated.'

Female private detectives have often had an uneasy relationship with the police. In Victorian times, Scotland Yard was reluctant to publicise the fact that it employed women to help solve crime and usually kept their identities a secret. By the 1920s the relationship appeared to be growing closer and Maud West talked openly about working undercover for the police.

Annette Kerner ended her 1950s memoir with an ode to the 'boys in blue', after she'd received public support from two senior officers at her fraud trial. Zena Scott-Archer found the police quite helpful, but 'I couldn't go to them and say, "I want to look at your files". I think my father would have been in a better position to do that because of the old boys' network, you know.'

In more modern times, the relationship seems to have become more antagonistic. 'The police don't like us,' declared Pat Storey, ABI president in 1990. If she went to the police station, 'I get absolutely no cooperation whatsoever. I'm a female, I'm a PI – on your bike. They don't want to know.'

But female PIs have always had to work alongside plenty of former police, who haven't necessarily looked favourably on their female colleagues. Barbara Macy, who took minutes at ABI meetings in the 1970s, describes the association then as 'mostly pompous men'. 'They're a bit like little boys with their toys,' explained Sally Isted, a PI in Hampshire, who attended several ABI seminars in the 1980s, 'and there's no question that they feel superior to us women … an awful lot of them are pretty chauvinist, but I suppose their world, the police, was like that.'

Jackie Malton can attest to the 'macho squad-room culture' of the police. She became one of only three women detective chief inspectors in the Met and experienced misogyny and homophobia throughout her career. When Jackie joined Leicester Police in the 1970s, male recruits were given a truncheon, the women received a handbag. Her 'welcome' into CID meant being subjected to 'station stamping'. Two officers grabbed her as she was leaving work one night; a third pulled down her underwear and stamped her with the CID ink stamp, while another group of men looked on. When Jackie joined the Flying Squad in the early 1980s, her male partner refused to work with a woman, and her nickname in the squad was 'the Tart'. Her experiences in the force inspired the groundbreaking police drama *Prime Suspect*.

As for private detectives, Jen Jarvie describes the modern ABI as 'brilliant and very supportive', but the first time she attended an AGM, 'everybody came up to my husband and asked, "Oh what area of investigation are you in?" It isn't a sexist industry. It's just that people say things like, "Crikey, you're a death investigator, a *death investigator*? So, you don't do *matrimonial* things? You don't do honey traps and surveillance?" And I say, "No, I generally look at dead bodies, I look at murder scenes". They are traditionally considered to be very manly roles.'

Jen fits investigations around the rest of her life, spending evenings and weekends working in a 'log cabin' in the garden looking at 'horrendous things, researching the inflicting of wounds, reading about the behaviour behind why someone injures a victim in such a horrendous way. I'm not doing this for sensationalism,' she explains. 'It is for that victim. It sounds dreadfully flowery, but the victim tells me – their remains or their injuries tell me. I'm giving them a voice.' Jen pauses for a moment. 'My dad died when I was 17. It was cancer, and it was tragic. But I knew the who and why. What if I didn't know? Last week I spoke to a lady. Her daughter was murdered twenty-nine years ago. It's never been solved. There is nowhere for her to go. All the doors are now shut.'

Jen, who has served on the ABI's Governing Council, says one of the benefits of the ABI is its Code of Conduct and desire to uphold professional standards. 'Without that,' she says, 'anyone could go to a victim and say, "I'll help you solve this". Jen has no time for 'armchair detectives' who trawl the internet on well-known murder or missing persons cases and make far-fetched assumptions. 'If you're a family of a cold case victim,' she explains, 'it's twenty years down the line. You've lost faith in the police, and someone comes along with the gift of the gab, saying, "I will get answers for you, I will find you justice." What do you do? At this point, desperation takes over rationale. That's why I do the work pro bono.'

'What?' I ask. 'You do the cases for free?'

'Yes. Because how do you charge? It would be like saying, how much is your loved one worth? What do you do, charge more if it's a child? Or if it's thirty years ago? Morally, I refuse to make a profit from other people's misfortune. This is the worst thing that has happened to them in their lives.'

'So, you don't charge them anything?'

'No.'

'But how can you afford to do that?'

'I'm a lecturer,' says Jen. 'I have a wage every month. It's a matter of justice. Families are more than willing to pay expenses, and for reports and forensics, but I don't get paid.'

'So, what do you get?'

'The satisfaction,' Jen says at once. 'I've got all these qualifications ... I teach, I lecture, but I want to actually give something back to someone.'

Female private detectives have often been motivated by a sense of justice – or injustice. They've rescued women and girls from conmen, unfaithful husbands, predators, peeping toms, blackmailers, drug dealers and white slavery. They've also spoken out about social injustice, whether the right to vote, the right to work or the unfairness of divorce laws as applied to women.

I ask Jen if she's aware of the women who have come before her. 'I'm a real historian with crime,' she says, gesturing behind at a row of books, including Dr Nell Darby's *Sister Sleuths*. 'I love knowing where we are now because of where we've been. I can well imagine women in the past having a bit more to prove, I can relate to that.'

Jen strikes me as a natural storyteller and a century ago newspapers would have been begging for tales from her 'casebooks', so I wonder what her relationship is like with the press.

'At first I was extremely cautious,' she explains. 'It was a little bit scary. There was an article in the *Sun* and before it came out, myself and my family felt a bit cringy, would they be calling me a "private dick"? But I've been really lucky.'

Press coverage also means people often send her packages – 'I'm slightly alarmed in case there are body parts' – such as copies of court papers and crime scene DVDs. But Jen is annoyed that the press call her a 'criminologist', confusing her lecturing job with being a private investigator.

She also describes one photo shoot when she was told to take her glasses off, 'I said, if I do that, then I can't see. There is a thing of, as a female, I did think, what will I look like?' Women private eyes have always been judged on their appearance and made acutely aware of how they present themselves. Dorothy Tempest was portrayed as a handsome lady detective in a crushed-strawberry costume and black hat. Annie Betts was stylish and aristocratic looking – until she became a store detective – while Matilda Mitchell had an 'altogether dominant face for a woman'. Kate Easton was pretty and plucky, and so was Maud West, while Zena Scott-Archer was both a 'pleasant faced housewife from Liverpool' and 'the Modesty Blaise of Wirral'.

Jen Jarvie has a direct link to her Merseyside forebear. In April 2022, she won the Zena Scott-Archer Award for Investigator of the Year. She's the third woman in the ABI's history to receive the honour, after Brenda Balmer in 1994 and Sarah Martin in 1998. Jen was nominated by Debbie Simpson, for 'her outstanding and relentless work' in helping to bring the cold case investigation into Ann Heron's death 'to its rightful conclusion'. But when the case featured in a Channel 5 documentary a few weeks later, Durham Constabulary insisted that Michael Benson 'is not and never has been a suspect in this case' and they were 'all but certain' he was living abroad at the time of the murder. They added it was regrettable the killer had not been found, but that Peter Heron had been 'designated as a suspect' in 2005 and 'this status has not changed'.

In January 2023, Jen teamed up with Jaz Khan, a former Detective Superintendent at West Yorkshire Police. 'He has thirty years' experience,' she tells me. 'We make a formidable team.'

Jarvie Khan Investigations now charge for some of their cases. 'We can afford to be choosy with some and still take them pro bono,' says Jen, 'but these are usually ones from vulnerable backgrounds or where the family are at a loss.' They are currently investigating the disappearance of 14-year-old Charlene Downes, who went missing from Blackpool nearly twenty years ago. 'The police don't look at a case as a PI would,' Jen explains. 'A PI brings fresh eyes.'

But myths about female private eyes remain and even in the twenty-first century, there is the assumption that women are incapable of 'manly roles' like murder investigations, and are far more suited to honey trapping.

TWENTY-FIRST-CENTURY DETECTIVES

When the new *Charlie's Angels* film opened in Britain in 2000, there was 'much discussion about the reality of being a sleuth', explained the BBC, 'and whether women might, by their very nature, be better at it than men'. This was the same discussion that had been held ever since the 1880s, when Frances Power Cobbe suggested women be employed to capture the 'demon of Whitechapel'. Now, as the three glamorous Angels demonstrated their 'martial arts, tech skills and sex appeal', the advantage possessed by female sleuths was being debated once again. Women, by their 'very nature', were prone to snooping, disguise and using feminine wiles. Female sleuths were 'sexy angels', and judging from reports in the British press, their primary job was catching adulterous men.

Rebecca Jane, who launched the Lady Detective Agency in Manchester in 2009, was a 'Sex Spy', according to the *Sun*, whose job was 'to catch the UK's men with their pants down'. Rebecca was a glamorous figure, as portrayed in her memoir, *The Real Lady Detective Agency*. She wore 'super high heels', stayed at five-star hotels, and drove a top of the range sports car with blacked-out windows.

Like many previous female private eyes, her initial dream had been to be on the stage, and she stumbled on detection through personal experience. When Rebecca was seven months pregnant her husband left, after just two months of marriage. She suspected he was having an affair and went through the *Yellow Pages* contacting private detectives.

But they were 'classic investigators, cold and hard', and they charged nearly £100 an hour. So, along with two friends, Rebecca set out to watch her husband herself.

At the age of 24, she formed her own agency, reading everything she could find about 'methods of detection: surveillance, background checking, DNA testing – you name it'. She launched a website, made use of all the latest gadgets, and went after cheating men like a moral force, much as Annette Kerner had done.

But while detection proved to be a 'dream job', Rebecca also had doubts. 'Some people claim this industry is all about making money from heartbreak and preying on the weak. What if they're right?' She enjoyed the 'rush of feeling' when she uncovered someone being unfaithful, but it also tarnished her faith in human nature.

For those who wanted a partner investigated before getting married, the twenty-first century saw the rise of arranged marriage detectives. The service had started in India, where Delhi alone boasted 3,500 firms, many run by women, who carried out pre-matrimonial investigations, looking into the character, assets, earnings, background and lifestyle of potential spouses.

When 'Sukhi' wanted to know more about her future brother-in-law, she hired British agency Lion Investigation Services. Detectives followed their target to a bar in the Midlands and kept him under surveillance all weekend. Before long, he was sending 'intimate and graphic pictures of himself' to a female agent. The company offered infidelity checks as well as 'integrity' and lie detector tests. If a potential spouse sounded too good to be true, it warned, 'then they probably are'.

Lion Investigation Services was set up in 2013 by 'Raj Singh', an ex-police officer who didn't reveal his real name. His agents were fluent in Punjabi and Urdu, and around 70 per cent of their clients were Asian. The company is now a franchise and 'the biggest and fastest growing Asian Private Investigation Firm' in the UK.

Traditionally, the British private detection industry has been overwhelmingly white. Most PIs have always been ex-police and the force has been mainly white – today, just 3 per cent of the police force in England and Wales are Asian, and less than 2 per cent are Black. There must have been men, and women, of colour who were hired by Scotland Yard and private inquiry agents to investigate crime and work undercover since at least Victorian times, but their stories still remain hidden and I haven't come across a single reference until modern times.

In the United States, Hattie Lawton, who worked for the Pinkerton National Detective Agency, has been described as the first mixed-race woman detective. She was the second female agent hired after Kate Warne, and Allan Pinkerton praised her as a 'brave, true-hearted woman', who dedicated her life to her country. But while she gathered intelligence about Confederate Army movements and made repeated trips into enemy lines, little is known about her identity today.

Internationally, there are several famous female figures, such as Rajani Pandit, 'India's Sherlock Holmes' and the 'Lady James Bond of India'. She started Rajani Investigative Bureau in the mid-1980s and claims to have solved over 75,000 cases involving missing persons, murder, family disputes and corporate espionage. 'I had access to more spaces that men couldn't penetrate,' she told the *New Indian Express*, in words that closely echoed Kate Warne in the 1850s.

In Kenya, ex-police officer Jane Mugo describes herself as the best private detective in the world. She lives in a 'secret' compound in Nairobi with ten bodyguards and a chef who tastes her food before she eats it. In 2021, Jane featured in a BBC documentary, *Kenya's 'Spy Queen'*, where she was portrayed as a 'real version' of James Bond.

Africa's most famous fictional private eye, meanwhile, is Alexander McCall Smith's Mma Precious Ramotswe, 'the only lady private detective in Botswana', who possesses intuition and intelligence in abundance. Mma Ramotswe is 'less a detective more an Agony Aunt', according to her creator, and she deals with 'very human problems in an affirmative kind of way'.

Human problems have always provided work for private eyes, particularly clients exploited in love, whether the victims of cheating partners, romance scams or marriage fraud. Victorian sleuth Antonia Moser was once hired by a lovestruck woman to follow a count across Europe, where she discovered he was already married. Maud West laid a trap for two bogus gentlemen who'd proposed marriage to two young French women in London.

Annette Kerner claimed to have helped a 'Mrs H' in the 1920s, who placed an advert in her local paper, 'widow, 50, travelled, living very much alone would like to meet a sincere friend of either sex with a view to mutual companionship'. She received a reply from Arthur Hafner, who introduced himself as a stockbroker and Oxford graduate, and he proposed a few weeks later. But then one evening, a man burst into Arthur's flat and saw the unwed couple together. He demanded money to buy his silence and Mrs H was persuaded to write a cheque for £200. She later went to the police and the conmen were convicted. 'Middle-aged, lonely, loveless women wanting companionship,' said the judge, 'are easy prey to such men as you.'

Marriage scams have existed for centuries. In 1895, five men were jailed for charging fees for fake introductions to 'high-class' ladies at the World's Great Marriage Association in London. A few years later, a woman on the Isle of Man placed an advert in a Yorkshire paper: 'intelligent, attractive young lady wishes to meet honourable gentleman; object, matrimony'. She started up a correspondence with a man from Leeds, promised a 'delightful tête-à-tête' if he sent £3 to cover her travel expenses, and then disappeared once she'd received the money.

Today, such scams have moved online. The perpetrators still use a mix of charm and threats, and modern criminal methods call for new forms of investigation.

ROGUE DATERS

I'm weaving my way around lunchtime shoppers at Brent Cross shopping centre in north London, on my way to meet a private eye. She's arranged a rendezvous outside W.H. Smith, and when I get there, she's already waiting, leaning against the window, small and slight, dressed all in black but for a multicoloured facemask.

Sam Cooper has been a professional investigator for nearly ten years. She's a former member of the ABI's Governing Council, and she runs a detective agency that helps people who fear they're being scammed online.

We walk up the escalators to an empty coffee shop and sit down in the corner.

'So,' I say, 'did you always want to be a private detective?'

'No,' Sam smiles, 'I originally wanted to be an air hostess, but I wasn't tall enough.'

Like a lot of PIs, she fell into the job by accident. At the age of 37 she was recently divorced, with two young children. Before her marriage, she'd been a secretary and worked in human resources, then she sold cosmetics online so she could work from home. Then one day, Tony Imossi, a private investigator and ABI president, asked, 'Have you ever considered being a PI?' Sam had known Tony for years, and had always been interested in his job, 'Maybe because I'm a bit of a busy body. The job sounded cool; I loved the intrigue that went with it. I think I've always wanted to appear a tough woman.' Sam opens a bottle of water and takes a sip. 'It's also a fantastic talking point, when people ask me what I do, and I tell them; straight away they want to ask questions.'

'And do you mind that?'

Sam smiles, 'I love it!'

She started by studying for the BTEC Level 3 award, then ABI members began to offer small jobs, such as a drive-by on a property, after which she filed a report. 'ABI members help each other,' she explains. 'There's an assignment list, and we're located all over the country.'

While Sam talks, I can see her eyes scanning people coming in and out of the coffee shop. 'Do you ever switch off?' I ask.

'Oh yes,' she says.

Sam Cooper is a very attentive listener, and she focuses closely on my replies to her questions. But I get the feeling she's providing only the information that is necessary, and not giving much away about her background or life before she became a PI. Her company has a registered address, but that's not where the agency is based, and she doesn't ever disclose where she lives. But at least she's agreed to meet me, because ever since I sat the BTEC exam I've been trying without success to find a PI who will let me watch her at work.

In 2018 Sam started her own firm, Private Investigations Ltd. One of her first cases was a client whose landlord had disappeared with rent money. She tracked him down and gave the address to the client's solicitor. 'I love tracing,' she says. 'I recently had a case with two people who'd lost contact forty-eight years ago. I reconnected them, and to me, that's the best.'

'So, how do you find people?'

'It's all about knowing where to look,' says Sam. 'I can take information and make sense of it, like you can take words and turn them into a book.'

'Did you always have this skill?'

'No!' she laughs. 'When people ask what skills make a good PI, my usual, flippant, answer is "I'm female and I'm nosey". But on the way here to meet you, I was thinking about it, and I realised, I like game playing, I love puzzles and I also love understanding how things work.'

Sam explains that she asks a series of questions before she agrees to take on a client who suspects their partner is cheating. She wants to know if they're married, if they live together, if they own property together and if they have children. If they do, then the outcome of the case may involve a legal battle. If the answer to everything is no, then she tells them, 'I can't help you. You *want* to know, but you don't *need* to know.'

Sam was recently approached by a woman whose partner is having an affair. 'She knows who he's having it with, she knows the address, but she needs photographic evidence. I asked her, why does she need the proof?'

Last week, a woman called about her ex-boyfriend. 'She doesn't trust him,' says Sam, 'but I can't help if it's only curiosity. They need a legitimate reason. People think because they're going to pay me, I have to do it.'

'What about tracing people,' I ask. 'How do you approach that?'

'Well,' Sam takes another sip of water, 'if I'm doing a trace, like finding an estranged father, then I have to explain that I can't give a client my findings until I have the consent from the person I'm tracing. If they say, "Oh, he'll never consent", then it suggests something is not OK. If you need to find someone, then why? I need to think about the potential risks of harm to the individual. I don't want to read about someone being attacked because I've traced them and shared their personal details.'

'But how can you tell if there is a legitimate reason?'

Sam shrugs, 'It's instinct.'

'If I asked you to trace someone, what would you say?'

Sam leans forward across the coffee shop table. 'I always need to check who my client is. So, the first thing I'd say is, "Caitlin, I need some ID from you".'

I laugh and put my notebook down. 'Do you think it's true that women make the best PIs?'

Sam nods. 'I've heard men in the industry say they can do surveillance better than women because they can sit in a car for hours and just pee in a bottle. I would say I can justify sitting in a car much better than a man. If someone asks what I'm doing …' Sam suddenly turns into the perfect imitation of a flustered woman, tilting her face and fluttering her hands, 'I just say to them, "oh, sorry! I think my husband's cheating on me, in that house over there …" Then I point in the opposite direction to the house I'm watching.'

I laugh again, she's very skilful at transforming her character and I think of all the female sleuths from the past who dreamt of making it on the stage. 'Did you ever want to act?'

'I *never* liked acting,' says Sam, 'but I like thinking on my feet. You can plan twenty-five scenarios about what will happen and what you're going to say on someone's doorstep, but only one will ever fit.'

'Is that quite scary?'

'If I overthink,' says Sam, 'that's when I scare myself.'

In 2018, she launched another company, Rogue Daters, after a client had been scammed for money by someone she'd met online. 'It made me remember back to when my kids were young,' says Sam, 'and wanting them to be safe and worrying about bringing someone else, a man, into the family home.'

Rogue Daters covers dating sites, as well as social media platforms such as Facebook, messaging services and games apps with chat functions. Some scammers are professionals, she explains, some are chancers, and some are organised crime. The usual targets are men or women over the age of 45. 'They will have been working, they may own property, their kids might have left home. They might be due their private pension or have inherited from a family member; they could be a widow or widower. They're re-entering the social dating world, but they weren't born into technology, they might not be as shrewd.'

Sam sees two types of clients. Some turn to her before they've been scammed, 'They have a doubt, a niggle in the back of their mind. They're wondering if the person is too good to be true.' Sometimes, it's family members who are concerned, or the client wants to prove to their family that they've found a genuine relationship. Then there are those who turn to Rogue Daters after they've already been exploited. 'It's hard to reclaim money,' says Sam, 'but I'll try. I make a report that they can take to the police. But I never give false hope. Someone came to me after they lost £300,000. Looking at the information the woman had, I could have stopped it before she parted with any money!' Sam sighs and finishes her bottle of water. 'I'm not after the scammers; they move on, my aim is preventative.'

She describes her clients as hurt, financially and emotionally, but 'they come to me and they trust me, I think that's lovely. They say, "You've given me hope; I needed to tell someone." I love the human interaction. I have no legal background, and I'm not a psychologist, I'm *not* emotionally attached but I do care.'

'What would you do,' I ask, 'if I told you my 86-year-old father is online dating and I'm worried he's been giving a woman money?'

Sam looks serious. 'I would ask, "What does your father think?" And I would need evidence that money has been sent.'

She doesn't want to go into the details of her processes, but she cites a 2020 report from Action Fraud, which has recorded a rise in romance fraud in the UK, with total reported losses of over £68 million. Sam says the true figure is higher as many people are too embarrassed to report what's happened. During Covid lockdowns, more people started using online dating agencies. 'They're at home,' says Sam. 'They're not socialising. They're looking for romance, for companionship.'

According to Crimestoppers, gay men are disproportionately targeted by romance fraudsters, making up 12.4 per cent of all victims in 2021. Scammers use dating apps such as Grindr and Tinder, asking for cash and trying to get personal information such as passports. There have also been threats of 'outing'.

In 2019 Pink Detective was launched 'specifically to cater for members of the lesbian, gay and transgender communities', reported *The Scotsman*, and offered protection to people being threatened with 'exposure' and blackmail. In one case, a client discovered that a man had filmed him with a camera hidden behind a wardrobe and then put it up on a pay-for-view website. The client had turned to private detectives rather than the police, the man was tracked down and 'persuaded to remove the footage'.

Other scammers use methods that are a century old. In 2022, 'Bradley', a 27-year-old in London, joined a dating website where he met a man called 'Alfie'. They exchanged numbers and swapped photos and then, explained *Pink News*, Alfie said he wanted to visit Bradley in London. But he was a carer for his mother, and couldn't afford the train fare, so Bradley sent him £150.

Alfie missed the train, and then he stopped responding to texts, so Bradley turned to PI Alison Marsh, who runs Miss AM Investigations in Oxford. She soon tracked Alfie down and discovered he'd used fake social media profiles and photographs to scam numerous men – just like the 'intelligent, attractive young lady' in the early 1900s who'd promised a 'delightful tête-à-tête' – asked for travel expenses and then disappeared.

Sam Cooper encourages people to run background checks early on, to know who they are connecting with online, such as searching their name online and running a reverse image search on their profile photo to see if it's been taken from somewhere else. Scammers tend to construct elaborate stories about their lifestyle. They may travel a lot, deal in gold or diamonds, describe themselves as a doctor, businessperson or soldier.

Then suddenly – like Mrs H and the stockbroker conman in the 1920s – they're in trouble and need urgent help. A business transaction has gone wrong, they're held up in customs, they need emergency medical care.

Scammers make their targets feel guilty if they don't part with their money, and Sam stresses that the victims aren't foolish, naive, or stupid, 'They've just let down their guard looking for love, companionship, romance'.

'Do you think I could come with you on a job?' I suddenly blurt out. 'Could I sit in the car while you're watching or following someone?'

'If you bring sweets,' Sam laughs.

'What sort of sweets?'

'Anything, as long as it's sweet. And crisps, bring crisps.'

'So, I could come on a job with you?'

Sam looks serious. 'I would have to get the OK from the client. I'd have to ask if they were OK if I had a journalist with me.'

'You wouldn't need to say journalist,' I say. 'I'd be doing it because of this book. I think journalist would make people run a mile.'

'Yes,' she nods, 'it would.'

I think of all the journalists who covered the exploits of Kate Easton, Maud West and Annette Kerner, and the reporters who went along for the ride with Zena Scott-Archer as she drove around Liverpool in her leopard-skin coat. But modern PIs, as Val McDermid discovered in the 1990s, are much warier of the press. Confidentiality and data protection are far more protected, and professionals follow the rules. I don't think many of Sam Cooper's forebears would go to the same lengths to find out if a client had a legitimate reason for an investigation, request consent from a person she's tracing or question why someone wanted photographic evidence of an affair.

Sam does appear in the media, and she asks her clients' permission before she shares their anonymous stories. She's been on BBC's *For Love or Money*, a consumer series focusing on online dating scams. She'd like to write a weekly column for a magazine or newspaper and a book on how to avoid being scammed online.

'What else would you do,' I ask, 'if you weren't a PI?'

Sam thinks for a while. 'I would love to be an usher in a courtroom. I did jury service, and I would love that.'

'An usher?' I'm surprised. 'I can imagine you more as a magistrate.'

She laughs. 'I love the end bit, when the jury find someone guilty and then they introduce extra evidence, and you see the verdict was right.'

'Do you think your work has changed your view on human nature?'

'No, because there are a lot of good people out there.'

'Has it made you tougher?'

'No,' says Sam. 'It's more that it's made me understand myself. I'm not flaky. People say, "You must be really brave". And I think, "Really, do you think so?" Although I'm definitely more ballsy than I've ever been; partly it's because of the job.'

She says there are more women in the field now, and it's slowly increasing. Sam recently spent a year as Membership Chair for the ABI, interviewing people applying to join. But overall numbers are still low. Of the 388 members listed in the ABI website directory, I estimate that roughly twenty-five are women – still around 6 per cent, just as it was twenty years ago.

The coffee shop is getting busy now and we can't talk without being overheard, so we end our chat and get up to leave. We go back down the Brent Cross escalator amid all the afternoon shoppers, and part outside W.H. Smith. 'Make sure you do let me see a copy of what you write,' says Sam. Then she adds with a slight smile, 'I don't want to come looking for you.'

★ ★ ★

On the bus home I wonder if any of Sam's clients will let me go on a job with her. It seems unlikely. The nature of her work means the cases are personal – tracing lost relatives, gathering evidence of affairs, investigating online romance frauds.

It's proving impossible to find anyone who will let me accompany them on the job. The case officer who I sat the exam with doesn't want to be identified, while Jen Jarvie deals with highly sensitive cold-case murders. I've already contacted ten female PIs in London, but only one replied, and, ultimately, she was not able to help. I've also emailed The Lady Private Investigators Ltd in Surrey, which describes itself as a 100 per cent woman-owned business, but they're too busy, 'We receive a lot of requests and interest from the media. It's tricky because we are a tiny company and do not have the luxury of time.'

So now I contact half a dozen more PIs, and while two initially agree to an interview, they then stop replying to my emails. If it's difficult finding out about female private eyes from the past, it's equally hard getting access to modern PIs. Gone are the days when I could have responded to an advert in a personal column, turned up at the given address, knocked on the agency's plate-glass door and greeted the female detective inside.

The job remains underground, and now with the internet, it can be even more anonymous. PIs don't welcome outsiders and considering the portrayal of 'private dicks' in the press, it's no wonder they aren't keen to talk. But I can't believe that, after all this time, I've failed to find a single female PI who will let me visit her at work.

37

THE ART OF SHADOWING

I'm walking down Cattle Market Street in Norwich, heading away from the city's medieval castle and down towards Rose Lane. I'm looking for No. 40 and it's not hard to spot. I can see a teal-coloured sign from a few hundred feet away. It could be a solicitor's office or a private health clinic, perhaps, set on a busy road alongside a petrol station, pub, tattoo parlour and a large block of flats and offices.

As I get nearer, I can read the sign – Taylor Investigations. The front windows are half-frosted and etched with the services on offer: Person Tracing, Asset Tracing, Surveillance, Background Investigations, Digital Forensics, Family Trees. It is both highly visible – a private inquiry agency right in the heart of an East Anglian city – and yet it's also discreet, and there is no mention of the word 'detective' at all.

I ring the buzzer and Jamie North, investigator and client account representative, lets me in. Inside it's cool and clean, an open-plan office with a map of the world painted on one wall, alongside a row of certificates. Jamie's boss, Charlotte Notley, is standing by a shelving unit, busy unpacking a hamper. 'Hmm,' she says. 'Does that look like cheese? I told them not to pack cheese.'

'What's the hamper for?' I ask.

'It's going to be a lucky prize dip,' says Charlotte. 'We have a stall at a business fair this weekend.' It's early July, we're in the middle of a heatwave and she doesn't want anything to melt.

It's been over a year since I passed my professional investigators Level 3 award, and I've finally found a woman who will let me visit her. Charlotte Notley is unusual, she's following in the footsteps of her trailblazing forebears by deliberately setting up shop where people can find her. She wants the public to know the ways in which a PI can help, to take away the air of mystery that's always been associated with private investigators and to bring the profession into the mainstream. Unlike her twentieth-century forebears, however, who freely invited journalists into their offices and regaled them with daring detective tales, she's asked me to sign a Non-Disclosure Agreement, to ensure any confidential information is kept out of this book.

Charlotte's been on Rose Lane for just under six months, and on opening day her team served eight legal documents and took on four cases. Before this, her agency was based in a business park on the outskirts of a nearby market town. Now she's just a short walk from Prince of Wales Road, home to most of Norwich's legal and financial service companies, while the offices opposite house solicitors and accountancy firms. I ask Charlotte why there's no mention of 'detective' on her shop front or on the windows.

'Because I *hate* the word,' she says.

'Really? Why?'

Charlotte shrugs. 'It just doesn't sit well with me. People say, "private detective" and then they say, "private dick". The image is of an old, disgruntled man with a chip on his shoulder and a jaded view of the world.'

The 31-year-old, who set up her company six years ago and is now on the ABI's Governing Council, couldn't be more different. I glance at an array of marketing flyers on a bookshelf, printed with the agency's motto: 'There's only one truth.' I pick one up. 'Are you looking for some-one?' it asks – using the same sort of question private detectives have been employing since the 1900s.

Taylor Investigations is carefully branded. The company logo is teal, like the sign outside, and the office is coordinated to match, from velvet-covered chairs to filing cabinets, penholders, mouse mats and Charlotte's bright-blue flip-flops and aqua nail varnish. She sits down at her desk, one arm resting on the top in a way that makes me think of a police officer. Every time I glance up, I see a huge, blown-up image on the back wall – a woman's face half-hidden behind a camera.

Charlotte is from Kent, and originally wanted to be a primary school teacher. Then she took sociology at A Level, which included a criminology module, '"Cor," I thought. "I really like this." They were the only lessons I turned up to.'

She was interested in the reasons why people commit crime and went on to study criminology at Sheffield University. In her first year, she witnessed an incident with another student and was interviewed by the police. 'They said you can recall information quite well. Have you ever thought of joining the police?'

She hadn't, but Charlotte later took a module in policing and crime, and again she was praised for her skill at retaining information and observing. 'I can keep rational,' she explains. 'If someone comes in with a gun, I don't panic, I don't react, I observe.'

'Like a Rottweiler,' I say. 'They like to assess what's going on first.'

Charlotte grimaces. 'I've been called a Rottweiler three times. Once by a man who owed a debt, and twice while serving papers. I've been told I'm hard or cold, and I've been called a "tart in sheep's clothing".'

'What?' I ask. 'Who said that?'

'It was a man at a networking event,' says Charlotte. 'He asked what I did and when I said I was an investigator he said, "Like a private dick". I said, "No, no one says that any more." Then he said, "So a tart in sheep's clothing then".'

However far female sleuths have come in the last century and a half, they're still reduced to honey trappers.

After university, Charlotte joined South Yorkshire Police but in 2015, after five years in the force, she put in for a transfer to be closer to home. As she waited to start her new posting, she decided she'd had enough. 'I have a short fuse. I don't like wasting time; I don't want to do something if I can't see the benefit.'

Charlotte had never come across any mention of private detective work, either during A Levels, at university or while in the police force. But one day, she was talking to a friend of her mother's, a process server who was also ex-police. She started looking into what he did 'and I thought, wow, there's a whole new industry out there that I knew nothing about'. So, Charlotte spent £30 on a logo design, £100 for a website and £20 for business cards, and along with a laptop and a sofa she was ready to run her business from home.

She got her first job through a networking business group. 'I was asked to serve divorce papers. My motto is, say yes to everything and work out how to do it later.' She'd taken a short online course and talked to a friend who'd completed the UKPIN diploma in private investigation, and she knocked on a door, handed a man the papers and left.

Her first person trace was a client in France, who contacted her through her website. His wife had died, and he wanted to find his first love in England. He provided some vague information about the woman's husband and his connections to Norwich, and it took Charlotte nearly five months to track the man down. When she did, she discovered his wife had died three years earlier. 'My client was crying on the phone,' she says. 'It was very emotional. But I was able to tell him that his first love had often spoken about him.'

Charlotte's wristwatch pings, and she glances at it before continuing. 'I charged £200 for that trace. At first, I wanted to help everyone, but is that economically viable for a five-month job? No.'

'Do you see yourself primarily as a businessperson?'

'No,' says Charlotte, 'not at all. But these days, I won't pick up a pen until a price has been agreed. I'm not social services or the cops; I am running a business. That's what I'm like now.'

Her watch pings again.

'What's that?' I ask.

'I get an alert when someone uses the live chat on our website.'

'How often does that happen?'

Charlotte starts scrolling through her phone, 'Since midnight, there have been thirty alerts.'

Taylor Investigations' website promises availability twenty-four hours a day, seven days a week. It lists their services and prices – a desktop trace starts at £60 plus VAT – and Charlotte is keen to disprove the idea that hiring a PI is very expensive.

A recent website inquiry came from a loan company with 200 debtors they wanted traced. But her work comes mainly through word of mouth, and especially through local business networking. The most common cases are process serving and personal tracing. 'There's been an increase in debt-related cases,' Charlotte says. 'We've recently served over £10 million in debt, and that was just on four people.'

When it comes to personal tracing then, like Sam Cooper, her first task is to check if it's a viable request, and she too relies on 'gut instinct'. A couple of weeks ago, a man wanted his ex-wife watched, alleging she was using drugs in front of their child. He said he'd paid £4,000 for a three-week surveillance with four people working twelve hours a day. Charlotte was suspicious; the cost for that would be nearer £20,000. She told him to go to a solicitor.

But she enjoys tracing. In one case, a client had been searching for her biological mother for eleven years and had hired four other PIs without success. It took Charlotte eighteen months. 'When I phoned to tell her, she cried, and I cried.' Over this past weekend, she's had a request from China – a family member has gone missing in the UK.

'Are there any jobs you won't do?'

'Honey trapping,' she says at once. 'Although there are people who would do that.'

'So, what will you be doing today?'

Charlotte gestures at her computer screen, 'I don't do surveillance myself these days, I'm too busy, most of my work is office based. So, I'll be answering a thousand emails. But,' she says, 'Jamie can take you out.'

Jamie North obligingly gets up from his desk. 'What would you like to do?'

'Shadowing,' I say at once. It's the classic job for a private eye, and I want to know how it's done.

Jamie fetches the agency's camera, and we leave the office and step back into the heat of the day. He joined Taylor Investigations two years ago. Having arrived for a business admin interview, he explained he really wanted to become a PI. Charlotte calls him 'Jamie the Enforcer'. He's also a semi-professional footballer, who plays for Gorleston Football Club.

Jamie is currently being trained by one of Charlotte's three surveillance experts, a senior investigator and ex-military man who can't be named. First, he spent the day shadowing Jamie, then he gave a full report on everything Jamie had done, where he went, who he'd met and what he'd eaten. 'It's crazy what he can pick up,' says Jamie. 'He took photos of every stage of my day, and at no point had I been aware I was being followed.'

Jamie's first proper case was a man who'd claimed he was incapacitated and unable to work. An Australian agency contacted Taylor's and wanted the man watched. Jamie spent two hours in a car, feeling conspicuous, sitting 100m from the target's house on a track road with only four houses. 'Then, it was so unexpected, the man came out of his house … and started walking his dog. I was ecstatic.'

Jamie believes his youth works in his favour; he's 27 and people never expect him to be a PI. 'If you have a trained background,' he explains, 'like a cop or the army, you stand out. It's the way you walk.' I've already noticed that Jamie has a remarkably relaxed way of walking; a leisurely stroll that would never draw undue attention. 'We'll pick someone,' he says. 'It's an awkward time, lunchtime, but let's see what happens.'

I've lost track of the direction we've taken, I've only been in Norwich once before, but we seem to be skirting away from the castle and now we're heading up a hill. 'Does it matter that I've got a notebook and pen in my hand?' I ask. 'Isn't that going to draw attention?'

Jamie shakes his head. He advises me to keep around 10 metres behind whoever I'm following and not to get too close. If the target stops, then it's fine to walk past them. 'Her,' he says.

Ahead is a woman in a bright red flowered dress, with blonde hair and carrying a white handbag. I'm not sure I want to follow a woman, but it's only an exercise, and despite what Jamie's just told me, I find myself speeding up. The woman keeps walking and then she seems to change her mind. It looks as if she's about to turn a corner. What if we can't see where she's going?

Normally surveillance would be done in pairs, Jamie explains, so at this point I'd move to the opposite side of the road for a better view. The woman turns left, and we continue uphill, dodging tourists and shoppers. But then suddenly she makes a right and my heart sinks – she's going into John Lewis. How am I going to follow someone in a busy department store? But, on the other hand, she will be hard to lose in her bright red dress.

Jamie has caught up with me and we enter the store, pausing by a rack of scarves. From the corner of my eye, I can see the woman heading left. We've lost her, I think, but Jamie knows the store layout and as we walk on, she soon reappears.

'Sometimes,' he says, 'it's good to stop and look at something.' We stand in front of a display of toys and Jamie appears to be very interested in a 3D puzzle. But I'm acutely aware that I'm supposed to be surreptitiously watching someone, and every time the woman glances our way, I have the impulse to duck my head.

'It's OK if people see you,' says Jamie. 'Once or twice, but not more than that.'

I'm looking at the puzzles, writing in my notebook and glancing up to check on the woman – and she's gone.

'At the cashpoint,' says Jamie quietly.

I look around, and there she is, further to the right, taking out money. If this was a proper job, then I should check the machine to see if she's left a receipt. I'd also have to make a report about what she was looking at, Jamie explains, what she bought and what it cost.

'What was she looking at?' I ask, because I've no idea.

'Suede shoes,' says Jamie.

'Oh,' I whisper, 'She's disappeared again.'

But Jamie nods to his left, and there she is, on an escalator heading upstairs.

I'm feeling disappointed. I thought I was observant and that it would be easier than this.

'Hey!' says a woman, moving to stand in front of us as we're about to leave John Lewis. Has she seen me acting suspiciously and wants to know what I'm doing? She has a name tag round her neck and seems to be selling beauty products. 'You have *such* beautiful eyes,' she says to Jamie. 'Sorry, but you really do have such beautiful eyes. I just had to stop you and tell you!'

Jamie gives me more advice as we set off walking around Norwich again. It's important not to panic. Phones get you out of trouble a lot – people don't think anything about someone being glued to their phone. We come to a busy retail street and pass a cheap shoe shop. If a shop is tight inside, says Jamie, it's better to stay outside and use the windows to watch.

'Can we follow someone else?' I ask.

Jamie nods. 'You choose.'

'Let's do a man,' I say. 'Him.'

Ahead of us is a man in his 40s, wearing shorts and carrying a rucksack on his back. Jamie falls back in order to shadow me, and I set off to follow. I hesitate as my target comes to a road. My impulse is to stand beside him but instead I hover nearby. The man seems impatient; he starts to cross even though the light is red. Again, I hesitate, then rush after him across the road. The man turns left into a Sainsbury's Local, and I follow him in and down to the end of an aisle. He starts looking at lunchtime meal deals.

This is going to be easy: I'm going to be able to say exactly what he's done and what sandwich he's bought for lunch. But then the man moves on and turns down another aisle. I follow, pause halfway and pick up an apple, then I can go to the till along with the man. But what if he isn't going to the till? I put the apple down, where has my target gone? He's back at the sandwiches again. He picks one up, puts it back, walks halfway down the aisle and then returns.

I glance behind me. Jamie is standing casually at the end of an aisle, apparently intent on his phone. When I look back, the man has disappeared. Where's he gone? I look down every aisle – and he's nowhere to be seen.

Furious with myself, we leave the shop. 'He was dithering,' I say. 'He was acting erratically.'

Jamie nods, 'Counter surveillance.'

'Sorry?'

'That's the way someone acts if they think they're being followed, and they want to throw you off.'

We both agree that the man didn't appear to think I was shadowing him, but I realise I wasn't properly focused. I was too busy imagining, who was the man? What was in his rucksack? Where was he going? I should have stayed outside the shop, and simply watched through the windows. Don't read into things, Jamie tells me. Just stick to the facts, such as what time the man went into the shop. But I have no idea what the time is at all.

'Let's do another,' I say.

There's a stocky, muscular man on the pavement ahead, wearing black trousers and a blue T-shirt, a phone in his hand. He's walking quickly so I speed up. He seems to be on a mission, rushing along Market Avenue, and when I glance right, I can see the road will soon lead down into an underpass. But if I felt uncomfortable following the woman, and a little uneasy following the man with the rucksack, now I'm intent on my job. It's nothing personal, I just need to follow this man.

My target reaches a crossing with traffic lights, and suddenly veers across the road. There's a car coming so I'm stuck, and when I eventually cross, it's just in time to see the man disappearing down an empty alleyway. I look behind for Jamie, but somehow, he's already on the same side of the road as me. 'You don't want to follow him down there,' he warns. 'He's going to a block of flats and you will stick out.'

Private detectives have always stressed how hard it is to shadow someone. Maud West found the job 'unpleasant' and Anne Summer described it as the 'most difficult and nerve wracking' part of her work. 'It is not every woman,' wrote police detective Lilian Wyles, 'who can undertake this arduous duty.' Barbara Macy warned me just recently that TV programmes make it look straightforward, 'People think that following people is easy, it isn't.'

But still, I can't believe how useless I've been. I've just failed to follow three different people round Norwich. It's also a bit addictive, however, and the challenge makes me want to do it again – and to next time succeed.

★ ★ ★

When we return to Taylor Investigations, Charlotte Notley is inspecting a group of very large parcels in the entranceway. 'Evidence boxes,' she says. 'Just arrived.'

'Evidence about what?' I ask.

'It's an insolvency case.' Charlotte picks up one of the boxes and checks it's secure. 'We often get hired by insolvency practitioners, to investigate the assets of a director when a company goes into liquidation, if there's suspicion of fraud or director wrongdoing. We also get instructed on provisional liquidations and we go in with a team under a search-and-seize order.'

Charlotte checks another box. 'This one is a huge multimillion-pound fraud investigation. When we got there, there were dozens of phones, even more computers, and lots of servers. We were on site for seven days, but we've been working on the case for nine months. We seize all the equipment and the digital data. I love that sort of job.'

Charlotte sits down at her desk, and I notice an invitation to a summer garden party from a local firm of financial planners has just arrived. I ask if anyone has come into the office since we've been out. 'Just our IT support person,' says Charlotte. 'People don't often come in. They say, "I walked past your office and I didn't have the balls to come in".'

'Why?'

'Because it's often personal,' Charlotte says, 'and because they're nervous. They've never spoken to a PI before; they don't know what questions they will be asked.'

Not long ago, a local solicitor did come into the office. 'She brought an old lady, who said there were people in her loft. We get a lot of "My neighbours are spying on me, they're bugging me". Some PIs have taken thousands of pounds off people to "debug" their homes.'

'We had one woman,' adds Jamie, 'she said her neighbours were firing lasers of her face into the sky.'

Private detectives have always received inquiries like these, and such clients are vulnerable to exploitation. Sydney Scott described people who were 'suffering persecution mania' in the 1940s, sending thirty-page letters 'explaining their woes in almost undecipherable handwriting'. May Greenhalgh was once summoned to a London suburb to find an elderly woman enveloped in white rubber sheeting with white rubber helmet and boots. She thought her neighbours were plotting to electrocute her by pushing live electric wires through the walls and floors.

In the 1960s, *Tatler* reported that every agency in Britain was constantly pestered by people with 'imagined problems and persecutions' and most firms received two such cases a week. Unscrupulous agencies took the client's money and 'pretended that they really had made a thorough search through Ealing for Napoleon or Jack the Ripper'.

'A lot of people who consult private investigators are barmy,' declared Zena Scott-Archer in the 1970s. 'I try not to take their money from them because their quest is futile.' One client wanted Zena to follow her husband because she believed he was having an affair with the woman next door. 'I asked her why she thought this, and she said, "My hat, which is always on the pillow of a night, is moved in the morning – isn't that proof enough?"' In another case, a woman insisted her friend was stealing all her new furniture and replacing it with exact replicas, including the kitchen sink.

Barbara Macy recalls a client who said that every time she went to T.J. Hughes department store in Liverpool, all the security guards converged on her and she was escorted from the building. Barbara was employed to follow her every day for a week, 'Nothing happened. I stopped doing it. I just didn't have the time.'

I'm just telling Charlotte about some of these cases when the office phone rings and Jamie answers it. 'She's in a meeting,' I hear him say. 'I'm an investigator, if I can help?'

The caller must be reassured. When Jamie puts down the phone, he explains a client wants him to serve divorce papers. The Divorce,

Dissolution and Separation Act 2020, which recently came into force and applies to England and Wales, is the first major change in divorce laws for fifty years. Petitioners who are married or in a civil partnership no longer have to prove any 'fault', provide evidence of adultery or unreasonable behaviour or wait until they've been separated for years. Instead, they produce a statement that the relationship has irretrievably broken down. If the couple agree about children, money and property, then they usually don't need to attend court either. But private detectives are still hired to serve papers, and there are regular requests for PIs to deliver divorce documents on the UKPIN forum.

Like most investigation agencies, Taylor's work is very varied. One client wanted surveillance on a CEO to find out where he took his morning coffee, so they could strike up a conversation and try to interest him in a contract. Another wanted to know someone's day-to-day route, so they could put up sandwich boards advertising their product. A TV company hired Charlotte to investigate someone in a documentary; a beauty brand was concerned about theft of stock; while a PR agency wanted investigations for people in the public eye. People often want to know who is behind an Instagram account or harassing them online, and she's also handling a current case for an African government.

Charlotte doesn't call herself 'Norfolk's Leading Woman Detective', as Kate Easton would have done, but people often come to her because she's a woman. 'I think they feel more comfortable,' she says, 'especially if it's family related. But half the time they say they've contacted me because they want a woman, and I have no idea why, it doesn't relate to the case at all.' Charlotte smiles and rests her arm on the desk. 'I understand the struggles of women in the industry, but I don't want to play on it, I don't want to give it airtime. I won't let being a woman define me, or the decisions I make in the business. People often say, "I can't believe how well you've done." Would they say that to a man? I don't play on being a woman, or that it's harder being a woman – although of course it is.' As far as she knows, she is one of only fifteen women to own and run a private detective agency in Britain.

Charlotte takes me upstairs to look at the second floor, where there's an office for an investigator and a meeting room with framed press reports on the wall. In the corner I spy a magnifying glass in an open wooden box. 'Where did you get that?'

Charlotte laughs, 'The Sherlock Holmes Museum in London.'

'You did?'

'Yes,' Charlotte nods. 'I bought it from the gift shop. I had a good look around the museum, then I put my business card in his study.'

'Really?' I laugh and pick up the magnifying glass.

'There's a noticeboard,' Charlotte explains, 'just as you go into Sherlock's study, with old-fashioned cards. So, I put one for Taylor Investigations right in the middle.'

She shows me a picture on her phone and there it is, an advert for a modern woman's detective agency nestling between fake Victorian memorabilia.

I put the magnifying glass back in the box, feeling I've come full circle. A year and a half ago, I was wandering around the Sherlock Holmes Museum on Baker Street trying to find clues to the history of private detectives. Now I've finally spent the day with a real-life PI.

'Do you think the job has changed you?' I ask.

Charlotte's watch pings and she smiles. 'I've become a lot more cynical.'

'A lot more cynical about what?'

'About everybody. I don't trust anyone. But,' her watch pings again, 'I love this job. The satisfaction when you crack a case is just amazing.'

38

THE BEST DISGUISE
IS A WOMAN

How do you find out the truth about female private detectives, when the nature of undercover work is to remain undetected? Historically, women have been very skilled at hiding themselves, and they've also been hidden by the men who employed them. And what a motley crew they were: Inspector Charles Field, who bored spyholes in doors; Henry Slater, the expert in secret watchings; Henry Clarke, imprisoned for perverting the course of justice; Maurice Moser, who stood trial for assaulting his partner; and Charles Kersey, convicted fraudster and trainer of lady detectives. All of them furthered their own careers by employing and promoting female sleuths, but the history of the women themselves is far more secretive.

Female detectives have always been a bit of a mystery, ever since the fictional 'Miss Gladden', who declined to reveal anything about herself, not even her name. Who was Mrs Jenkins, 'the pioneer of female detectives' who helped catch the American coiners in the 1850s? Or what about Clubnose, employed by Scotland Yard to infiltrate criminal gangs, equipped with her magic whistle? Were these women real or just creatures of journalistic fantasy?

As the nineteenth century progressed, female detectives became more visible. Their names, and sometimes their images, appeared in the press, their words reported as they gave evidence in court trials.

By the early twentieth century, women were launching their own detective agencies, writing true crime tales in the nation's best-selling newspapers, and soon they became household names. But as high profile as they were, the women had such a habit of embellishment that their identities can be just as difficult to unravel. 'All detective stories are games of let's pretend,' writes Julian Symons, and female sleuths have certainly loved to pretend. They've changed their names, their class and their backgrounds. They've lied about their ages, places of birth and marital status. They've disguised themselves while out on a job and taken on a whole new persona for the press.

'What you do in this world is a matter of no consequence,' Sherlock Holmes tells Dr Watson in *A Study in Scarlet*. 'The question is, what can you make people believe that you have done.' And these female sleuths asked people to believe in all sorts of far-fetched things. Private detection was the perfect place in which to reinvent themselves.

When I set out to investigate Annette Kerner, the self-styled Mrs Sherlock Holmes of Baker Street, I didn't know that a lot of her memoir would turn out to be nonsense. Yet her ambitions, motivations and experiences closely echo those of so many other women who came before and after her. They had different social backgrounds and worked in very different times – whether the position of women, attitudes to divorce, the state of formal policing or laws about privacy. But from the 1850s to the present day, they have had an awful lot in common.

Few ever expressed a burning desire to be a private detective. Instead, they often fell into the job by accident – agreeing to help police constable husbands or solicitor friends, starting out as copying clerks, typists, secretaries, assistants and then sometimes buying the agency. Many initially dreamed of acting, others did have a stage career, however short-lived. Sleuthing gave them the chance to hone their performance skills, because being a private detective meant playing at being different people all the time. 'It is more than acting,' Annette Kerner explained. 'It is like having to write your own script and act it, all on the spur of the moment.'

Some of the women were driven by circumstances and desperate for work, others were attracted to the job because of the human element. But whatever their reasons, they all loved being a private detective, however difficult, mundane, tiring or dangerous. It gave them respect, excitement and confidence – they became their own boss, hiring men, giving orders and sending their male agents into the field. Where else could they have found this sort of work?

But fighting crime didn't fit with a lady's true nature – she was too sensitive, emotional and irrational – and female detectives were repeatedly asked if they were up to the job. Male sleuths were never asked if their work was hindered by the fact they were men, nor what particular masculine skills they brought to the job. No one asked what their wives thought, whether they had children or who did the housework. Detection didn't sit well with women's assigned role as wife and mother – and yet real private detectives have always managed to balance investigation with domestic life, and some turned it into a family affair.

Female sleuths not only had to prove their capabilities, they also had to defend their morals. There has always been a sleaziness associated with the job, and particularly women's role within it. Did undercover work really suit a woman who was 'morally all that she ought to be'?

The British press were happy to encourage female sleuths – printing their adverts, serialising their tales, telling readers they were the 'best known' and 'most famous' lady detective in the world. But they also derided, patronised and laughed at them, cast aspersions, questioned their morals and sexed them up. Male sleuths might be gumshoes or derring-do action heroes, women were grandmotherly Miss Marples or honey trappers.

Private detection was a distinctly male profession and the 'female toughs' who succeeded showed themselves 'capable of a man's work'. They were also portrayed as versions of a man – 'Miss' or 'Mrs' Sherlock Holmes, or a 'female James Bond'.

Modern PIs are still subjected to assumptions and prejudice. Charlotte Notley describes attending a General Data Protection Regulation (GDPR) conference when a man told her, 'I think you have the wrong room. The beauty conference is down the corridor.' At the same time, however, there has always been a belief that women are actually *better* at private detection than men.

Ever since Victorian times, we've been credited with being more observant and painstaking, paying closer attention to detail and being more likely to diffuse conflict. We can 'penetrate' domestic spaces and find it easier to pass unnoticed, especially if we're older. Female PIs still have the element of surprise in their favour because no one suspects what they do for a living. Women sleuths have been deliberately subverting other people's low expectations for over a century, in order to do the job.

They have also relied heavily on feminine intuition or 'mother wit' – an instinct, 'gut feeling', hunch or 'sixth sense' that tells them what to do. A woman's powers of intuition were a great asset, argued Victorian Antonia Moser, while May Storey insisted a woman could 'feel the presence of the wrong-doer'. Zena Scott-Archer credited her first successful job as 'a guts thing', the modern-day case officer uses her instinct to come to conclusions; Sam Cooper trusts her instinct when she decides to take on an investigation, and so does Charlotte Notley. But a 'woman's instinct', as Agatha Christie argued in the 1920s, 'is in any case a very debatable thing. We use the phrase glibly enough, but when we really come down to facts, what, after all, does it mean?'

In the nineteenth century, instinct was a peculiarly feminine trait, a miraculous gift that enabled the 'power of seeing implications'. Sherlock Holmes may have possessed a 'kind of intuition', but it was not of the feminine variety. Modern scientists are still intrigued by the idea of intuition, and just as eager to search out differences between men's and women's brains. Women are apparently hardwired to be more intuitive: our brains move back and forth between the right side, where intuition operates, and the more logical left side of the brain. Men, on the other hand, stay in the logic zone.

However, the notion of a 'male' and a 'female' brain is a myth, argues Gina Rippon in *The Gendered Brain*. It has been used to justify misogyny since the nineteenth century, and to promote the theory that 'male' brains are ideally suited to science. But brains change and adapt. They're influenced by our surroundings, experiences and how we're brought up. Our brains are continually making guesses, responding to information and coming up with predictions – even in adulthood.

So, do women really have better intuition because our brains are wired differently, or is 'feminine instinct' a result of the societies in which we live? Modern PIs often define intuition as the ability to make rapid decisions, but they too see it as a skill that is characteristic to women.

If women *are* so well suited to the job of private detection, if we are so observant and intuitive, then why has the number of female investigators declined so markedly over the past century? Was it really the incessant work, the uncertain and unsociable hours and the potential for danger? Or were women just squeezed out by men who felt threatened by their capabilities?

'It is said that men are jealous of women treading on their grounds,' wrote Antonia Moser in 1905, 'and that they try in every way to thwart any effort a woman may make out of the beaten track.' There has certainly been rivalry. Antonia fought a bitter battle with her former mentor, Maurice Moser, and one male sleuth was so enraged at Kate Easton's employment that he warned the very woman he was supposed to be watching. Tracking down criminals was 'regarded as a man's job', May Storey complained, 'and men, I might add, have taken good care to see that such work remains in their own hands'.

Today, however, the number of women does seem to be growing. Membership of UKPIN, the open network group, is 20 per cent female, according to Philip Smith, and he estimates the same applies to the industry in the UK as a whole. 'I'm delighted to say that over the past twenty-plus years, there has been a steady year-on-year increase in female entrants,' says Ian D. Withers, a founder of the World Association of Professional Investigators (WAPI), formed in 1999. 'In the United States, the female PI ratio has increased at an explosive rate, with some of the very best and most skilled PIs being the ladies'. In 2000, only 2 per cent of WAPI members were female, now it's 10 per cent, while membership of their open eGroup has grown from zero to 20 per cent.

'There has definitely been an increase in interest from women,' says Glyn Evans, Secretary General of the Institute of Professional Investigators (IPI). 'I've seen the numbers coming in from our courses.' In 2022, an impressive 30 per cent of those starting the IPI's Skills for Justice Level 3 Professional Investigators Course were women. 'They come from all walks of life,' explains Glyn. 'They might have left school and be wondering what to do, they might have watched Miss Marple on TV and think they fancy trying it. Some have a natural talent for detection, others see it as a stepping stone to the police or law enforcement, and for many, the work fits their work/life balance. Women might also think, just like their male counterparts, that it's quite a sexy business – which it's not.'

The IPI's newer members include Verity Henton Private Investigations, launched by two former policewomen in Essex in 2020. Sam Hutchinson and Emma Coles say they are 'trying to change the face of the industry' and report a 'massive' increase in client inquiries, partly because many people 'just don't trust the police'. The reputation of the Met Police, the largest force in the UK, is particularly dire when it comes to protecting women and girls. In Baroness Casey's recent review into the culture of the Met, following the abduction, rape and murder of Sarah Everard by serving police officer Wayne Couzens, she condemned the force as institutionally misogynistic, racist and homophobic.

Will lack of trust in the police lead more people to private investigators – and especially female PIs? And if the numbers of women in private detection continue to rise, could female sleuths regain the place they once held? Will a new generation of women see death investigator Jen Jarvie on TV or walk past Charlotte Notley's very public agency in Norwich and think, 'I could do that'?

'The world of security has evolved,' explains Siti Subaidah Naidu, former president of the World Association of Detectives, 'and the tools and technology used in information gathering have advanced. Today we see more and more women entering into areas of information security, cyber security, business continuity, and internal controls.' The industry is also less dominated by ex-police – who now make up around 65 per cent of PIs – and there is far more variety when it comes to women sleuths in popular culture.

One thing, however, has remained the same. PIs in Britain are still not licensed. Private detectives have been calling for regulation ever since Harry Smale formed the BDA in 1913 and vowed to make it a clean profession. The issue of licensing has been raised each time there's a scandal, whether phone hacking or police corruption.

The latest came in October 2022, when several public figures announced they were suing Associated Newspapers Ltd over 'gross breaches of privacy'. Prince Harry's lawyers have alleged 'abhorrent criminal activity', including investigators hired to bug homes and cars, and record private phone conversations. There are also claims that PIs obtained details of medical records on other complainants, intercepted live phone calls and monitored bank accounts and phone bills. Associated Newspapers has dismissed the allegations as 'preposterous smears'.

So why has regulation still not happened? Tony Imossi, current ABI Secretariat and former president, gives two reasons. 'First of all,' he says, 'it's a relatively small industry, and secondly, it's too difficult to regulate. Nobody really understands what we do, and how to catch the bad guys.' But Tony believes that data protection has provided a new opportunity.

'We have to wake up to the fact this is what we do for a living, day in and day out, we process personal data, this is our bread and butter.'

The existence of GDPR means there's an increasing need for codes of conduct, and for the past three years the ABI has been working on a draft code for investigators, along with the Information Commissioner's Office. 'Although it's a voluntary scheme, code membership is the closest to regulation this industry has ever got,' says Tony. Code members, for example, will be audited once a year by an accredited independent body, and they will have to show the lawful reasons for their investigations. Tony believes the success of a code will rest in the hands of the legal profession, which represents the largest source of instructions for investigators.

The old rivalry between the IPI and the ABI has tempered over the years, and both want the profession regulated, but the IPI argues the code is not inclusive enough and benefits the ABI. 'We're all in favour of anything that brings professionalism to the business,' says Glyn Evans. 'The problem is, it's all voluntary, it's not enforceable and its focus is data protection. It doesn't include tackling and eradicating rogue traders, for example.' WAPI has similar concerns and wants to see 'a more equitable alternative option'.

It is still remarkably easy to become a PI in the UK, or at least to call yourself one. In Spain, private detectives need a three-year university degree to get a licence, while the Republic of Ireland introduced business licensing in 2017. But in the UK, there are no requirements at all.

I studied the Level 3 and the diploma to try to understand the job, not to start an agency, but already I've been offered work. I received a message from someone looking for a 'woman private eye' to find their child. They'd already paid two PIs, and now they wanted 'an honest person'. At a recent book festival, a man in the audience asked for my business card and explained he was a solicitor and often employed PIs. But it's also a hard industry to break into – a lot depends on networking. There is no set route and few, if any, opportunities for work experience.

When I first started researching this book, I assumed the job of a private detective meant following people and finding evidence of affairs. But it's an industry with such breadth and variety, whether corporate investigations, tracing missing people, probate, computer forensics, family trees, criminal defence, digital and crypto currencies, online catfishing or cold-case murders.

I've been surprised at the passion with which the women talk about their work. They may complain about the grind and the hours spent sitting in cars or sifting through information, but they also cite the buzz and excitement, and the satisfaction they get when a puzzle is solved. Private investigators 'are not peeping toms,' says Siti Subaidah Naidu. 'We don't walk around like spies or secret agents like the movies portray. Our role is to help businesses make informed strategic decisions, to help build families, not destroy them. It is a respectable profession.'

But I don't know if I'm cut out to be a PI. If I can't even manage to shadow someone for more than fifteen minutes in Norwich, then I should probably stick to investigating women from the past. Although, if I had a call from Rogue Daters or Taylor Investigations asking for help preventing a romance scam, reuniting a parent and child or solving a multimillion-pound fraud, I'd probably leap at the chance. And I wouldn't need to conceal myself or don a deerstalker hat or trench coat and trilby, because I already have the best disguise – I'm a woman, and as the history of private detection shows, I therefore have a distinct advantage when it comes to making private inquiries.

SOURCES

The main sources available on each private detective are listed below, with a brief selection of newspaper articles. Other sources include birth and death certificates, census records, wills, electoral rolls, marriage certificates, the 1939 Register, baptism records, deed polls, probate records, trade directories and Post Office directories.

I'm grateful to Professor Louise A. Jackson, author of 'The Unusual Case of "Mrs Sherlock": Memoir, Identity and the "Real" Woman Private Detective in Twentieth Century Britain', in *Gender & History*, Volume 15, Issue 1, January 2003; Dr Nell Darby, author of *Sister Sleuths: Female Detectives in Britain* (Pen & Sword, 2021); and Susannah Stapleton, author of *The Adventures of Maud West, Lady Detective: Secrets and Lies in the Golden Age of Crime* (Picador, 2019). Their work provided information and inspiration for many of the chapters below.

Useful Websites

Ancestry: www.ancestry.co.uk
The Association of British Investigators: www.theabi.org.uk
The British Newspaper Archive: www.britishnewspaperarchive.co.uk
British Pathé: www.britishpathe.com
Find My Past: www.findmypast.co.uk
FreeBMD: www.freebmd.org.uk
Newspaper Archive: newspaperarchive.com
The Proceedings of the Old Bailey, 1674–1913: www.oldbaileyonline.org
'Secret Sleuths', Dr Nell Darby: substack.com/profile/1380015-dr-nell-darby
Women's Rights Collection, The Women's Library, LSE: digital.library.lse.ac.uk/
    collections/suffrage

Prologue

Kerner, Annette, 'I Trapped the "Con" Man at the Back Door of the Bank', *The People*, 25 September 1949.

Kerner, Annette, 'The Case of the £100,000 Trickster' from *Woman Detective* (Werner Laurie, 1954).

Chapter 1

Doyle, Arthur Conan, 'A Study in Scarlet', in *The Complete Sherlock Holmes Long Stories* (John Murray, 1959).

Horsburgh, Frances, 'Lesley Takes Sherlock Under Her Umbrella', *Aberdeen Press and Journal*, 16 August 1974.

The Sherlock Holmes Museum: www.sherlock-holmes.co.uk

Chapter 2

Bluemoon College: bluemooncollege.co.uk

Imossi, Tony, 'Licensing Investigation in the Private Sector' (ABI, 2019).

'Private Investigators', Home Affairs Committee Fourth Report, 2012–13: publications. parliament.uk/pa/cm201213/cmselect/cmhaff/100/10002.htm

Chapter 3

Banerjee, Jacqueline, 'Inspector Bucket Points the Way': www.victorianweb.org/authors/dickens/bleakhouse/bucket.html

Dickens, Charles, 'A Detective Police Party', *Household Words*, Volume 1, Number 18, 27 July 1850: Dickens Journals Online: www.djo.org.uk

Dickens, Charles, 'On Duty with Inspector Field', *Household Words*, Volume 3, Number 64, 14 June 1851: Dickens Journals Online: www.djo.org.uk

'Evans V. Robinson – Crim.Con', *The Times*, 4 April 1855.

Goddard, Henry, *Memoirs of a Bow Street Runner* (Quaystone Books, 2022).

Kesselman, Bryan, *Paddington Pollaky, Private Detective* (The History Press, 2015).

'A Memoir of Inspector Field', *The Illustrated Times*, 2 February 1856.

'My First Capture of Coiners by the First Female Detective', told by ex-chief inspector Cavanagh, *Penny Illustrated Paper*, 4 August 1894.

Potter, Russell, 'Inspector Charles Frederick Field': w3.ric.edu/faculty/rpotter/chasfield.html

Slater, Michael, *Dickens' Journalism Volume II: 'The Amusements of the People' and Other Papers: Reports, Essays and Reviews, 1834–51* (J.M. Dent/Orion Publishing Group, 1996).

Takayanagi, Dr Mari, 'Jane Campbell: Parliamentary Divorce Pioneer': thehistoryofparliament.wordpress.com/2016/10/05/jane-campbell-parliamentary-divorce-pioneer

The Vidocq Society: www.vidocq.org

'The Word Detective': www.word-detective.com/2009/11/detective

Chapter 4

British Transport Police History Group: www.btphg.org.uk

'Capture of a Thief at Bishopsgate Station', *Suffolk Chronicle*, 8 December 1855.

'Clever Arrest by a Female Detective', *Newcastle Guardian*, 24 April 1869.

Coles, Nigel, 'Sarah Batcheldor', research based on report in *Liverpool Standard*, 28 July 1835.

Dickens, Charles, *Bleak House* (Penguin Classics, 2003).

Enss, Chris, *The Pinks: The First Women Detectives, Operatives, and Spies with the Pinkerton National Detective Agency* (TwoDot, 2017).

Pinkerton, Allan, *The Expressman and the Detective* (W.B. Keen, Cooke & Co., 1874).

Pinkerton, Allan, *The Spy of the Rebellion: True History of the Spy System of the United States Army during the Civil War* (CreateSpace, 2016).

'Plodd in the Square Mile': www.ploddinthesquaremile.co.uk/the-stations-of-the-city-of-london-police

Police History Society: www.policehistorysociety.com

'Stealing Sugar from the West India Dock', *Morning Advertiser*, 17 January 1860.

'Walks Through the Grand Exhibition', *Morning Advertiser*, 8 May 1851.

'A Welsh Relieving-Officer Superseded by his Wife', *Liverpool Mercury*, 1857.

Chapter 5

Ellis, Edward, *Ruth the Betrayer; or, The Female Spy* (Gale digital collections, the British Library, 1863).

'A Female Detective', *Leicester Daily Post*, 17 March 1877.

Forrester, Andrew, *The Female Detective* (British Library Crime Classics, 2014).

Hayward, William Stephens, *Revelations of a Lady Detective* (British Library, 2013).

'Studies from Life – "Clubnose"', *Chamber's Journal of Popular Literature, Science and Arts* (W&R Chambers, 1879).

Chapter 6

Allen, Grant, 'Power of Women's Intuition', *Toronto Saturday Night*, 12 July 1890.

'A Chat with a Woman Police Spy', *Newry Telegraph,* 24 July 1894.

Cobbe, Frances Power, 'To the Editor of the Times', *The Times*, 11 October 1888.

Davidson, Mrs H. Coleman, *What Our Daughters Can Do for Themselves: A Handbook of Women's Employments* (Forgotten Books, 2018).

'Female Detective', *Leytonstone Express*, 1 December 1877.

'The May Magazines', *Glasgow Herald*, 11 May 1893.

Merrick, Leonard, *Mr. Bazalgette's Agent*, with an introduction by Mike Ashley (The British Library, 2013).

Pirkis, Catherine Louisa, *The Experiences of Loveday Brooke, Lady Detective* (Hutchinson & Co., 1894).

Rennison, Nick, *Sherlock's Sisters: Stories from the Golden Age of the Female Detective* (No Exit Press, 2020).

Ward, L.F., 'Female Intuition', in L.F. Ward, *The Psychic Factors of Civilization* (Ginn & Company, 1893).

'Women as Detectives', *Aberdeen Evening Express*, 18 October 1888.

Chapter 7

Ally Sloper's Half-Holiday, 18 October 1890.

'The Barrett Affair', *Leeds Times*, 2 March 1895.

'County of London Prisoners for Trial, England & Wales, Crime, Prisons & Punishment, 1770–1935': www.findmypast.co.uk

'The Divorce Conspiracy', *Derby Daily Telegraph*, 2 April 1895.

'Police Intelligence', *London Evening Standard*, 8 July 1892.

'Police Intelligence', *London Evening Standard*, 7 February 1895.

'Sensational Sequel to a Divorce Case', *Westminster Gazette*, 14 January 1895.

'The Strange Sequel to a Divorce Case', *Lloyd's Weekly*, 27 January 1895.

Trial of Ellen Lyon, Old Bailey Proceedings Online, March 1895.

Chapter 9

Papers relating to the Mosers' and Williamsons' divorces can be found at the National Archives: Court for Divorce and Matrimonial Causes, later Supreme Court of Judicature: Divorce and Matrimonial Causes Files, J 77: Reference numbers J 77/447/3639, J 77/484/14738, J 77/433/3201.

'Female Detectives at Work', *Flintshire Observer*, 6 March 1890.

Higginbotham, Peter, 'The History of the Workhouse': www.workhouses.org.uk

Moser, Maurice, *Stories from Scotland Yard*, recorded by Charles F. Rideal (Gale, Making of Modern Law, 2010).

Showalter, Elaine, 'Victorian Women and Insanity' in *Victorian Studies*, Volume 23, Number 2 (1980): www.jstor.org/stable/3827084

Wagner, A., and Antony Dale, *The Wagners of Brighton* (Phillimore & Co. Ltd, 1983).

'Women as Detectives', *St James Gazette*, 3 August 1889.

Chapter 10

Papers relating to Antonia Moser's bankruptcy and businesses can be found at the National Archives: BT 226/2488, BT 31/13518/114126, BT 31/18658/100808.

Antonia Moser's case stories appeared under 'The Adventures of a Woman Detective' in the *Weekly Dispatch*, 1907:
'The Case of the Foreign Nobleman', 2 June.
'The Gentleman Cracksman', 9 June.
'The First of the Gold Brick Swindle', 23 June.
'A Case of Identity', 30 June.
'The Lady Who Disappeared', 7 July.
'A Criminal by Instinct', 14 July.

Other stories and letters by Antonia Moser:
'Wife's Strange Story', *London Daily News*, 24 October 1902.
'Watching a Wife', *Sheffield Independent*, 5 March 1909.
'A Millionaire as Burglar', *Reynolds's Newspaper*, 4 July 1909.
'Women's Suffrage', *Harrow Observer*, 29 March 1912.
'The Suffering of Women', *The Referee*, 7 April 1912.
'Women As Detectives, "Often Better than a Man"', *The London Standard*, 4 January 1913.
'Man's Duty Towards Woman', *Pall Mall Gazette*, 20 August 1913.
'A United Demand', *The Vote*, 12 June 1914.
'Capital v. Labour', *West London Observer*, 24 January 1919.

Crawford, Elizabeth, 'Suffrage Stories: "Laura Grey": Suffragettes, Sex-Poison and Suicide', *Woman and her Sphere*: womanandhersphere.com

Crawford, Elizabeth, *The Women's Suffrage Movement: A Reference Guide 1866–1928* (Routledge, 2000).

Chapter 11

'A Baronet's Divorce Action', *The Belfast Newsletter*, 21 June 1904.

Cox, Alex, '5 Defiant Suffrage Statements Found in the 1911 Census', July 2020, www.findmypast.co.uk/blog/discoveries/suffragettes-in-the-1911-census

'The Lady Detective', *American Register*, 27 November 1910.

'Lady Detective', *Lloyd's Weekly*, 19 May 1907.

'Madeleine Lucette', The D'Oyly Carte Opera Company: gsarchive.net/whowaswho/L/LucetteMadeleine.htm

'Maud West Woman Detective', *San Francisco Call*, 3 August 1913.

'My Work as a Lady Detective', *London Mainly About People*, 5 February 1910.

'Tea Party Damage', *Evening News*, 23 May 1913.

'Why I Shadow People', *Pearson's Weekly*, 4 May 1911.

Chapter 12

'Female Detectives at Work', *Leicester Daily Post*, 4 March 1890.

'Lady Detective's Adventures', *The People*, 25 January 1914.

'Lady's Visit to West-End Store', *Pall Mall Gazette*, 8 March 1913.

'The Secret Service at Selfridges', *Daily Herald*, 10 March 1913.

Tickell, Shelley, *Shoplifting in Eighteenth-Century London* (The Boydell Press, 2018).

'We Take Off Our Hat To', *The Sketch*, 28 January 1914.

Chapter 13

'Baronet's Divorce Suit', *Sheffield Daily Telegraph*, 20 June 1903.

Darby, Nell, 'The Clairvoyants Who Failed to Tell Their Own Fortunes': criminal-historian.wordpress.com

'Indignant Palmist', *Mirror*, 11 August 1904.

'Lady Detective and Wizard', *Mirror*, 18 August 1904.

'Married Lady's Letters from Lover', *Manchester Courier*, 20 June 1903.

McDonald, Brian, *Alice Diamond and the Forty Elephants: The Female Gang that Terrorised London* (Milo Books, 2015).

'The Palmists' Trial', *Daily Mirror*, 6 October 1904.

'Professional Cards', *The Stage*, 16 November 1911.

'Provincial Theatricals', *The Era*, 3 November 1906.

'Provincial Theatricals', *The Era*, 15 January 1910.

'Society Wizards in Court', *Mirror*, 4 October 1904.

'Trial of West-End Palmists', *Penny Illustrated Paper*, 15 October 1904.

'Trial of the West End Palmists', *St James Gazette*, 4 October 1904.
'West-End Palmists', *The Globe*, 18 August 1904.
'West End Wizards', *Manchester Courier*, 10 August 1904.

Chapter 14

Jackson, Louise A., '"Lady Cops" and "Decoy Doras": Gender, Surveillance and the Construction of Urban Knowledge 1919–59', *London Journal*, Volume 27, 2002.
Jackson, Louise A., *Women Police: Gender, Welfare and Surveillance in the Twentieth Century* (Manchester University Press, 2006).
'A Lady Copper', *Free Church Suffrage Times*, 1 July 1915.
Lock, Joan, *The British Policewoman* (Robert Hale, 1979).
Newman, Kathryn, 'A Policing Pioneer', *Newsletter of Lancashire Archives*, June 2019.
Orczy, Baroness, *Lady Molly of Scotland Yard* (House of Stratus, 2008).
Staveley-Wadham, Rose, 'Policing Pioneers: A Look at the History of the Women's Police Service', The British Newspaper Archive blog, 25 February 2021.
'Training School for Women Police', *Common Cause*, 1 October 1915.
'Women Police Marching Single File in Hyde Park', *Leeds Mercury*, 10 December 1914.

Chapter 15

'Divorce since 1900', UK Parliament: www.parliament.uk/business/publications/research/olympic-britain/housing-and-home-life/split-pairs
'Girls Trained as Detectives', *Sunday Post*, 24 April 1927.
International Police and Detective Directory 1922, San Francisco General Efficiency Company (Forgotten Books, 2019).
'Ju-Jitsu UK History': bjjagb.com/jujitsu-uk-history
'The Woman in Blue', *Britannia and Eve*, 1 December 1931.
'A Woman Detective on her Work', *Weekly Dispatch*, 8 May 1925.
'Women Private Investigators', *British Pathé*, 1927.
'Woman 'Tecs of Baker Street', *The Graphic*, 30 April 1927.

Chapter 17

'Alleged Shoplifter for Trial', *Dundee Evening Telegraph*, 10 September 1928.
'Bogus Detective Agency', *Sunderland Daily Echo*, 7 May 1912.
'"Detectives" who blackmail and cheat their clients', *Weekly Dispatch*, 19 January 1936.
'Love Affair Leads to Arrest of Wanted Man', *Sunday Post*, 29 November 1925.

Marsden, Michael, 'The Work of Private Detectives', *The Lancashire Evening Post*, 22 April 1935.
'Memory Feats of a Woman Sleuth', *Daily Mirror*, 20 October 1934.
'Shoplifting Charge', *Norwood News*, 14 July 1933.

Chapter 18

Articles by May Storey, 1932:
    'Sleuthing is a Great Career for Girls', *Birmingham Gazette*, 9 January.
    'Give the Woman Sleuth a Chance', *Sunday Mercury*, 6 March.
    'Drama in a Midland Mansion', *Sunday Mercury*, 1 May.

Articles by May Storey, 1933:
    'The Legion of the Lost', *Sunday Mercury*, 5 February.
    'A Cracker Party as I Saw it', *Sunday Mercury*, 12 February.
    'The Worst Man I Ever Tackled', *Sunday Mercury*, 26 February.
    'Wife's Lover Thrashed with Whip', *Sunday Mercury*, 12 March.
    'Wily Women Criminals', *Sunday Mercury*, 11 June.
    'Tragedies of our Divorce Laws', *Nottingham Journal*, 12 July.

Billington-Grieg, Teresa, 'The Truth About White Slavery', *English Review*, June 1913.
'Burradon and Northumberland Past': www.burradonhistory.co.uk
'Girl Detectives of the "Yard"', *Sunderland Daily Echo*, 17 August 1933.
'The Girl Victim', *Sunday Dispatch*, 8 October 1933.
'Her Lost Speech', *Reynolds's Newspaper*, 9 December 1934.
Lammasniemi, Laura, 'Anti-White Slavery Legislation and its Legacies in England' in *Anti-Trafficking Review*, Issue 9, 2017: www.antitraffickingreview.org
'May Storey', The National Portrait Gallery, www.npg.org.uk/collections/search/person/mp165710/may-storey
Oram, Alison, 'Experiments in Gender: Women and Masculine Dress': www.english-heritage.org.uk/learn/histories/women-in-history/experiments-in-gender

Chapter 19

Bean, Henry, 'People Today', *News Chronicle*, 24 November 1938.
Christie, Agatha, 'Does a Woman's Instinct Make Her a Good Detective?', *The Star*, 14 May 1928.
Christie, Agatha, *Murder, She Said*, edited and introduced by Tony Medawar (HarperCollins, 2019).

Christie, Agatha, *The Murder at the Vicarage* (HarperCollins, 2016).

Keene, Carolyn, *The Secret of the Old Clock: Nancy Drew Mystery Stories* (Simon & Schuster, 1930).

'Life of a Woman Detective', *The Recorder*, 28 January 1932.

'Modern Girls Who Take to Crime for Kick to Be Got in it', *Kingston Gleaner*, 25 June 1931.

'Secrets of a Woman Detective', *Sunday Pictorial*, 3 April 1938.

West, Maud, 'War Spies I Caught', *Sunday Dispatch*, 22 November 1931.

'Woman's 33 Years as a Detective', *Adelaide News*, 29 December 1938.

Chapter 20

'An Assiduous Worker for a War Fund', *The Sketch*, 7 August 1918.

'A Bankrupt Who Earned £12 Per Week', *Acton Gazette*, 17 July 1914.

Bland, Lucy, *Modern Women on Trial: Sexual Transgression in the Age of the Flapper* (Manchester University Press, 2013).

Kerner, Annette, *Further Adventures of a Woman Detective* (Werner Laurie, 1955).

Kohn, Marek, *Dope Girls: The Birth of the British Drug Underground* (Granta Books, 2003).

'The Ladies' Guild', *The Stage*, 3 April 1924.

Lalwan, Rory, 'Jewish community in Soho': www.sohomemories.org.uk/page_id__41.aspx

'Miss Annie Symons', *Tatler*, 7 August 1918.

O'Day, Rosemary, 'The Jews of London: From Diaspora to Whitechapel', Fathom at LSE: fathom.lse.ac.uk/Features/122537

'Our Portrait Gallery', *The Stage*, 4 September 1924.

'Persecuting the Jews', *Lisburn Standard*, 9 August 1890.

'War Worker', *Sunday Mirror*, 21 July 1918.

Chapter 21

Papers relating to Annette Kerner's divorce can be found at the National Archives: J 77/3567/621 Divorce Court File: 621.

Trixie Etheridge's police warrant can be found at: MEPO4/351.

Annette's casebook tales in *The People*, 1949:

    'The Case of the Haunted Murderer', 18 September.

    'I Trapped the "Con" Man at the Back Door of the Bank', 25 September.

    'Divorce Was My Business Too', 2 October.

'I Set a Telephone Trap for the Blackmailer', 9 October.
'How I Trapped the Rogues Who Prey on Film-Struck Girls with Flattery', 16 October.
'I Put My Microscope on Her Broken Romance and Solved it', 23 October.

Jackson, Stanley, 'Mrs Sherlock Holmes', *Melbourne Argus*, 20 November 1946.
'"People in Camera": Home Guard Police Fight Crime Wave', British Pathé, 1946.
Smith, Ron, 'Pathé': fomphc.com/wp-content/uploads/2019/03/
   Pathe-News-Guide.pdf
'Women's Realm', *West Australian*, 4 October 1946.

Chapter 22

Annette Kerner's bankruptcy papers can be found at the National Archives:
   B 9/1476, and BT 226/5611.

'Ex-detective Cleared,' *Daily News*, 11 March 1952.
'Film Studios Club', *The Stage*, 18 August 1949.
'I'm No Nark, She Says', *Daily Mirror*, 11 March 1952.
'She Lost £500 at a Sitting', *Daily Mirror*, 2 June 1934.
'Woman Private Detective Cleared', *Marylebone Mercury*, 14 March 1952.

Chapter 23

Carteret, 'From a Londoner's Notebook', *West London Observer*, 9 July 1954.
'Echo Bookshelf', *Liverpool Echo*, 16 March 1954.
'Marriage and Divorce', Hansard, HL Deb, 24 October 1956: api.parliament.uk/
   historic-hansard/lords/1956/oct/24/marriage-and-divorce
'Meet Britain's Famous "Mrs. Sherlock Holmes"', *Sydney Morning Herald*, 1 April 1954.
'Private Eye', *Oxford Reference*: www.oxfordreference.com
'She Hunted Dope Pedlars and Blackmailers', *Marylebone Mercury*, 10 December 1954.
Taohy, Ferdinand, 'Private Detectives Are Thriving', *Britannia and Eve*, 1 June 1950.
Thompson, Victor, 'Personal Piece', *Daily Herald*, 8 May 1957.
'Woman Detective', *Birmingham Daily Post*, 18 March 1954.

Chapter 24

'Cecilia Green': www.russellflint.net/russellflint-cecilia.html

Craig, Zoe, 'When Wardour Street Was "Film Row"':
londonist.com/london/history/when-wardour-street-was-film-row

'Death Sentence Verdict for Road Accident', *Westminster & Pimlico News*,
19 October 1962.

'Film Justice Talk for Children', *Kinematograph Weekly*, 25 June 1953.

'Jack Finberg', *Kinematograph Weekly*, 19 June 1952.

'Jules Simmons Joins Louis Jackson', *Kinematograph Weekly*, 13 February 1941.

'Justice – and the Price of a Punch on the Nose', *Daily Mirror*, 11 June 1964.

London Beatles Store: www.beatlesstorelondon.co.uk.

'Men and Movements', *Kinematograph Weekly*, 3 November 1927.

Shirin Simmons: www.shirinsimmons.com/about.html

'Threadbare Boy', *Westminster & Pimlico News*, 20 July 1973.

'Verse and Worse', *Fulham Chronicle*, 1 March 1974.

Chapter 25

'Flying Squad's 80 m.p.h. Car', *Evening Telegraph*, 19 August 1927.

Graves, Charles, 'Private Detective, 1949', *Nottingham Evening Post*, 4 August 1949.

Jackson, Louise A., 'Interview with Mrs Zena Scott-Archer', 17 July 2000.
School of Cultural Studies, Leeds Metropolitan University.

'The Liverpool Blitz', Imperial War Museum: www.iwm.org.uk

'Liverpool Memories': www.liverpoolbidcompany.com/1940s-day-3-of-liverpool-
memories

'Merseyside Roundabout', *Echo*, 24 August 1951.

Petersen, Christian, 'Business Booming for the Private Detective', *Sunday Dispatch*,
1 May 1949.

'Private Sleuths Wage War on Swindle Agents', *Weekly Overseas Mail*, 12 January 1952.

Shelmerdine, Eric, 'Zena Scott-Archer', *ABI Investigator's Journal*, February 2009.

Smith, Noel E., 'Helmets, Handcuffs and Hoses: The Story of the Wallasey Police and
Fire Brigade': www.museumofpolicingincheshire.org.uk

Chapter 26

Chandler, Raymond, *The Long Good-Bye* (Hamish Hamilton, 1953).

'Detection for Her Is the Spice of Life', *Woman's Magazine*, 28 February 1959.

Elgin, George, 'Mrs "Private Eye" Has No Use for Fists and Guns', *Evening Express*,
11 June 1953.

'Have You Seen an Author?' *Daily Dispatch*, 2 May 1955.

'Her Perquisite', *Weekly Dispatch*, 5 December 1954.

Manifold, Charles, 'The Debs', *The People*, 7 July 1956.

The Private Investigator, Volume 1, June 1956.

'Private Sleuths Wage War on Swindle Agents', *Weekly Overseas Mail*,
    12 January 1952.

Waterhouse, Keith, 'On with a Tiara and Off to Work Goes Melodie',
    Daily Mirror, 29 August 1953.

'Zena is a Private Eyeful', *Reynolds's News*, 10 June 1956.

'Zena of Many Disguises', *Daily Herald*, 2 June 1954.

Chapter 27

'Comedian's Extra Turn', *Daily Record and Mail*, 30 September 1918.

United Kingdom Professional Investigators Network: ukpin.com

'Woman Agent Sues Dominic', *Sunday Mirror*, 1 May 1960.

Chapter 28

Lawrie, Belle, 'It's Not a Job for Women, Says Woman "Private Eye"', *The Journal*,
    12 October 1962.

Oughton, Frederick, *Ten Guineas a Day: A Portrait of the Private Detective*
    (John Long, 1961).

Peploe, Mark, 'The World of the Private Detective', *Tatler*, 1966.

Chapter 29

Cleave, Maureen, 'The Very Public Life of a Lady Private Eye', *Belfast Telegraph*,
    24 July 1965.

Dobson, Jean, 'Anne, the Private Eye, Clues Up the Fashion Set', *Daily Mirror*,
    28 February 1967.

Evans, John, 'Playing a Squalid Game of "I-Spy"', *Coventry Evening Telegraph*,
    2 January 1969.

Hills, Ann, 'Detection', *The Times*, 1 December 1967.

Howe, Hannah, 'Anne Summer: An Inspirational Woman':
    hannah-howe.com/tag/anne-summer

Marriott, Valeen, 'The Red-Headed Private Eye Who Knows What Goes on at the
    Bottom of a Hotel Bed', *Leicester Chronicle*, 27 December 1968.

'Private Investigators Bill', Hansard, 30 April 1969:
    api.parliament.uk/historic-hansard/commons/1969/apr/30/private-investigators
Summer, Anne, *But I Couldn't Do That!* (Souvenir Press, 1968).

Chapter 30

Adams, Penny, 'Britain Leads the World in Top-Class Women Sleuths – Who Laugh at
    Danger', *Herald Express*, 1 October 1970.
Brough, Harold, 'Zena and the Case of the Missing Thump', *Daily Post*, 7 July 1987.
'The Case of the Private Detective Who Met a Bigamist on a Train', *Frederick
    News-Post*, 30 June 1975.
'Crime is My Business', *Woman's Own*, 30 November 1974.
'Going Out with the Gumshoes', *Telegraph Sunday Magazine*, 31 July 1977.
Hamilton, Alex, 'Tales of a Private Eye', *Guardian Miscellany*, 30 April 1975.
James, P.D., *An Unsuitable Job for a Woman* (Faber & Faber, 1972).
'Meet a Sleuth Named Zena', *Daily Mail*, 23 November 1970.
'No Two Days Alike for "Sherlock" Zena', *Colorado Gazette Telegraph*, 22 August 1975.
Whited, Charles, 'Private Eyes Are "Nice Guys"', *News-Herald*, 28 November 1974.

Chapter 31

'The Art of Nosing Around', *Sunday Times Magazine*, 10 October 1982.
Bell, Lynne, *Sydney Morning Herald*, 28 August 1972.
Bowers, Fergal, 'Not Like the Telly 'Tecs', *Evening Herald*, 7 January 1986.
Checkland, Sarah Jane, 'The Elementary Rules of Spying', *The Times*,
    7 November 1983.
Diamond, Donagh, 'Sleuths with an "Eye" for Fashion', *Evening Herald*,
    28 January 1989.
Ellis, Edna, 'The Mrs Sherlock Holmes of Merseyside', *Liverpool Echo*, 18 March 1982.
'Englishwoman Will Receive Top Sleuth Post', *Las Vegas Sun*, 15 September 1981.
'Femininity, My Dear Watson', *Daily Mail*, 6 October 1981.
Gillingham, Syd, 'Zena Certainly is an Extraordinary Private Eye', *My Weekly*,
    November 1982.
Grafton, Sue, *'A' is for Alibi* (Holt, Rinehart and Winston, 1982).
'24 Hours in the Life of Zena Scott Archer: The Mrs Sherlock Holmes of Merseyside',
    Liverpool Echo, 18 March 1982.
Jones, Sylvia, 'Seedy Side of the Real Mike Hammers', *Daily Mirror*, 28 August 1986.
Mara, Sandra, *No Job for a Woman* (Poolbeg, 2008).
O'Kelly, Ita, 'Keeping a (Private) Eye on the Antics of Adulterous Husbands', *Irish
    Independent*, 27 February 1986.

Paretsky, Sara, *Indemnity Only* (Hodder, 1982).

'Private Eyes Share Ideas at Grand Lake Gathering', *The Joplin Globe*, 10 October 1985.

'Super-Sleuth Zena: The Female Touch Tracks Them Down', *The Wirral Globe*,
23 October 1980. Taylor, Carolyn, 'The Private Eye Who Wears a Leopard Skin
Coat', *Liverpool Echo*, 23 April 1981.

'The Top Private Eye is a Lady!', *Evening Star*, 13 October 1981.

'Where Marlowe is Non-starter and Sam Spade is Trumped', *Yorkshire Post*,
27 April 1981.

World Association of Detectives: www.wad.net

Chapter 32

Henderson, Alexandra, 'Love Spy', *Sunday Times Scotland*, 29 January 1995.

Judah, Hettie, 'Trust Me. I'm Just a Nice Little Old Lady', *Guardian*, 27 May 1999.

'Just Another Day in the Search of the Sleuth', *Daily Post*, 15 November 1994.

Larner, Tony, 'Yvonne Eyes Her Private Success', *Birmingham Weekly Mercury*,
29 November 1998.

McDermid, Val, *Dead Beat* (HarperCollins, 1992).

McDermid, Val, *A Suitable Job for a Woman: Inside the World of Women Private Eyes*
(Harper, 1995).

Miller, Peter, 'How to Set a Man Trap', *Sunday Life*, 17 July 1994.

'Real-life Miss Marple Detects Career in TV', *Daily Post*, 31 May 1999.

'A REAL-LIFE Miss Marple Has Been Named Britain's Top Private Eye', Feminist
Majority Foundation Blog, 26 May 1999.

'Real Miss Marple Wrinkles out the Bad Guys', *News of the World*, 30 May 1999.

Roberts, Jan, 'For Your Eyes Only', *Chronicle*, 12 December 1990.

Quartly, Jill, 'She Sleuths to Conquer', *Birmingham Post*, 11 March 1992.

Quartly, Jill, 'The Women Detectives Who Make Men Look Clueless', *Evening Sentinel*,
10 September 1991.

Chapter 33

Bird, Lyndsay, *Zena: The Housewives' Detective* (Matador, 2023).

'Sherlock Holmes Is Back in Baker Street', *The Sphere*, 2 June 1951.

'Sherlock Holmes Pub', British Pathé, 3 February 1958.

Sherlock Holmes Pub, London: www.londonspubs.com/sherlock-holmes-pub-london

Chapter 34

'Ann Heron Update – Discussion with Jen Jarvie', *The Unseen Podcast*, 29 April 2021:
   podtail.com/en/podcast/the-unseen-podcast/ann-heron-update-discussion-
   with-jen-jarvie

Corrigan, Naomi, 'Was Violent On-the-Run Prisoner Responsible for Ann's Death?',
   TeesideLive, 2 January 2022.

'Detective Agency Launches After Chance Meeting at York St John': www.yorksj.
   ac.uk/news/2023/jarvie-khan-investigations

Malton, Jackie, *The Real Prime Suspect*, with Helene Mulholland (Endeavour, 2022).

The Mysterious Murder of Ann Heron, Channel 5, August 2022.

Ridley, Mike, 'Murder Mystery', *Sun*, 5 April 2021.

Chapter 35

Barns, Sarah, 'Sex Spy', *Sun*, 22 July 2017.

Bhatia, Sidharth, 'Interview: "In an Increasingly Confrontational World, We Need
   Some Happiness and That's What My Books Provide"':
   thewire.in/books/alexander-mccall-smith-ladies-detective-agency-interview

Female Detectives, BBC World Service, 21 November 2020:
   www.bbc.co.uk/worldservice/people/highlights/001121_private.shtml

'India's First Woman Private Detective', *Huff Post*, 25 June 2017.

Jane, Rebecca, *The Real Lady Detective Agency* (HarperCollins, 2013).

'Kenya's Spy Queen', *BBC Africa Eye*, 25 January 2021.

Lion Investigation Services: lioninvestigations.co.uk

Parmar, Sheetal, *Undercover with the Asian Marriage Detectives*, BBC Asian Network,
   25 February 2016.

Prasad, Blessy Mathew, 'The Under "Cover" Life of a Private Eye', *New Indian Express*,
   10 October 2016.

Tiwari, Anuj, 'Meet Rajani Pandit', *India Times* (online), 18 June 2022.

Chapter 36

'Blackmail': www.pinkdetective.co.uk

Davis, Rachael, 'Meet the Catfish Hunter Who is an Expert at Spotting the Tell-Tale
   Signs You're Being Duped by a Fraud Online', *MyLondon*, 11 December 2021.

Hope, Lynsey, 'Conline Dating', *Sun*, 5 May 2020.

Milton, Josh, 'It's Not Just the Tinder Swindler: Sinister Romance Scammers are
   Ruining LGBT+ Lives', *Pink News*, 11 February 2022.

Miss AM Investigations: missaminvestigations.co.uk

'Pink Panthers Put a Tail on Anti-Gay Prejudice', *The Scotsman*, 28 February 2019.

Rogue Daters: www.roguedaters.co.uk

'Romance Scams on the Up During Lockdown': www.actionfraud.police.uk/fauxmance

'Tackling Romance Fraud', Crimestoppers: crimestoppers-uk.org/news-campaigns/campaigns/tackling-romance-fraud

Chapter 37

Briggs, Stacia, 'My Unusual Job: What's it Like to Be a Private Detective in Norfolk?' *Eastern Daily Press*, 24 March 2022.

Taylor Investigations: www.taylorinvestigations.co.uk

Chapter 38

The Baroness Casey Review: www.met.police.uk/police-forces/metropolitan-police/areas/about-us/about-the-met/bcr/baroness-casey-review

Institute of Professional Investigators: ipi.org.uk

Rippon, Gina, *The Gendered Brain: The New Neuroscience that Shatters the Myth of the Female Brain* (Vintage, 2020).

Sandford, Daniel, and Tom Symonds, 'Elton John and Prince Harry Sue *Daily Mail* Publisher over "Privacy Breach"': www.bbc.co.uk/news/uk-63164654

World Association of Professional Investigators: wapi.org

SELECT BIBLIOGRAPHY

Bingham, Adrian, and Martin Conboy, *Tabloid Century: The Popular Press in Britain, 1896 to the Present* (Peter Land Ltd, 2015).

Bredesen, Dagni A., 'On the Trail of the First Professional Female Detectives in British Fiction' (2010): thekeep.eiu.edu/women_faculty/3.

Clarke, Clare, *British Detective Fiction 1891–1901: The Successors to Sherlock Holmes* (Palgrave Macmillan, 2020).

Davies, Caitlin, *Bad Girls: The Rebels and Renegades of Holloway Prison* (John Murray, 2019).

Davies, Caitlin, *Queens of the Underworld* (The History Press, 2021).

Iron, Glenwood (ed.), *Feminism in Women's Detective Fiction* (University of Toronto Press, 1995).

Levine, Philippa, '"Walking the Streets in a Way No Decent Woman Should": Women Police in World War I', *The Journal of Modern History*, Volume 66, Number 1 (1994): www.jstor.org/stable/2124391.

Lombroso, Cesare, and Guglielmo Ferrero, *Criminal Woman: The Prostitute and the Normal Woman* (Duke University Press, 2004).

Nown, Graham, *Watching the Detectives: Life and Times of the Private Eye* (Grafton, 1991).

Rivers, Aileen A., *A Brief History of the Private Detective* (Association of British Investigators, 2009).

Seys, Genevieve L., '"Petticoated Police", "Intimate Watching" and "Private Agency(ies)": Reading the Female Detective of Fin-de-siècle British Literature' (2016): digital.library.adelaide.edu.au/dspace/bitstream/2440/113262/1/01front.pdf.

Shpayer-Makov, H., 'Revisiting the Detective Figure in Late Victorian and Edwardian Fiction: A View from the Perspective of Police History', *Law, Crime and History*, Volume 1, Number 2 (2011): pearl.plymouth.ac.uk/handle/10026.1/8867.

Stone, Lawrence, *Road to Divorce: England, 1530–1987* (Oxford University Press, 1990).

Symons, Julian, *Bloody Murder: From the Detective Story to the Crime Novel* (Penguin, 1985).

Wade, Stephen, *Plain Clothes and Sleuths: A History of Detectives in Britain* (The History Press, 2007).

Wyles, Lilian, *A Woman at Scotland Yard* (Faber & Faber, 1952).

ACKNOWLEDGEMENTS

Thank you to all the PIs who agreed to speak with me, the organisations who represent them and everyone who provided documents from their own research and allowed me to use personal photographs.

I'm indebted to Lyndsay Bird for her interviews, diary transcripts and wealth of photographs and press articles on Zena Scott-Archer – and to Marion Smith for her warm, witty emails and for allowing me to quote from her sister's diaries and use family photos.

Thanks to Martyn Goddard for allowing me to use his *Telegraph* photographs of Zena; the British Library Board and the British Newspaper Archive (www.britishnewspaperarchive.co.uk) for allowing the reproduction of their newspaper images; Richard Graham for answering numerous questions about Antonia Moser; Eric Shelmerdine for sharing his memories of Zena and providing documents and video clips; Professor Louise A. Jackson for sharing information on Inspector Wilson and the Werner Laurie archives; Alan Stephenson for his photo of Princes Building; and Dr Clare Clarke for her research into Maurice Moser. Her book, *Mr and Mrs Sherlock Holmes: The True Adventures of Moser and Moser, Victorian London's Most Scandalous Detective Duo*, will be published in 2024.

Thanks also to Plodd in the Square Mile; the Research Group of the British Transport Police History Group, and especially Martin Mckay; the Police History Society and especially Barry Walsh; Keith Foster, Nigel Coles, Alan Moss (www.historybytheyard. co.uk), Martin Baggoley and Dave Allen (bowstreetpolicestation.weebly.com); Martin Edwards, president of the Detection Club and archivist at the CWA; Susan Leggett at Bob O'Hara Public Record Searches for once again accompanying me on a very long journey into the past, and to Laura Perehinec, Publishing Director at The History Press, for putting women at the forefront.

INDEX

Note: *italicised* page references indicate illustrations

Alexander, Florence 90
American Register 80, *168*
Andrews, Eamonn 222
Argyll, Duchess of 203
arranged marriage detectives 266
Asian Private Investigation Firms 266
Asquith, Herbert 74–5
Association of British Detectives (ABD)
    200, 212, 214, 225, 227, 230,
    235–6, 251
Association of British Investigators (ABI)
    56–7, 235, 244, 245, 255, 256, 257,
    258, 260, 261, 269, 295
    training courses 17–18, 55, 56–7
    women in *176*, 235–6, 241–2, 255,
    256, 257, 260, 270, 275
The Avengers 218

Baker Street 11, 13–15, 107–8, 137, 181–3
Balmer, Brenda 244, 262
Barrett, Gertrude 49–51
Barrie, Gus (Samuel Harris) 202
Bell, Florence 128
Bendit, Dr Laurence J. 162
Betts, Annie (*née* Lange) 95–7, 99–100,
    262
Billington-Greig, Teresa 124
Bird, Lyndsay 250–4
Bluemoon College 17, 18, 21, 58, 113
Bluemoon Investigations 55, 56

Bond, James (fictional spy) 211, 212, 219,
    226, 233, 267, 291
Boström, Mattias 183–4
Bow Street Runners 25–6, 202
Britannia and Eve 107, 119, 160
British Detective Association (BDA)
    117–21, 136, 195, 200
Brooke, Loveday (fictional detective) 48,
    166, 231
Brough, Harold 229
Bryanston Street case 26–9
Butt, Clara 138

Calvert, Leonard and Charlotte 26
Campbell, Jane 26
Canon Street Murder (1866) 72
Carey, Elsie ('Lady Jack') 128
Cavanagh, Chief Inspector Timothy 24
Chandler & Co (TV show) 242
Chandler, Raymond 160, 200, 245
Chang, Brilliant 'Billy' (Chan Nan)
    142–4, 162
Charlie's Angels (film and TV show) 233,
    265
Christie, Agatha 132, 245, 292
Churchman cigarettes 127–8, *172*
City of London Police 32, 33
Claridge's 9, 150
Clarke, Clare 69
Clarke, Henry John 50–1, 289

Clayton, Will 55–6, 57–8, 113
Clifford, Naomi 183
Clubnose (Margaret Saunders) 39–41
Cobbe, Frances Power 44–5, 75
cocaine 110, 125, 142, 143
Colborne-Malpas, Yvonne *176*, 202–3
Coles, Emma 293
College for Feminine Undergraduates of
    Crime Investigation 107–8, *171*
Conan Doyle, Arthur 14, 15, 243, 245
Cooper, Sam *180*, 269–75, 292
Courts, Harriet 96
Crime Writers' Association's (CWA)
    161–2, 164
Criminal Investigation Department (CID)
    62, 105, 125, 126, 143, 213, 260
Cummings, Kathleen 214

Daily Mail 97, 98, 196
Daily Mirror 96, 120, 131, 153–4, *176*, 188,
    198, 221
Daily Telegraph 48, 82, 86
Darby, Nell 98, 261–2
Davies, Madame Clara Novello 138, 140,
    163
'death grip' 107, *171*
death investigations 257–63
Detection Club 133
Diamond, Alice 90, 100
Dick Barton – Special Agent (radio serial)
    160
Dickens, Charles 24, 71–2
disguise 9, 47, 86, 90, 91–2, 132, 147,
    149–50, 214, 220, 265, 296
    Annette Kerner 153, 161, 183
    as a man 86, 91, 108, 124, 149–50
    on the railways 31, 91
    store detectives 90, 120
    Zena Scott-Archer *177*, 191, 195, 229,
        236, 246–7, 255
divorce 159, 214, 219
    case numbers 118–19, 200, 213, 228
    document serving *170*, 201–3, 279,
        286–7
    legislation 26, 28, 43, 65, 76, 109, 119,
        125, 148–9, 222, 228, 261, 286–7
    obtaining evidence 26–7, 44, 49–51,

    52, 65–6, 81, 83, 91, 98, 118–19,
        132, 142, 147, 197–8, 227–8
The Divorce, Dissolution and Separation
    Act (2020) 286–7
The Divorce Reform Act (1969) 222
Docker, Lady Norah Royce 162–3
document serving *170*, 201–3, 205–9, 232,
    244, 254–5, 278, 279–80, 286–7
Downes, Charlene 263
Dr No (film) 211
Drew, Nancy (fictional character) 134
drugs 10, 77, 110, 124, 125, 142–4, 154,
    162
Dunaway, Sarah 33–4

Easton, Kate Augusta Mead 79–86,
    109–10, *168*, 189, 254, 262, 293
Echo 45–6, 215, 246
Eglin, George 198
Ellen, Harriet 67
Elliot, George 72
Elliott, Harry 85
Ellis, Edward 41
Etheridge, Trixie (Beatrix) 146–7
Evans, Glyn 293, 295
Evans, John 222
Evans, Ormwold and Mary Sophie 26–8

Fabian, Robert 160
The Female Detective (Forrester) 41, 42
feminism 231, 236–7
Field, Charles Frederick 23, 24–5, 26–7,
    28–9, 33, 118, *165*, 289
Fielding, John and Henry 25
Finberg, Jack Gerald 141, 188, 189
Finberg, Maurice (*né* Feigenbaum) 140,
    149, 154
Finberg, Ruth 141, 188–9
Finlay, Janet 199
The Firearms Act (1920) 110
First World War 101, 117–18, 138–9, 142,
    191
Flying Squad 191–2, 260
Forrester, Andrew 41
fortune telling 95–7, 100, 105
Forty Elephants 90, 100
Foulkes, Samuel 34

Foyle, Christina 128
Freemasons 67
Frost, George 'Jack' 162
Fyson, Susanna 186

gambling 10, 126, 143, 152–6
Gardner, Tony 222
General Data Protection Regulation
    (GDPR) 291, 294–5
Giuliani, Laura 246
Gladden, Miss (fictional detective) 41, 42,
    231, 289
Goddard, Henry 25–6, 202
Gower, Pauline 128
Grafton, Sue 237
Grant, Lindy 242
Great Coram Street murder (1872) 72
Great Exhibition (1851) 33
'Great Turf Fraud' 62
Greenhalgh, May *174*, 198–9, 286
Griffiths, Jackie 244
Grocott, Sarah 23, 27–8
Grosvenor, Lady Henrietta 26
guns 78, 110, 163, 218, 231, 232, 244

Haig, Field Marshall Sir Douglas 141
Halton, William 117
Hancock, Matt 57
Harmsworth, Sir Alfred 97
Harry, Prince 294
Hartopp divorce case 91
Hayward, Tom 93, 94, *169*
Heron, Ann 258–9, 262
Heyward, William Stephens 41–2
Hobson, Win *175*, 233, 251
Holmes, Sherlock (fictional detective) 11,
    15, 61, 109, 142, *165*, 183, 196, 251,
    290, 291, 292
  'India's Sherlock Holmes' (Rajani
      Pandit) 267
  'Lady Sherlock Holmes' (Annie Betts)
      100
  'Miss Sherlock Holmes' (May Storey)
      127
  'She-lock Holmes' (Lindy Grant) 242
  Sherlock Holmes Museum 13–15, 182,
      288

Sherlock Holmes pub *179*, 249–53
Sherlock Holmes Society *179*, 249,
    250
  see also Kerner, Annette; Scott-Archer,
      Zena Philippa
Howes, Audrey 147
Humphries, Ada Alice 92–3
Hutchinson, Sam 293

Imossi, Tony 269, 294–5
India 266, 267
Institute of Professional Investigators
    (IPI) 293, 295
*The International Police and Detective
    Directory* 109
Inverclyde, Lord 132
Isted, Sally 260

'Jack the Ripper' 44–5, 75
Jackson, Professor Louise 183, 184, 214
James, P.D. 230–1
Jane, Rebecca 265–6
Jarvie, Jen *179*, 257–63, 275
Jarvie Khan Investigations 263
Jews 140, 183, 186, 191
Joyes, Elizabeth 31–3
ju-jutsu 107, 123, *171*

Karloff, Boris 161
Keiro, Professor and Madame 95–9, 115
Kelly, Hannah 100
Kempton, Freda 142
Kenya 267
Kerner, Annette ('Mrs Sherlock Holmes')
    9–11, 15–16, 18, 137–44, 145–50,
    151–7, 159–64, *173*, 181–9, 242,
    267–8
  and Brilliant 'Billy' Chang 142–4, 162
  in disguise 153, 161, 183
  memoirs 15–16, 149–50, 156–7,
      159–61, 183–4, 189, 290
Kerner, Henry Isidore 149, 153, 156, 164,
    188
Kersey, Charles Henry 107–11, 118, 181,
    289
Khan, Jaz *179*, 263

Lady Molly of Scotland Yard (Orczy) 104
The Lady Private Investigators Ltd 275
Lavender Guthrie, Joan ('Laura Grey')
 77
Lawton, Hattie 267
Leslie, Ernest 44
Lewis & Lewis (solicitors) 97, 98
Limehouse 142–3
Lincoln, Abraham 36
Lion Investigation Services 266
Liverpool 28, 32, 34, 35, 62, 124, 125,
 126, *177*, 185, 192–3, 215, 232–3,
 247, 286
 see also Scott-Archer, Zena Philippa
Lloyd's Weekly 51, 52, 82, 83, 115, *166*
Lock, Joan 104
Lombroso, Cesare 47, 69
London Evening Standard 63, 76
London Mainly About People 84, 85
Lyon(s), Ellen 51, 115, *166*

Macy, Barbara *175*, 231–3, 238, 251, 260,
 285, 286
Malton, Jackie 260
Mara, Sandra 237–8
Marks & Spencer 120, 186, 226
Marlowe, Phillip (fictional character)
 200–1
Marple, Miss Jane (fictional character)
 132–3, 184, 226, 239, 241, 244,
 245, 291, 293
Marriott, Valeen 222–3
Marsh, Alison 273
Martin, Annie 105
Martin, Sarah 262
The Matrimonial Causes Act (1857) 28
The Matrimonial Causes Act (1923) 109
The Matrimonial Causes Act (1937) 119,
 222
May, Theresa 17–18
Mayfair Detective Agency 137, 146–50,
 155–6, 163, 164, 185
McCall Smith, Alexander 267
McConnell, Sir Robert and Lady Elsie 81
McDermid, Val 243–4
Merken, Peter 211, 212
Merrick, Leonard 47–8

Metropolitan Police 23, 61, 102, 103–4,
 107–8, 118, 126, 146, 153, 191,
 293–4
Metropolitan Police Women Patrols
 103–4, *170*
Metropolitan Women Police Association
 184
Meyrick, Kate 162
Mitchell, Matilda 89–94, 115, *169*, 262
Molock, Violet Emily (*née* Williams) 120
Montagu, Arthur 44
Moser, Charlotte Antonia ('Antonia';
 previously Williamson) 61–70, 71–8,
 82, 86, 109, 115, *166*, *167*, *168*, 254,
 267, 292, 293
Moser, Maurice 61–70, 71, 72, 73, 74, 75,
 82, 118, *166*, 289, 293
Mr Bazalgette's Agent (Merrick) 47–8
Mugo, Jane 267
Muir, Alec 162
Mullins, Claud 162–3

Naidu, Adil 246
Napier, Sir Archibald Lennox M. 98
National Portrait Gallery 128
Naylor, Detective Inspector Lilian 104
New Realm Film Company 156
'New Woman,' the 48
Newton, Judith 35
Norstac Inquiry Office 241
North, Jamie 277, 281–4, 286–7
Notley, Charlotte *180*, 277–81, 285–6,
 291
Novello, Ivor 138
Nown, Graham 183

O'Callaghan, Sheila 133
O'Donnell, Peter 219
online scams 269, 272–4
opium 10, 110, 124, 142, 143, 154
Orczy, Baroness 104
Oughton, Frederick 213–14

Page, Raissa 214, 242
palmistry 96, 97, 98
Pandit, Rajani 267
Paretsky, Sara 236–7

Parsons, Eddie 10, 147, 163
Pathé News 108, 146, 150, 161, 181, 182, 185, 249
Paul, Jennifer Sarah 242
Payne, Violet 143
The People 93, 149–50, 153, 159
Pink Detective 273
Pinkerton, Allan 36, 160, *165*, 267
Pinkerton National Detective Agency 36–7, 117, *165*, 267
Pirkis, Catherine Louisa 48
Pollaky, Ignatius Paul ('Paddington Pollaky') 25
'private dicks' 160, 209, 235, 276, 278, 279
'private eye' 159–60
Private Investigations Ltd 270
The Private Investigator 200
prostitution 33, 102, 142, 143, 153, 221

Quartermain, Barrie 211–12

railways 31–2, 33, 91–2, 98, 101, 105
Recordon dictating machines 148
Redford, Jessica 244
Regent Street 95, 96, 99, 107, 142
Regent Street Polytechnic 162
regulations 17–18, 19, 56, 294–5
Revelations of a Lady Detective (Heyward) 41–2
Reynolds's Newspaper 34, 75, 115, *167*, 200
Rideal, Charles 66
Rippon, Gina 292
Rivers, Aileen A. 183
Robinson, Howard 9–11, 150
Robinson, William Frederick 150
Rogue Daters 272
romance fraud 267–8, 272–4
Rous, Lady Marye Violet Isolde *173*, 198
Rumper, Mary Ann 44
Ruth the Betrayer; or, The Female Spy (Ellis) 41
Ryley, Madeleine Lucette 80

St Giles Workhouse Infirmary 68, 69
Sangster, Louisa 65
Scotland Yard 62, 63, 78, 93, 161, 191–2, 200, 250

ex-detectives become private investigators 117, 118, 150, 153, 198
female detectives work with 10, 37, 40, 102, 105, 109, 110, 125, 142, 259
in the media 66, 104, 160
Scott-Archer, Zena Philippa ('Merseyside's Mrs Sherlock Holmes') *174*, *175*, *178*, 191–6, 197–203, 215, 225–33, 244–7, 250–6, 259, 262, 286, 292
disguises *177*, 191, 195, 229, 236, 246–7, 255
and the media *177*, 197–8, 199–200, 225–7, 229, 235–6, 238–9, 242, 244–5, 247, 252
and professional organisations *176*, 195–6, 200, 209, 215, 225, 227, 230, 235–6, 246, 255, 256
and Terry Wogan 238–9
Scott, Sydney *174*, 191–2, 194, 195, 196, 250, 252–3, 286
Second World War 136, 153, 192
Selfridges 89, 92
The Sex Disqualification (Removal) Act (1919) 103
shadowing 84, 85, 105, 111, 118, 128, 197–8, 277–88
Shelmerdine, Eric 245
Sherlock Holmes Museum, Baker Street 13–15, 182, 288
Sherlock Holmes pub *179*, 249–53
shoplifting 89–90, 92–3, 94, 97, 100, 120–1, 125, 128, 146
Simmons, John Raymond 186–7
Simmons, Jules (*né* Symons) 185, 186
The Sketch 93, 140–1, *169*
Slater, Henry (*né* George Tinsley) 43, 44, 45–6, 48, 49, 51, 53, 63, 65, 289
Smale, Harry 117–18, 119, 121
Smith, Caroline 44
Smith, Philip 205, 206, 208, 293
Sorrell, Rosemary 241–2
spiritualism 110
Stapleton, Susannah 85, 86, 132, 135–6, 184
Stokes, Fred 163

Stone, Lawrence 26
store detectives 89–90, 92–3, 94, 97, 100,
    109, 120, 146, 155
Storey, May 123–9, *172*, 292
Storey, Patricia 241, 243
Subaidah Naidu, Siti *178*, 245–6, 294, 296
suffrage 44, 48, 74–5, 76, 77, 78, 84, 86,
    100, 101, 103, 105
Summer, Anne *176*, 217–23, 231, 242,
    284–5
Sunday Dispatch 124, 131, 160, 196
Sunday Pictorial 132, 134
Sunday Post 108, 110
Sunday Telegraph 177, 229
surveillance 20, 58, 126, 197–8, 205, 208,
    232, 242, 271, 280–2
Symons, Barnett (Ben) 185–6, 189
Symons, Julian 133, 290

Tatler 140, 211, 212, 213, 286
Taylor Investigations *180*, 278–88
television and radio 160, 199, 218, 233,
    236, 238–9, 241, 242–3, 244, 247,
    252, 267, 274, 285, 293
Tempest, Dorothy 97–9, 115, *169*, *170*,
    202, 262
Thackeray, William Makepeace 71–2
Thompson, Victor 164
The Times 28, 44–5, 76, 212, 218, 220,
    235, 243
tracing 18, 208, 245, 270, 271, 275, 277,
    280, 281
Tripp, June 132
Twiby, Yvonne 243–4
Tyler, Walter 32, 33

UK Private Investigators Network
    (UKPIN) 205, 208–9, 279–80, 287,
    293
Upperley, Paulowna 51–2, 115

Verity Henton Private Investigations 293
Vers, Jacques 9
Vick, Sir Russell 162
Vidocq, Eugène-François 25
Vinson, Christine 246
The Vote 76, 77

Wackerman, Miss Vanderbilt 68
Wagner, Reverend Henry Michell 64
Wagner, Sarah Antonia 64
Walsh, Melodie 198
Ward, Lester Frank 45
Warham, Catherine 92–3
Warne, Kate 36–7, 96, *165*, 267
Weekly Dispatch 71, 72, 73, 82, 108, 198
Werner Laurie (publishers) 156
West, Maud (*née* Edith Maria Barber)
    85–7, 109–11, 115, 129, 131–6, *168*,
    172, 184, 186, 189, 254, 262, 267,
    284
Wheelwright, Edith 84
white slavery 102, 121, 123–4, 142
Whitechapel murders 44–5, 46, 63
Whiteleys 100, 147
Wigglesworth, Francis 83–4
Wilks, Welburn 63–4, 69, 74
Williams, Hyman 151–2, 154
Williamson, Charles Wilks 71–2
Williamson, Edward James Clarendon
    64–5, 69
Wilson, Professor David 244
Wilson, Janet 242
Winant, Ursula 157
Withers, Ian D. 293
Wogan, Terry 239
Woman Detective (Kerner) 156–7, 159–61,
    184
Women Police Volunteers (WPVs) 101
Women's Business and Legal Agency 75
Women's Freedom League 75, 84
Women's Social and Political Union
    (WSPU) 74, 77, 107
World Association of Detectives (WAD)
    235–6, 238, 245–6, 251
World Association of Professional
    Investigators (WAPI), 293, 295
Wyles, Lilian 103, 105, 141, 143, 160, *170*,
    213, 285

Ziska, Madam 100
Zodiac, Professor 99